Football

STEPS TO SUCCESS

Greg Colby

HUMAN KINETICS

Library of Congress Cataloging-in-Publication Data

Colby, Greg, 1952-
  Football / Greg Colby.
     pages cm. -- (Steps to success)
  1. Football. I. Title.
  GV950.7.C64 2013
  796.33--dc23

                          2012049045

ISBN-10: 1-4504-1170-3 (print)
ISBN-13: 978-1-4504-1170-7 (print)

Acquisitions Editor: Justin Klug
Developmental Editor: Cynthia McEntire
Assistant Editor: Elizabeth Evans
Copyeditor: John Wentworth
Graphic Designer: Keri Evans
Cover Designer: Keith Blomberg
Photographs (cover and interior): Jason Allen
Visual Production Assistant: Joyce Brumfield
Photo Production Manager: Jason Allen
Art Manager: Kelly Hendren
Associate Art Manager: Alan L. Wilborn
Illustrations: Jody Roginson Creative Services
Printer: Versa Press

We thank Urbana High School in Urbana, Illinois, for assistance in providing the location for the photo shoot for this book.

Human Kinetics books are available at special discounts for bulk purchase. Special editions or book excerpts can also be created to specification. For details, contact the Special Sales Manager at Human Kinetics.

Printed in the United States of America   10 9 8 7 6 5 4 3 2 1

The paper in this book is certified under a sustainable forestry program.

Human Kinetics
Website: www.HumanKinetics.com

United States: Human Kinetics
P.O. Box 5076
Champaign, IL 61825-5076
800-747-4457
e-mail: humank@hkusa.com

Canada: Human Kinetics
475 Devonshire Road Unit 100
Windsor, ON N8Y 2L5
800-465-7301 (in Canada only)
e-mail: info@hkcanada.com

Europe: Human Kinetics
107 Bradford Road
Stanningley
Leeds LS28 6AT, United Kingdom
+44 (0) 113 255 5665
e-mail: hk@hkeurope.com

Australia: Human Kinetics
57A Price Avenue
Lower Mitcham, South Australia 5062
08 8372 0999
e-mail: info@hkaustralia.com

New Zealand: Human Kinetics
P.O. Box 80
Torrens Park, South Australia 5062
0800 222 062
e-mail: info@hknewzealand.com

E5478

Football

STEPS TO SUCCESS

Contents

Climbing the Steps to Football Success

Football is a game of yards and inches. Those who play football most successfully possess strength, speed, skill, drive, and competitive spirit. *Football: Steps to Success* will take you on a journey to becoming a more complete, more successful football player. The journey will require hard work and perseverance. It isn't a quick trip. You will climb a staircase that leads to one mastered skill after another on your way to becoming a complete player.

Each of the 13 steps builds on the previous steps. The first two steps provide an overview of the positions and responsibilities for offense and defense. Step 3 then moves into the fundamental skills all players, regardless of position, must learn and understand to be successful on the field.

Steps 4 through 7 go into great detail about the key skills of passing, catching, running the ball, and tackling and blocking. Steps 8 and 9 focus on defending running plays and pass plays. Step 10 addresses special teams, with instruction on how to master kicking and punting the ball. Depending on your position, you might choose to skim or skip some of these steps, but I advise reading all of them. A defensive player who understands what a running back is trying to do will be in better position to stop him. A quarterback who knows blocking patterns will be able to see blitzes early and save a broken play. A punter who can read defenses is going to be better prepared to adjust his timing.

Building on the foundation of these key skills, steps 11, 12, and 13 move into strategy and play calling, covering offensive football, defensive football, and special-team play. In these chapters, the fundamental skills learned are put into play to move the ball on offense, stop the offense on defense, and gain yardage and points through special teams. Again, all players, regardless of position, will benefit from this information.

The *Steps to Success* is a proven method that provides a systematic approach to learning football skills, techniques, and strategies. Approach each of the steps in this way:

1. Read the material covered in the step to understand why the step is important to football success.

2. Follow the technique photos that show how to execute each skill.

3. Review the missteps in technique and use this information to avoid or correct common errors.

4. Execute the drills. Drills help you improve your skills through repetition and purposeful practice. Read the directions and the success checks for each drill.

5. At the end of each step, answer the review questions to make sure you are ready to move to the next step.

As you progress through the 13 steps, you'll encounter many challenges and will be asked to do a lot of hard work, but your effort will be rewarded with better play, safer execution, and solid teamwork—in other words, *success*.

The Sport of Football

The purpose of *Football: Steps to Success* is to provide readers with a fundamental knowledge of the game of football, including rules, definitions, techniques, and skills needed to play successfully. In this introduction, we'll cover the basic format and definitions of the game, as well as the fundamental rules that govern its play. As anyone who knows football will tell you: The game is far too complex to even mention all the rules, strategies, schemes, and variations in one short introduction. For more detailed information after reading this introduction, please turn to the drills themselves, and also to the glossary at the end of the book, which is a thorough compilation of basic information on nearly every football term.

At the end of the introduction we'll discuss drills, which are focused sessions of practice that most coaches use to instill skills in their players and prepare them for games.

PLAYING THE GAME

Football is a game played between two teams of 11 players each. The object of the game is for the offensive team to take the football and either carry or pass it into the goal area (end zone) of the opposing team. The defensive team tries to tackle the offensive man who has the ball before he can move it to the end zone, which is called a touchdown and is worth 6 points. In the early days of football, the player who scored was required to touch the ground with the ball in order for the score to count. That is no longer a requirement.

Each game is started by one team kicking the ball to the other team. Once a player catches the kicked ball, the play continues until that player is either tackled or crosses one of the restraining lines (sidelines or goal line). After the player is tackled on the kickoff, the offensive team has four plays to move the ball 10 yards. Each time the offense moves the ball 10 yards—this is called getting a first down—they earn a new set of four downs. The offense often chooses to punt (kick) the ball to the defense on the fourth down if they're not confident of earning a first down. If they do punt, the receiving team now becomes the offense, and they have four downs to gain 10 yards. Each time a team scores a touchdown (crosses the opponent's goal line with the ball) or kicks a field goal (place kicks the ball between the uprights of the goal post), the next series of downs is started by a kickoff. Each half of the game is also begun with a kickoff.

Once a play is started, the offensive players can block the defensive players to prevent them from tackling the offensive man carrying the football. A block entails physically preventing the opponent from getting to the ball carrier. The blocker may use his hands, arms, or shoulders to physically hit the defender. However, the blocker may not grab the defender outside his arms (the frame) or block above the shoulders with the hands or arms. In certain circumstances, the blocker also may not block below the defender's waist or in the back.

When tackling, there are fewer restrictions for defensive players. They may pretty much use their arms and hands in any way, except they may not grab the ball carrier's face mask or the collar of his shoulder pads. Blocking or tackling illegally results in a penalty. Penalties usually take the form of the offending team having the ball position moved in their direction a specified number of yards—from 1 to 15 yards or more—by the official. A penalty may also result in the number of downs available being increased or reduced.

The offense may either run the ball or pass the ball in order to gain yardage. If they choose a running play, the quarterback may hand the ball to any teammate except the five offensive linemen, or he may carry the ball himself. On a pass play, the quarterback may throw a pass to any of his teammates except the five offensive linemen or have the pass thrown to him after he hands or passes the ball to a teammate. A pass is any ball thrown overhand or underhand to another player forward toward the line of scrimmage. If the pass is thrown sideways or backward from the line of scrimmage, it is called a lateral. A pass that is not caught before it hits the ground is considered incomplete and results in the end of the play. On an incomplete pass, the offense uses one of their four downs and must try their next down from the same spot. If a lateral is thrown or pitched and lands on the ground, it is considered a free ball for either the offense or defense to pick up and gain possession. A pass must be thrown from behind the line of scrimmage on the offensive team's side. If a player throws a pass once he has crossed the line of scrimmage, it is a penalty on the offensive team.

Strategy comes into play when the offensive team tries to figure out the best way to move the ball down the field. Some of the strategy for the offense involves finding ways to line up to be able to run the play as effectively as possible. This may then be countered by the defense trying to line up against the offense in such a way to put them in the best position to stop the play. This back and forth continues throughout the game. The same type of strategy may involve the offense trying to run plays at specific defensive players they feel they can exploit. Similarly, the defense will try to line up their players to get the best physical match-ups they can versus the offensive players.

The strategy also includes running certain kinds of plays in certain situations and in certain parts of the field. Likewise, the defense can choose to run specific defenses at certain times to counter the offense's attempt to run certain plays. This may include all manner of movement by the defense, as well as "blitzing" to beat the offensive blockers. We'll explain blitzing and spend much more time discussing strategy and schemes later in the book.

The football field (figure 1) is 120 yards (360 feet) long and 53-1/3 yards (160 feet) wide. The outside lines on the long sides are called sidelines. The outside lines on the short sides are called end lines. Ten yards from the end lines are the goal lines. The goal lines mark the beginning of the goal area of each team. The field is marked off by hash marks at every yard and yard lines at every 5 yards. The hash marks are located 20 yards from each sideline. Each play starts from a point somewhere on or between these hash marks. The area between the goal lines and the side lines is the field of play. A player is considered out of play (out of bounds) when he touches or crosses the sideline. He is considered in the end zone when he touches or crosses the goal line.

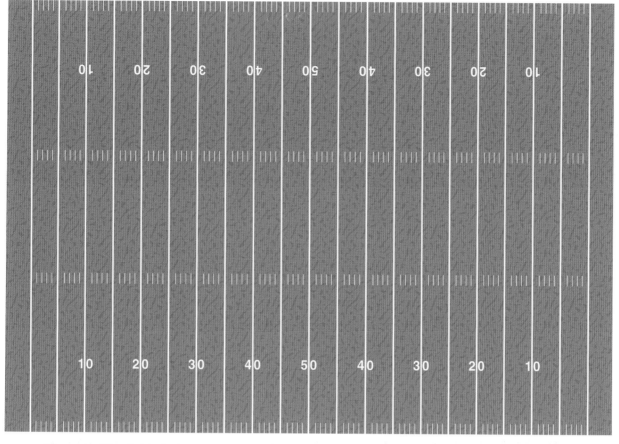

Figure 1 The field of play.

GAME RULES

The rules of football vary slightly depending on the level being played. In this discussion, we'll cover the general rules that pertain to all levels of play.

Field and Equipment

The first rule of football sets the field dimensions and markings, as stated earlier and shown in figure 1. It also defines the type of equipment required to play. Fields at all levels have the same dimensions with the exception of the distance from the sidelines to the hash marks. At the high school level and below, the distance from the sidelines to the hash marks is 53 feet, 4 inches. At the college level, it is 58 feet. At the pro level, the hash marks are 70 feet 9 inches from the sidelines. The outside dimensions and yard-line markings are the same at all levels.

Many rules in football have developed over time to ensure that participants have adequate protection to reduce the number and severity of injuries to participants (including the officials). The basic protective equipment required includes a helmet; mouth guard; shoulder pads; hip pads, including a pad for the tail bone; thigh pads; knee pads; and shoes with nonmetal cleats less than half an inch long.

There are very specific safety requirements for helmets. Helmets must meet National Operating Committee on Standards for Athletic Equipment (NOCSAE) standards. This should be clearly marked on each helmet.

No player may have any metal or hard material on him that is not sufficiently padded to prevent it from injuring others. This usually applies to braces or casts that may be worn for injury prevention.

The uniform includes pants and a jersey. The jersey must have a number on the front and back that falls into one of two categories: eligible and ineligible numbers. These refer to the jersey numbers of the offensive players who are allowed to line up in a specific position and who are allowed to catch a pass or not. Eligible numbers are those from 1 to 49 and from 80 to 99. Ineligible numbers are from 50 to 79. Offensive linemen must wear ineligible numbers, whereas running backs, quarterbacks, tight ends, and receivers must wear eligible numbers. Defensive players can wear any number. Traditionally, the home team wears a dark-colored jersey and the visiting team wears a light-colored jersey.

Blocking

Blocking is obstructing an opponent by contacting him with any part of the blocker's body. The frame of a player's body is at the shoulders or below, other than the back. This designation is used to determine if a blocker has his hands in the proper position. Anytime the blocker's hands are outside the player's frame, he is considered to be holding the player, which earns a penalty.

Types of blocks include the following:

- Below the waist: Initial contact is made below the waist with any part of the blocker's body against an opponent other than the ball carrier.

- Chop block: This is a high–low combination block by any two offensive players against an opponent.

- Clipping: This is a block in which initial contact by the blocker is either from behind or below the waist.

The blocking zone is a rectangle centered on the snapper that extends 5 yards laterally and 3 yards longitudinally in each direction. The blocking zone disintegrates when the ball leaves the zone.

Downs

A down is an opportunity for the offensive team to take the ball and run a play in an attempt to advance the ball as many yards as possible or, ideally, into the end zone. The offense can run the ball, pass the ball, or kick the ball on any of their down opportunities. The offense has four plays (downs) to move the ball at least 10 yards. If they succeed, they receive four more downs. If they fail, the opposing team takes possession of the ball and receives four downs to move 10 yards. In many cases, when the offense fails to move the ball 10 yards on its first three downs, they will choose to punt the ball to the opponent to force the opponent to start their series of downs farther away from their goal line. The offense can use their fourth down attempt to get the ball past the 10-yard mark, but if they fail, the defense takes over possession of the ball at that spot. Depending on how close this spot is to the offense's goal, this may not be an acceptable risk in most situations. The offense also could kick a field goal if they are close enough to the defense's goal.

Fair Catch

A fair catch is the act of catching a scrimmage kick by the receiving team without the option of running with it after the catch. The receiving player gives a valid fair-catch signal by waving his hand above his shoulders. Players from the opposing team are not allowed to hit or tackle the player who calls for a fair catch. Once the receiving player gives the fair-catch signal he is not allowed to run with the ball once he catches it. The rule allows him one step after the catch as part of the catching motion. The player who signals for the fair catch is also not allowed to block anyone in the event he does not catch the ball. Anyone else who may catch the ball is bound by the fair-catch signal, even if he is not the player to give the signal. In other words, if two players are in a position to catch a kick and one of them gives the fair-catch signal, neither player is allowed to run with the ball once its caught.

A fair catch can be used in a couple of situations. First, if the kicking team's coverage men are getting close to the receiving player, the receiving player can call a fair catch to protect himself from being hit and perhaps dropping the ball. A second situation is when the ball is kicked very short, giving the receiving team good field position at the point where it's caught. By using a fair catch in this situation, the receiving team ensures they have good field position without risking the returner fumbling the ball when he's tackled.

Kicking

There are several types of kicks in football.

The punt is a kick in which the player drops the ball and kicks it before it strikes the ground. This is usually used on the fourth down of the offensive team's series when the offense decides they cannot reach the down marker (10-yard mark) on a run or pass play.

A drop kick is a kick in which the player drops the ball and kicks it as it touches the ground. (Although this is a legal kick in football, it's almost never seen anymore.) The drop kick can be used instead of a place kick or a free kick.

A place kick is usually called a field goal or a point after touchdown (PAT). This is a kick by a player in which the ball is positioned either on a tee or on the ground and held by a teammate while the kicker kicks it off the ground or tee, depending on the level of play. High schools and below may use a tee. College and professionals must kick off the ground.

A free kick is made at the beginning of each half of play or after a touchdown or successful field goal. The ball is kicked from the scoring team's restraining line (40-yard line in high school; 35-yard line in college and professional). The ball must be a place kick or drop kick. If a place kick, the ball is kicked off a tee placed on the restraining line. Though allowed, the drop kick is no longer used by anyone because of the difficulty of this skill. All members of the kicking team (except the kicker and a holder) must be behind the restraining line until the ball is kicked. The receiving team must line up at least 10 yards from the restraining line prior to the kick. A free kick is also used after a safety by the team who was tackled for the safety. The kicking team may use a kick, drop kick, or punt. This kick is made from the kicking team's 20-yard line.

The point after touchdown (PAT) is a scrimmage kick that may be either a place kick or a drop kick. The PAT kick occurs after a touchdown and is kicked from the 3-yard line. A successful PAT kick results in 1 point.

The field goal is a scrimmage kick that may be either a place kick or a drop kick. A ball that goes through the uprights of the goal is worth 3 points for the kicking team. A field goal is kicked when the offense feels they cannot reach the down marker (make a first down) and believe their kicker can make the kick from that location. A field goal is traditionally kicked on fourth down but may be kicked on any down.

Neutral Zone

The neutral zone is the space between the two lines of scrimmage, extending from one sideline to the other.

The line of scrimmage is an imaginary line for the offensive and defensive teams. This line is even with the point of the ball closest to that team and extends from one sideline to the other. The line of scrimmage for each team is divided by the neutral zone, which is the length of the football.

Prior to the football being snapped to start a play, the offensive players must align on their side of the line of scrimmage and not move forward for at least 1 second prior to the snap. The defensive players must be aligned on their side of the line of scrimmage and may not be in or across the neutral zone prior to the ball being snapped.

In college and professional football, the defensive player is allowed in the neutral zone prior to the snap as long as he is back on his side before the ball is snapped. Below the college level, any movement into the neutral zone is considered encroachment and is a penalty. If any offensive player is in the neutral zone prior to the snap, it is considered off sides and is a penalty.

Snapping the Ball

The snap of the football, which begins a play from scrimmage, is either handing or passing the ball from its initial position on the ground (as placed by the official) with a quick and continuous motion of the hand or hands. The snap may be either between the legs or not, although except for a few specialty plays, it is usually between the legs. The player snapping the ball (the offensive center or punt and field goal snapper) may not pick up or move the ball prior to the snap. He may rotate the ball to get it in the desired position as long as he does not pick it off the ground in doing so.

Passing

The football may be passed either overhand or underhand. A pass may be forward, backward, or lateral. A pass that is exactly parallel to the line of scrimmage is considered a backward pass or a lateral. A forward pass that is not caught before it hits the ground is considered incomplete and results in a new down. A lateral or backward pass that hits the ground is a free ball and is treated like a fumble and can be advanced by the first player from either team who gains possession of the ball.

Tackling

Tackling is grasping or encircling an opponent with the hands or arms. This is usually done by the defensive team to the ball carrier. The tackler may grab any part of the ball carrier's body except the face mask or the side or back collar of the shoulder pads.

Periods, Time Factors, and Substitutions

Each game consists of four quarters of noncontinuous play. The length of each quarter depends on the level of play. High schools play 12-minute quarters. College and professional teams play 15-minute quarters. If the score is tied at the end of regulation, there may be one or more additional overtime periods to determine the winner. In professional football, the first team to score is the winner. In college and high school, each team gets an opportunity to run plays to score, regardless of what the opponent does on their turn.

Each team is allowed 11 players on the field at a time. Between plays, players may be substituted as wished.

Each team is allowed three time-outs per half of the game. Each time-out lasts approximately 1 minute. The officials may call a time-out if a player on either team appears to be injured. That player must be taken out of the game for at least one play.

The offensive team has either 25 or 40 seconds to run a play once the official marks the ball in play. The exact time depends on the level of play and the game situation. Failure to snap the ball before the 24- or 40-second clock runs out results in a 5-yard delay-of-game penalty against the offense.

DRILLING FOR SUCCESS

In general, each core skill or technique needs to be repeated correctly multiple times by players before it is fully learned. If a drill can be designed in a way that achieves this in a short period of time, the drill will usually produce substantial positive rewards. If a group of 8 to 10 players needs to work on a specific skill, say catching punts, the coach can set up a drill that involves everyone at the same time. One group of two or three players can catch punts directly from the punter. Another group of two or three players can catch simulated punts thrown by the coach or another player. If you're fortunate enough to have a ball-throwing machine, use it to punt balls to the remaining two or three players. Players rotate between the three groups to get each type of punt. With this setup, in a 5-minute period each player should catch between 15 and 20 punts.

When setting up these types of drills, the coach should use key words so the next time he wants to run the drill, all he has to say is the name of the drill and the players will know how to line up and what to do. The coach should keep his coaching points and corrections brief and to the point, again using key words that tell players what they need to correct. Coaches should try to avoid long, drawn-out explanations or corrections when running drills. These are best delivered during team meetings, when there's more time to go into detail.

Another key element in setting up an effective drill involves the original teaching of the drill. Make sure each drill has a clear objective to be achieved. Two or three distinct coaching points should be emphasized. The coach should be as descriptive in his explanation of what he wants as possible. Coaches should not assume players will automatically understand what they are trying to convey. Keep it simple. Don't worry about speed of movement or speed of repetitions until players can perform the skill correctly. If possible, learn the drill prior to practice in a meeting or a walk-through. That way, players have a chance to digest what they need to learn before they try to execute the drill.

Key to Diagrams

TB	Tailback		**E**	End
FB	Fullback		**T**	Tackle
QB	Quarterback		**ILB**	Inside linebacker
WR	Wide receiver		**OLB**	Outside linebacker
T	Tackle		**FS**	Free safety
G	Guard		**SS**	Strong safety
C	Center		**CB**	Corner back
TE	Tight end		**N**	Nose tackle
⬭	Offensive player		**LLB**	Left linebacker
▭	Center		**RLB**	Right linebacker
⬬	Ball carrier		**LIB**	Left inside linebacker
◖⬭	Shading for block		**RIB**	Right inside linebacker
←	Running path		**D**	Defensive player
◄·····	Ball path (pass or kick)		**LB**	Linebacker
├─	Block		**DB**	Defensive back
‖	Handoff		**S**	Strongside linebacker
├---	Alternate blocking path		**W**	Weakside linebacker
◄---	Alternate running path		**M**	Middle linebacker
●──	Step		**R**	Returner
			K	Kicker
			H	Holder

Offensive Positions and Responsibilities

A football team consists of three units—offense, defense, and special teams—each with its own responsibilities and requirements. Each unit contributes to the outcome of a game in its own way. The job of the offense is to maintain possession of the ball, gain yardage, and score points. The job of the defense is to stop the offense from gaining yardage and scoring points and to try to take possession of the ball. All other responsibilities fall to the special teams.

The special-teams unit consists of six teams: the punting team, the punt-return team, the kickoff team, the kickoff-return team, the PAT (point after touchdown) and field-goal team, and the PAT and field-goal block team. Each special-teams unit has its own unique responsibility relating to the game situation. The punting team and punt-return team take the field on fourth down (or on another down on very rare occasions) when the offense elects not to attempt to make a first down or a field goal and thus must kick (punt) the ball to the opponent. The kickoff and kickoff-return teams take the field after a score (be it a touchdown, a field goal, or a safety). The PAT and PAT block teams take the field for the extra-point kick after a touchdown. The field-goal and field-goal block teams (usually the same players as on the PAT teams) take the field (usually on fourth down) when the offense decides to kick a field goal (worth 3 points) instead of running a play or punting the ball.

In step 1 we discuss the basics of the offense. Defensive basics are discussed in step 2. The essentials for special-team units are covered in step 13. In this first step, you'll learn about each position on offense, including the position's primary responsibilities as well as tips to help fulfill them.

Because the offense is charged with gaining yards and scoring, the importance of a strong offense is obvious. An offense that scores multiple touchdowns makes winning much easier. By moving the ball (i.e., gaining yardage) on each play, the offense can also help the defense and special-teams units. This happens in two ways. First, by moving the ball the offense retains possession of the ball, which gives the defense and special teams units a chance to rest and recover. Second, moving the ball helps establish good field position, which means (in the simplest terms) advancing the ball to the opponent's end of the field. Maintaining good field position allows a team to score more often and prevents the opponent from scoring as often as they would like.

A football team's offensive unit is made up of 11 players: five linemen, one quarterback, up to three running backs, up to two tight ends, and up to five wide receivers. The running back, tight end, and wide receiver positions vary in how many are playing at any one time, depending on the offensive scheme being employed. Figures 1.1 through 1.3 show three offensive formation alignments; note the number of running backs, tight ends, and wide receivers in each alignment.

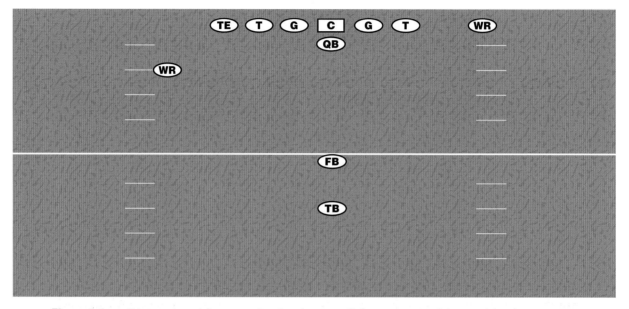

Figure 1.1   21 personnel (two running backs, one tight end, two wide receivers).

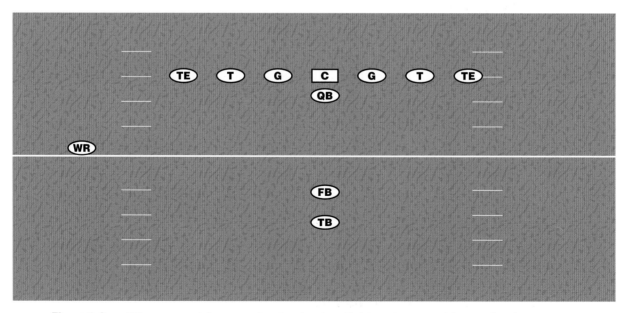

Figure 1.2   22 personnel (two running backs, two tight ends, one wide receiver).

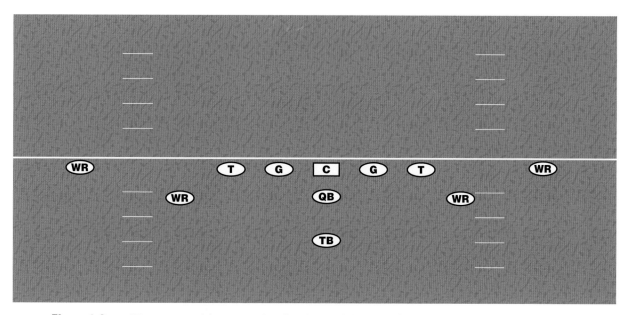

Figure 1.3   10 personnel (one running back, no tight end, four wide receivers).

Note the terminology used to name each formation. Many naming systems are used; the one we use here is one of the most simple. This system uses two numerals to name the personnel used in the formation; for instance, the first numeral in the 21 personnel is 2, and the second numeral is 1. The first numeral designates the number of running backs, including any fullbacks, to be used in a play. The second numeral designates how many tight ends are included in the play. You can then calculate the number of wide receivers to be used in the play by subtracting from five the total number of running backs and tight ends. For example, in 21-personnel formations, there are two wide receivers—five minus three. In 11-personnel formations, there are three wide receivers. Within each personnel grouping, various alignments can be used. Again, the terminology may vary from team to team.

The number of players on field on offense is always 11. To avoid having too many or too few players on the field for a play, coaches clarify personnel groups during practice sessions. Each player must know his personnel group and must know if he is a starter or a backup at his position. Each backup player must know when (and when not) to replace the starter at his position. This should always be controlled by the coach. Players should never substitute themselves without the coach's consent. Practice personnel organization by changing from one personnel group to another during practice. Each player learns to listen to the "call" for each play. The coach might call for backup players either by individually rotating players in or doing it as a group. For example, the first-team players might run several plays, followed by the second-team players running several plays. Or the coach may substitute these two groups in mass between plays.

The 11 players on offense for any given play must line up in correct formation (also called alignment), which must be taught in practice. To avoid players lining up in wrong formation, coaches must have the offensive unit work on correct alignment repeatedly during practice. Coaches can promote the learning of correct alignments by limiting the number of alignments used.

Now let's look at the basic alignments and responsibilities of each position on offense.

MISSTEP

There are too many or too few offensive players on the field.

CORRECTION

The coach must make sure all players know their personnel group. Changes and substitutions must be worked on during practice.

MISSTEP

A player lines up in wrong formation.

CORRECTION

The offensive unit must repeatedly practice correct formations. Promote learning by limiting the number of alignments used.

OFFENSIVE LINEMEN

The offense must have five offensive linemen (figure 1.4) on the field at all times. The offensive linemen consist of a center, two guards, and two tackles. Their primary job is to block defensive players to prevent them from tackling the player with the ball.

Figure 1.4   Offensive linemen: center, two guards, two tackles.

On a running play, the offensive line might block to give the running back an unobstructed path. On a pass play, the offensive line might prevent defenders from getting to the quarterback before he can throw the pass.

Offensive linemen are usually the largest players on a team. Because bigger generally means stronger, the bulk of these players helps the offensive line drive defenders away from the ball carrier. The bulk of the linemen also makes it more difficult for defenders to get around them. The bigger the offensive linemen, the better they can block defenders—*if* they maintain sufficient ability to move. Offensive linemen don't require great running speed, but they do need "quick feet." This means they can move short distances quickly. Quick feet also entails good reaction—the ability to adjust to the unpredictable movements of the defensive players. Offensive linemen also need flexibility in the lower body to get into a good football stance, move on the snap with quickness and agility, and react to the defense.

Overall strength, in both upper and lower body, is critical for offensive linemen. In essence, the offensive line must push very large defensive players out of the way—and they must do this at least 70 times a game, which means they also need great stamina.

Offensive linemen require physical and mental toughness as well. They cannot allow themselves to be pushed around, and must do their job in virtual obscurity. Offensive linemen seldom get the accolades that quarterbacks and running backs get. But without the offensive line, other offensive players would not be able to function.

Center

The center (figure 1.5) begins each offensive play by snapping the football. The snap must be a quick and continuous backward motion from the ball's starting position on the ground. The snap may be either through the center's legs (the usual method) or not. Prior to snapping the ball back, the center may not move the ball either forward or up. The center may make calls to other linemen to inform them how the defense is aligned or to tell them which blocking scheme to use based on the front.

Figure 1.5 Position of the center.

The center must be able to recognize the defensive scheme and direct other linemen accordingly. He must be able to snap the ball accurately every time whether the quarterback is under center or in shotgun position. He must then be able to step to the correct defensive man to block. The act of snapping and stepping simultaneously is unique to the center and should be foremost in mind when choosing who will play this position. The center need not be the biggest lineman, but he should probably be the most athletic.

Offensive Guard

The offensive guards (figure 1.6) line up on either side of the center. Guards must not only block defenders in their initial area but are many times asked to pull left or right to block defenders in other areas. This requires enough agility to move quickly from their aligned spot to other areas, usually ahead of the ball carrier. Speed and athleticism are prerequisites for this position. Guards are often a little smaller than tackles for this reason.

Figure 1.6 Position of the guards.

Offensive Tackle

The offensive tackles (figure 1.7) line up outside their respective guards. Tackles are often taller and heavier than guards and centers because their primary blocking responsibility is in their immediate area. Defensive ends are often tall and thus require taller blockers to negate their height on pass plays. Tackles also protect the defense's outside pass-rush lanes on pass plays and so benefit from a longer arm span to reach the rusher coming outside. Tackles may also be asked to pull outside or inside to lead a play, so agility is also important.

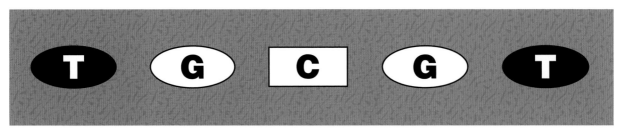

Figure 1.7 Position of the tackles.

In many cases, the left tackle should be the more talented and accomplished of the two tackles because he'll be protecting the right-handed quarterback's blind side on pass plays. Because the quarterback can't see a threat coming from his back, he cannot react when a defender is coming from that side. This duty to protect the quarterback is why left tackle is the highest-paid line position in professional football.

TIGHT END

The tight end is a hybrid player, a combination of an offensive lineman and a wide receiver. On many plays, be it a run or a pass play, the tight end is asked to block as if he were a lineman. This requires a player bigger and stronger than most wide receivers. On other plays, the tight end may be asked to run a route on a pass play, which requires quickness, agility, and an ability to catch the ball.

Tight ends usually line up on the line of scrimmage outside an offensive tackle. Their alignment has much flexibility, however, because rules allow them to be just about anywhere behind the line of scrimmage as long as seven other men are on the line. Tight ends are sometimes used as extra backs, usually to block. They may also be moved around to change the offensive formation on the run, making it more difficult for the defense to react.

Figures 1.8 through 1.11 show possible tight-end alignments. Alignment usually relates to what he will be doing on the play. For example, if lined up in the backfield, he will usually have a blocking responsibility. If he lines up split away from the offensive line, he will usually be involved in a pass pattern. If he lines up next to the offensive tackle on the line of scrimmage, he may either block or release downfield for a pass.

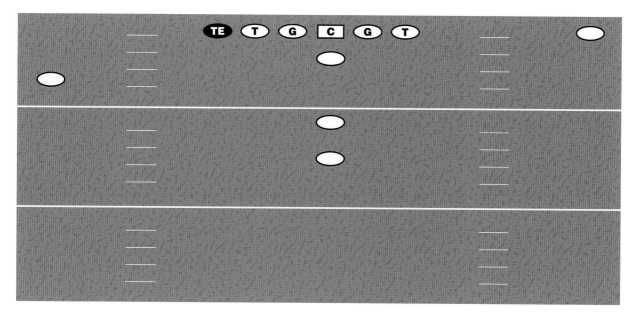

Figure 1.8   Tight end aligned on the line of scrimmage at the end of the offensive line (normal alignment).

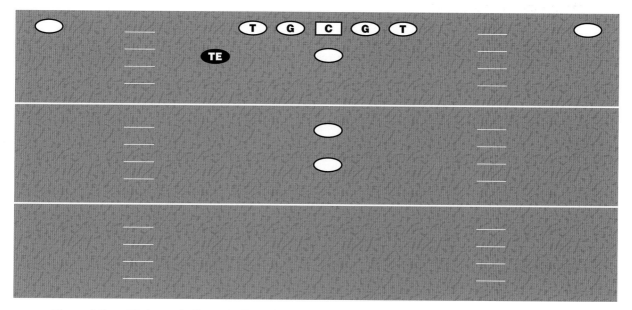

Figure 1.9   Tight end aligned off the line of scrimmage at the end of the offensive line.

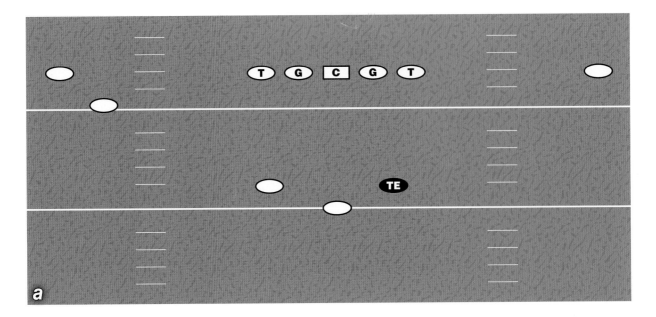

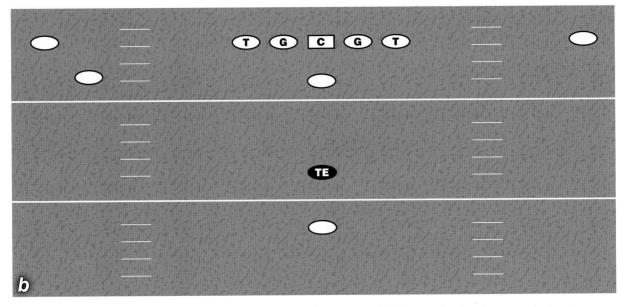

Figure 1.10 Tight end aligned in the backfield: *(a)* even with the running back or quarterback in shotgun formation; *(b)* behind the quarterback. The tight end can be aligned anywhere in the backfield, but is usually in the same position in which a fullback would align.

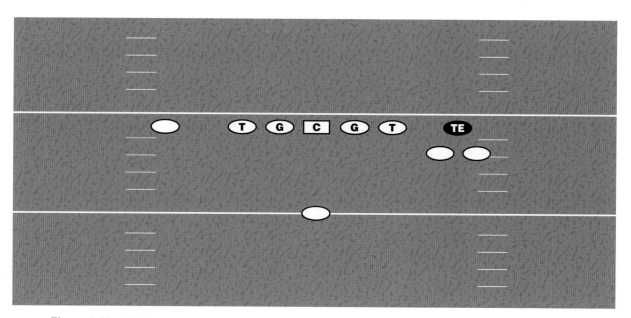

Figure 1.11   Tight end split out away from the line of scrimmage.

WIDE RECEIVER

The wide receiver lines up outside the offensive line either on the line of scrimmage or 1 to 2 yards off the line. The wide receiver's primary responsibility is to run pass routes and catch passes. The wide receiver must be an excellent runner with good speed and good hands to catch passes. The best receivers tend to be tall with excellent speed, although many different talent levels and body types have had great success at this position. Wide receivers might be asked to block on occasion, but this is not what they are known for.

RUNNING BACK

The two types of running backs are the tailback and the fullback. Traditionally, the tailback is the faster, quicker, and sometimes smaller of the two. He is the one with the primary responsibility to carry the ball on most run plays. He needs to be able to accelerate quickly to hit holes in the offensive line. He also needs the abilities to quickly recognize openings and to abruptly change direction to avoid tacklers. Overall speed is a plus as well. For the tailback, size is not as important as running ability. The ability to catch passes adds to his utility.

The fullback is usually stronger than the tailback and is often regarded as a blocker. Many teams use their fullback to block for the tailback on run plays and to protect the quarterback on pass plays. The best fullbacks, though, have good strength and size and can run the ball. In short-yardage or goal-line situations, the fullback might be called on to carry the ball the few yards needed to gain the first down or score. A fullback is sometimes required to gain 1 or 2 yards against a defense that knows he is coming and where he will be.

QUARTERBACK

The quarterback might be the most important offensive player. Often, he calls the offensive plays in the huddle and executes any play checks at the line of scrimmage. He is usually the player who handles the snap from the center and must get the ball to the running back on run plays or to the receiver on pass plays. He must have strong leadership skills, confidence, an ability to see and read defenses and make the correct play call at the line of scrimmage, the ability to handle the ball from the snap to the handoff without mishap, and of course the ability to throw passes with speed and accuracy. Quarterbacks come in many sizes, but taller quarterbacks can see receivers downfield better on pass plays (linemen tend to be tall!).

On offense, the quarterback is the coach on the field. He instills confidence in his teammates and controls what happens in and out of the huddle. Sometimes the offensive play called in the huddle is not the best one to run against a particular defensive alignment. In such a case, it's the quarterback's job to change the play call at the line of scrimmage (before the snap) and call a better play. This requires a player who can recognize defensive alignments and make sound decisions within a matter of seconds.

On run plays, the quarterback must take the center's snap and hand the ball to the running back smoothly (and sometimes with deception), which requires good eye–hand coordination and timing and a firm handling of the ball. This allows the running back to take the ball with confidence without having to look at it—he needs to keep his eyes on the running hole.

An effective quarterback must be able to throw several kinds of passes: the long pass (the bomb), the timing pass, the deep-out pass, the touch pass, and the throw-away pass. The stronger the quarterback's arm, the better chance he'll throw all these passes effectively. That said, many great quarterbacks do not have cannons for arms but are still very effective. We'll talk more about the quarterback and types of passes later in the book.

Offensive schemes in football tend to cycle. The option-run scheme was very popular and successful 20 to 30 years ago. The option required quarterbacks to be good runners, but some of them were not as good at passing the ball. As the option became less popular, offensive schemes began to highlight passing quarterbacks, which is still the norm for most teams. In recent years, however, some excellent running quarterbacks have allowed some coaches to put the quarterback run back into their offensive playbooks.

The physical qualities required at each offensive position depend partly on the offensive scheme a team is using—the team's way of doing things. This being the case, coaches must either design a scheme to fit their players or recruit players to fit their scheme.

Quarterback Under Center

When the quarterback aligns directly behind the center, he takes the ball directly out of the center's hands on the snap (figure 1.12). The quarterback should place his hands between the center's legs. His hands should be touching at the base of the palms with the fingers of each hand pointing directly away from each other, at least as wide as the ball. If the quarterback is right-handed, he should have his right hand on top and laid flat on the center's crotch. The left hand should have the fingers extended at an angle toward the ground.

As the center snaps the ball up to the quarterback's hands, the quarterback keeps his hand pressed against the center until the ball makes contact with his upper (right) hand. When the ball makes contact, the quarterback closes his bottom (left) hand onto the ball to secure it.

MISSTEP

The quarterback drops the ball on the snap.

CORRECTION

The quarterback's hands must stay in contact with the center's crotch until the ball makes contact with the top hand.

Figure 1.12 Quarterback securing the snap from the center.

Quarterback From the Shotgun Position

In the shotgun position, the quarterback aligns 4 to 5 yards behind the center to receive the snap (figure 1.13). Instead of the center snapping the ball directly from his hands to the quarterback's hands, the center passes the ball between his legs and sends it through the air to the quarterback.

The quarterback keeps hands about belly level, slightly apart, with fingers pointing to the outside. He watches the ball as it leaves the center's hands and travels through the air to his own hands.

Figure 1.13 Quarterback lined up in shotgun position.

MISSTEP

The quarterback drops the shotgun snap, even though the snap is on target.

CORRECTION

The quarterback must see the ball as it comes to his hands. This is the same skill that's needed when a receiver is catching a pass. The quarterback should watch the ball until it makes contact with his hands.

SUCCESS SUMMARY

In step 1 we have described the three basic units on a team—offense, defense, and special teams—and focused on the offense. We have discussed the responsibilities for each position on offense and highlighted factors that lead to success. We have also covered some basic offensive personnel groups and offensive formations to show how each position fits into overall schemes.

In step 2 we discuss the defense. We'll focus on the positions on defense and their responsibilities and touch on possible defensive personnel groups and alignment schemes. First, however, answer the questions that follow to check your understanding of the offensive basics we've introduced in step 1.

Before Taking the Next Step

1. What are the three basic units on a football team?

2. What are three offensive personnel groups that might be used in a game?

3. How many wide receivers are there in a 21 personnel offensive formation?

4. How many running backs are there in a 21 personnel offensive formation?

5. How many tight ends are there in an 11 personnel offensive formation?

6. If you are a player, which offensive position best fits your size, speed, and abilities?

Defensive Positions and Responsibilities

As we mentioned in step 1, the main job of the defense is to prevent the offense from scoring. A secondary job of the defense is to try to get the ball back for their own offense. In many ways, the defense must react to what the offense does. The defense rarely knows what will happen on each play, which means players must be able to react quickly; all players on defense must work in coordination to defend any play the offense might run. This takes a thorough knowledge of defensive responsibilities. It requires reading what the offense is doing—on both alignments and specific plays—and reacting quickly and properly.

Defensive teams consist of three position areas: the defensive line, made up of the defensive tackles and defensive ends; the inside and outside linebackers; and the defensive backs (safeties and cornerbacks).

The makeup of a defense depends on its overall scheme. The 4-3, 4-2, 5-2, and 3-4 are common defensive schemes. The 4-3 defensive scheme (figure 2.1) has four linemen, three linebackers, and four backs. The 3-4 defensive scheme (figure 2.2) has three linemen, four linebackers, and four backs. The 4-2 scheme (figure 2.3) has four linemen, two linebackers, and five backs. The 3-3 stack scheme (figure 2.4) has three linemen, three linebackers, and five backs.

We'll now discuss the position groups in ways that can apply to each of these schemes.

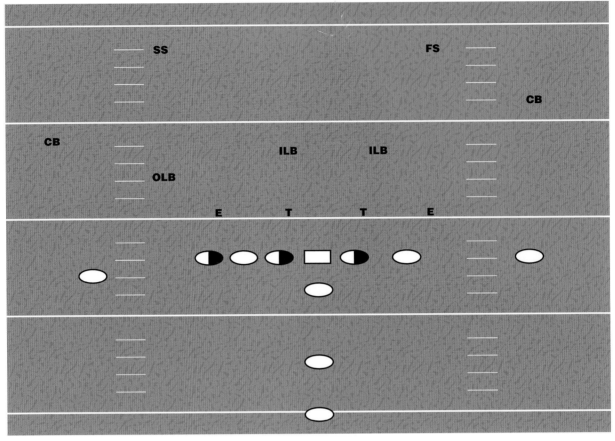

Figure 2.1 4-3 defensive scheme.

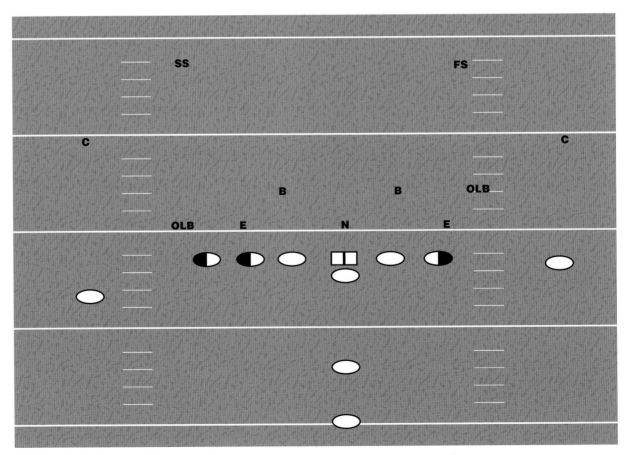

Figure 2.2 3-4 defensive scheme.

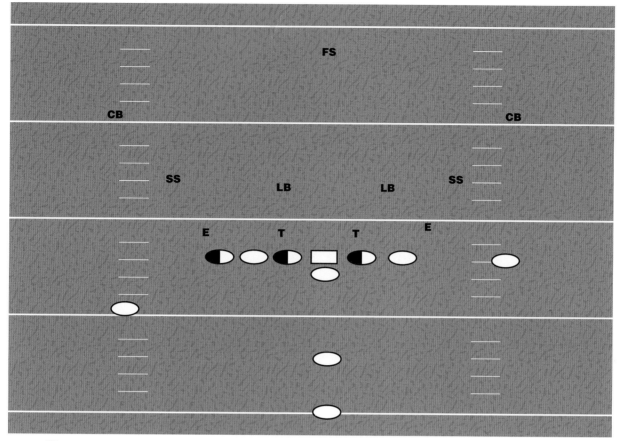

Figure 2.3   4-2 defensive scheme.

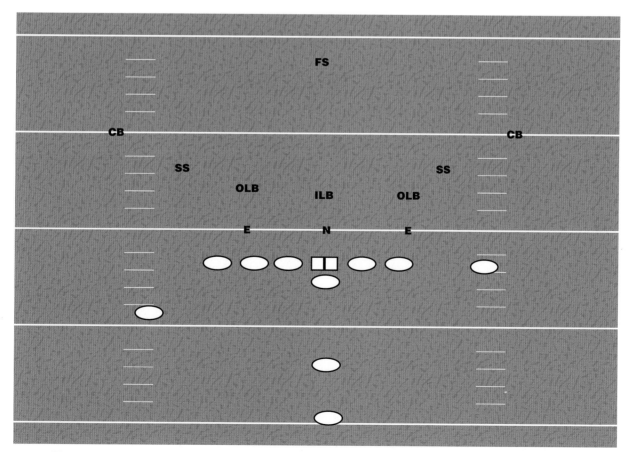

Figure 2.4   3-3 stack scheme.

DEFENSIVE LINEMAN

Defensive linemen line up directly in front of the offensive linemen. Their primary responsibility is to take on the blocks of the offensive linemen, hold their ground, and tackle any ball carrier who tries to run by their gap. Defensive linemen typically line up directly on the line of scrimmage in a three-point stance. They are usually assigned to defend a particular gap—the space between two offensive linemen. Their job also includes rushing the quarterback on pass plays, either to prevent the pass by sacking the quarterback or to pressure the quarterback into a poor throw. Many coaches use a common nomenclature system (figure 2.5) to designate the alignment positions of defensive linemen.

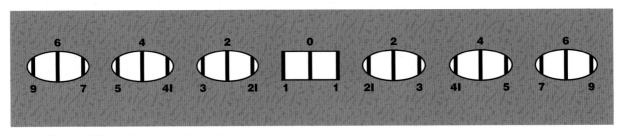

Figure 2.5   Defensive line alignments.

Any alignment head-up to an offensive lineman is an even number: 0, 2, 4, or 6. Most alignments on the offensive lineman's shoulder are odd numbers: 1, 3, 5, 7, or 9. The only exceptions are when a player aligns on the offensive guard's inside shoulder, which is known as a 2I (2 inside) technique. Likewise, an alignment on the offensive tackle's inside shoulder is known as a 4I (4 inside). You can use any numbering or lettering system you want to designate these alignments.

To further use this system, a defensive lineman who lines up on the offensive guard's outside shoulder is known as a 3-technique lineman. One who is aligned on the offensive center's shoulder (either side) is a 1 technique. A defensive end who lines up on the offensive tackle's outside shoulder is known as a 5 technique. This system is a quick and easy way to designate an alignment and subsequently a player's technique.

Defensive Tackle

Those players aligned on the offensive guards or center are also sometimes called defensive tackles. A defensive lineman who consistently lines up on the offensive center may be known as the nose tackle. Using the numbering system shown in figure 2.5, these defensive linemen can be known as 0 technique, 1 technique, 2I technique, 2 technique, or 3 technique.

These players require good size and strength. They are primarily run defenders, responsible for any run that comes to the inside-run gaps. Initial quickness out of the stance is critical in that the defensive lineman must attack the offensive lineman before the offensive lineman can establish his blocking momentum. This get-off quickness comes in part from the player's natural ability to see the ball movement on the snap and react instantly by coming out of his stance to attack the offensive lineman lined up over him. The quickness needed can also be developed to a certain extent. Defensive linemen should spend a great deal of practice time seeing the ball snapped and moving out of the stance as quickly as possible. The more times they can practice this basic move, the more ingrained it will become so that in a game it comes naturally without thinking. Proper footwork is critical in developing this skill. In a later chapter we'll discuss proper footwork for defensive linemen.

Players who can play with a low center of gravity (knees bent) and use their hands effectively do well as defensive tackles. They must be able to attack offensive linemen using their hands rather than their arms. This involves leading with the hands coming out of the stance, a skill not natural for everyone. The defensive lineman should "punch" the offensive blocker. The punch with the hands is important to stop the blocker's forward movement and maintain a position near the original spot at which the defensive lineman lined up. The defensive lineman uses his hands to hold the offensive lineman away from him. If the defensive lineman uses his forearms or shoulders to hit the offensive lineman, he allows the offensive lineman to get close to his body and grab his jersey, pads, or body to hold on to as he blocks. This makes it very difficult for the defensive lineman to disengage from the block and pursue the ball carrier. By using his hands to hold the offensive blocker away from his body, the defensive lineman puts himself in position to make a play on the ball carrier.

Physical toughness is very important for defensive linemen. Defensive linemen have to hit and be hit by offensive linemen on nearly every play. This constant pounding can wear out a player who is not used to it or cannot handle it. The defensive lineman will often be double-teamed, attacked by two offensive blockers at once, and must be able to hold his ground. This takes tremendous strength and toughness. The defensive lineman must fight to maintain his position. If he's not able to, the offensive lineman will create a large hole for the ball carrier to run through.

Defensive tackles need good reaction time and quickness as they change direction after coming out of the stance. A popular type of block for an offense to use is called a trap block, in which the offensive lineman aligned over the defensive tackle does not block him. Instead, the offensive lineman goes to block someone else, leaving the defensive lineman temporarily unblocked. The defensive lineman must then quickly determine who will block him and where he will come from. He must react quickly and not allow the blocker to get a good angle on him. This involves a very quick change of direction by the defender in order to prevent the trapping blocker to hit him unprepared.

Defensive tackles are typically not considered the most effective pass rushers on the defensive line, although they certainly can be. There are several reasons for this. First, defensive tackles tend to be bigger and weigh more, so they may not be as fast as the defensive ends. Second, the area they are forced to pass-rush in is more limited in space, and there may be an extra offensive lineman nearby to help block. It is possible to isolate a defensive lineman on a single pass blocker if you have one who's skilled in pass rushing.

Defensive End

The defensive linemen who line up on offensive tackles or tight ends are considered defensive ends. They might be called 5 techniques, 6 techniques, 7 techniques, or 9 techniques based on where they line up and who they line up on. If they consistently line up on offensive tackles (4 techniques, 5 techniques), they must have excellent size and strength, primarily because the offensive tackles tend to be the biggest and strongest of the offensive linemen. If the defensive ends line up on tight ends consistently (6, 7, or 9 techniques), size is not as important as quickness and overall speed. This is because tight ends tend to be smaller than tackles and because the defensive end might have more space to defend. Both types of defensive ends need good speed because they are usually outside pass rushers with farther to go to get to the quarterback, and the best chance to beat the slower offensive tackles. Defensive ends need good initial quickness similar to the tackles, but overall speed is more important at this position.

MISSTEP

The defensive lineman lines up in the wrong gap and is not able to defend the gap.

CORRECTION

To line up correctly, the defensive lineman must understand the defensive scheme call and remember his gap responsibility.

MISSTEP

During a play, the defensive lineman allows the offensive lineman to get between him and his gap.

CORRECTION

To keep the offensive lineman from getting between him and his gap responsibility, the defensive lineman must properly execute his defensive run technique. This is covered in step 8.

LINEBACKER

Linebackers must have good size and strength to defend against the run, as well as overall speed and quickness to defend against the pass. Linebackers are usually assigned a run gap to defend. They must defend the run first, pass second.

Inside linebackers tend to be a little bigger (they take on offensive linemen as blockers), whereas outside linebackers can be a littler smaller because they generally take on wide receivers and tight ends as blockers. In some defensive schemes, the inside linebackers might have different attributes from each other as well. For example, if a scheme has the defensive linemen in front of, say, the left inside linebacker, lined up in the same position relative to the offensive line every play, then the two inside linebackers may have slightly different abilities. The alignment shown in figure 2.6 (under shade front) has the left inside linebacker lined up behind a 3 technique and a 5 technique. The right inside linebacker is lined up behind a 1 technique, a 5 technique, and a 9 technique outside linebacker.

Because the left linebacker (LLB) has an uncovered offensive lineman in front of him, he will need to be able to take on that lineman's block by himself. This is usually a size mismatch, so the left linebacker will need more size and strength if he's going to be in this alignment very often. The right linebacker (RLB) has no uncovered offensive lineman who can come out to block him. He is protected by the alignment of the defensive linemen. Because he is protected, he will not need to have the size and strength of the right linebacker. Coaches must look at the defensive scheme

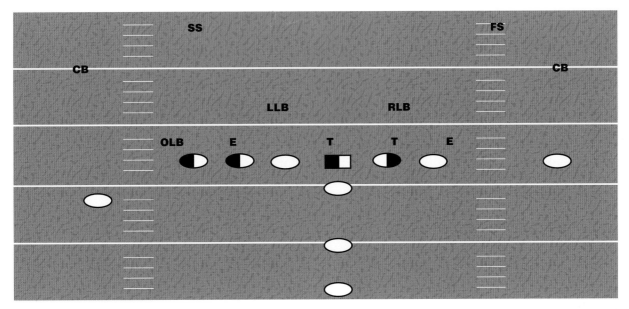

Figure 2.6   Under shade front.

or alignment that is used consistently in order to determine the size and strength needed by the inside linebacker.

Outside linebackers (OLB) may have more space to cover to defend passes and thus need better speed in general than inside linebackers. Because outside linebackers may be taking on the blocks of the tight end or wide receivers more often, size is not as critical for them as for the inside linebackers. But if an outside linebacker will be lining up consistently on a tight end (such as in figure 2.6), he will need more size and strength than if he's lined up off the line of scrimmage, as shown in figure 2.7.

In most cases, the offensive player whom the outside linebacker is responsible for is larger than the offensive player blocking the inside linebacker. This means the outside linebacker benefits from being faster and possibly more agile than the inside linebacker. Again, much depends on the defensive scheme being used—which is why coaches need to assess players' abilities when setting up their schemes. The scheme a coach teaches should exploit the abilities of his players to maximize chances for success.

If a defense is functioning well, the linebackers will make most of the tackles, so they must be sure tacklers also excel at getting off of blockers. This takes good change-of-direction skill (agility), strength, and technique. Linebackers are sometimes considered the best all-around players on defense because they're asked to defend against the run at the line of scrimmage as well as defend against the pass plays in the backfield. This requires speed and agility.

MISSTEP

The linebacker does not attack the line of scrimmage on a run play.

CORRECTION

The linebacker must press (run toward) the line of scrimmage once he identifies a run play, being sure to press toward the gap he is responsible for.

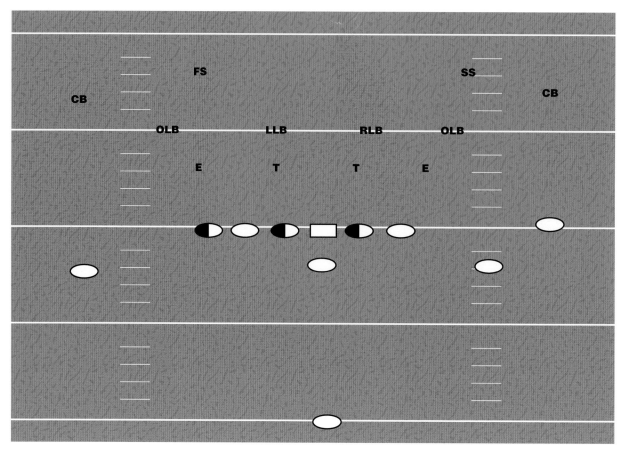

Figure 2.7 Flex front.

MISSTEP

The linebacker drops back to defend a pass when the offense is executing a run play, or he moves to defend a run when the offense is executing a pass play.

CORRECTION

The linebacker must read his run-pass key on every play. The key will tell the linebacker if the play is a run or pass play. The linebacker must focus on his run-pass key consistently at the beginning of each play.

DEFENSIVE BACK

The two kinds of defensive backs are safeties and cornerbacks. A defense's overall scheme and coverage philosophy will determine the requirements for each position. For example, on a team that plays primarily zone pass defense, safeties can be bigger, more physical players. If the team plays primarily man-to-man coverage, safeties must be more athletic to cover the athletic wide receivers. The same applies to a lesser degree with the cornerbacks.

Generally, safeties align behind the linebackers and are involved a great deal in defending the run game. They often have equal responsibility for defending the run and the pass. They must have good size—not linebacker size, but bigger than cornerbacks.

Cornerbacks must have excellent speed and agility. They are primarily involved in defending the pass, usually in the open field against the fastest players on offense— the wide receivers. Cornerbacks don't have to be as physical as other defensive players but must be sure open-field tacklers. Overall size is not as critical for the cornerback, although you don't want too much of a size mismatch between the cornerback and the offensive players. Cornerbacks also need short memories! Because their primary responsibility is usually the deep-pass zone, they are constantly challenged to stop the long bomb. When a cornerback gets beat deep, the result is always a big play for the opponent, often a touchdown. Everyone knows the corner got beat. If he worries about it, he'll lose focus and likely will get beat again. He must be able to shake off the bad play and focus on the next one.

Again, the required attributes of the cornerback are influenced by the defensive pass scheme being used. If a defense uses more blitzes with man-to-man pass coverage, the corners (and safeties) will need more movement skills. This includes overall running speed, but even more important is change-of-direction speed (agility) because the defender must stay close to the receiver throughout the play. If the defense is more of a zone pass scheme, the cornerback might be able to get away with being a little less athletic because he will be defending an area of the field rather than running right with the receiver throughout the play. He will need good reaction time to break on the thrown ball once he sees it. Reaction time is a skill that can be improved by working on signals that tell defenders when the ball will be thrown and where it is likely going.

MISSTEP

The defensive back doesn't stay in his assigned zone because he misreads the play as a run and moves up to defend the run.

CORRECTION

The defensive back must read his run-pass key consistently and accurately. This is covered in detail in step 8.

MISSTEP

A receiver runs a route near but not into the defensive back's zone, and the defensive back leaves his zone to cover the receiver.

CORRECTION

The defensive back must understand where his zone is and recognize when a receiver is in or out of it. He must not leave his zone open.

MISSTEP

The defensive back responsible for a deep zone allows a receiver to get behind him.

CORRECTION

Any defensive back covering a deep zone must make sure no offensive player ever gets behind him.

SUCCESS SUMMARY

In step 2 we have looked at the defensive unit, including the characteristics, alignments, and skills needed for success at each defensive position. There are many possible combinations of the three basic defensive groups—defensive line, linebackers, and defensive backs. There are also many alignments and responsibilities possible. The majority of these are directly influenced by the kind of offensive system the defense is facing. Coaches must know their players. This allows them to fill defensive positions with the players best suited for them. Also, the better a coach knows his players, the better he can work with them to improve the abilities they require to succeed in their positions.

In step 3 we'll look at the fundamental skills and abilities that every player needs for success in football, regardless of the position he plays. Before moving to step 3, check your understanding of the basic defensive concepts introduced in step 2 by answering the questions that follow.

Before Taking the Next Step

1. What are the three basic position groups on a defense?

2. What are three defensive schemes?

3. Who is primarily responsible for stopping running plays?

4. Who is primarily responsible for stopping pass plays?

5. Who must help stop both running and pass plays?

6. If you are a player, what defensive position do you feel best fits your size, speed, and abilities?

Fundamental Skills for All Positions

In this step we look at fundamental physical and mental skills essential to playing successful football. Although some skills are more important to specific positions, several fundamentals are common to all positions. We will discuss these first and then cover skills specific to offensive and defensive positions. In succeeding steps, we'll cover these skills in more detail in relation to each position.

We can classify fundamental football skills into two categories: general physical movement skills and skills related to a position, such as how a particular player gets into a stance before the start of the play. These fundamental skills are crucial for success at each position. The majority of practice time should be spent on mastering these essential core fundamentals.

CORE FUNDAMENTALS

The fundamentals required of all football players regardless of position are running speed, change-of-direction speed (agility), lower-body flexibility, and eye–hand coordination.

Running Speed

In football, speed is generally measured by a player's time in running the 40-yard dash. This distance was likely established because the average play lasts about as long as it takes to run a 40-yard dash. How much speed a player needs to be successful depends on his position and his level of play. For example, at the college level, an offensive lineman who can run a 40-yard dash in the low 5 seconds can be successful. At the high school level, this time can increase slightly and still lead to success. Table 3.1 shows recommended times for high school and college players for each position group. Keep in mind these figures are not etched in stone. Many excellent players have been slower than the times suggested here.

Table 3.1 Recommended Times by Position for the 40-Yard Dash

Position	High school (seconds)	College (seconds)
Offensive lineman	5.3 to 6.0	5.0 to 5.4
Tight end	4.8 to 5.2	4.6 to 4.8
Quarterback	4.6 to 4.9	4.5 to 4.9
Running back	4.5 to 4.8	4.4 to 4.6
Wide receiver	4.5 to 4.8	4.4 to 4.6
Defensive lineman	4.9 to 5.2	4.8 to 5.0
Linebacker	4.7 to 5.0	4.6 to 4.8
Defensive back	4.5 to 4.9	4.4 to 4.6

These speeds help players perform their position skills more efficiently. In general, the faster a player is, the better. A player can never be too fast!

We are born with the majority of our running speed potential. Muscle fiber makeup has a great deal to do with speed and endurance. We all have two basic types of muscle fibers: fast twitch and slow twitch. Fast-twitch fibers are associated with muscle contraction speed. The higher the percentage of fast-twitch fibers we have, the faster we can move. Slow-twitch fibers are associated with a muscle's ability to contract repeatedly. The higher percentage of slow-twitch fibers we have, the longer we can work.

We cannot change the percentage of fast-twitch or slow-twitch fibers we are born with, but we can develop those that we do have. In general, to develop fast-twitch fibers, we need to work the muscles involved in shorter, more powerful movements. Running short sprints (10, 20, 30, 40 yards) repeatedly can help develop fast-twitch fibers (see speed drill 1, described later in the chapter). Track athletes are usually adept at this type of training. For more information on fast-twitch fibers, refer to a good book on training for track and field.

Another way to develop speed is to work on running form (figure 3.1). The basic tenets of running form include leg movement, arm movement, and body angle. Leg movement refers to both the angle at which you move your legs and the rate at which you take strides. In reference to the angle, the important factors to remember include knee height when striding, foot and leg extension prior to bringing the foot down to the ground, and the pull exerted on the ground by the foot as the body passes over it. Many drills will develop good form, but one of the best is the claw drill described later in the chapter.

For best efficiency, keep legs moving in a straight line in the direction you are moving. In other words, try to point the toe and knee in that direction. As you finish driving the leg back and begin to lift it to come forward for another stride, bring your foot up to your butt as you drive the knee forward to approximately parallel to the ground in front. As your knee approaches that parallel position, your foot reaches ahead as far as possible prior to coming down on the ground again. As your foot contacts the ground in front, pull the foot backward powerfully. This is called the claw action because you are trying to "claw" at the ground quickly by pulling your foot back behind your body.

The upper body is important to running speed in several ways. The arms need to swing forward and back in close to a straight line in the direction being run. Any side-to-side rotation of the arms causes rotation of the entire body and reduces forward movement.

Figure 3.1   **GOOD RUNNING FORM**

1. Legs move in straight line in direction you want to move
2. Knee and toe point in direction you want to move
3. Front foot "claws" the ground quickly
4. Arms swing in a straight line in direction being run

5. Front hand is even with shoulders, back hand is even with back pocket
6. Elbows remain bent
7. Maintain a slightly forward lean

Arm swing is also critical to running speed. The rate at which you swing your arms affects your stride length. The shorter the arm swing, the shorter the stride length. The longer the arm swing, the longer the stride length. The general rule is to swing the arms so the hand is even with the shoulders in front and with the back pocket in back. Arms should stay at about a 90-degree angle as they swing. The elbow should not straighten during the arm swing because this can shorten the arm swing and thus shorten the stride length. A good mental picture for the arm swing is to drive the elbows on the backswing as if trying to punch a bag behind the body.

Body angle is important in that you need a slight forward body lean to enable the stride length to remain long. When you lean back, you tend to take shorter strides, causing you to slow down.

Each of these core skills works in conjunction with other skills. A player may lack one skill but make up for it with another stronger one. One skill that can help make up for a lack of running speed is change-of-direction speed, also called agility.

Speed Drill 1   Repeated 10-Yard Sprints

This simple drill emphasizes explosive movement (fast-twitch fibers) and is also a good conditioning drill.

Players start in a three-point stance. On command, they sprint 10 yards as fast as they can. They immediately turn around, assume the three-point stance again, and sprint back 10 yards as fast they can. The focus is on explosive movement out of the stance and through the 10 yards to develop fast-twitch response. For conditioning, run this drill 3 to 5 times in a row (a total of 6 to 10 sprints), rest briefly, and then repeat, running 5 or 6 sets (a total of 10 to 12 sprints).

Success Check

- Focus on exploding out of the three-point stance.

- Sprint hard through the 10 yards.

Speed Drill 2   Claw Drill

Players stand with one hand on a wall, chair, or partner for balance. They work one leg at a time—the leg opposite the support leg.

Players raise knees waist high. Using a quick, circular motion, they claw at the ground with the foot, brushing the foot across the ground with toe pulled up. They then pull the heel as close to the butt as possible. From this point, they pull the knee forward and up, and repeat the motion. They make one continuous circular motion, emphasizing the powerful and quick clawing of the ground. Run 8 to 10 repetitions of the drill on one leg, switch legs, and repeat. Do several sets on each leg.

Success Check

- Perform one continuous circular motion.

- Focus on powerfully clawing the ground with the foot.

Change-of-Direction Speed (Agility)

Change of direction is the ability to run in one direction, stop moving in that direction, quickly change direction, and regain top running speed.

Agility is enhanced when you move with your center of gravity low and knees bent in a football position. Before you can stop moving in one direction and start moving in another, you need to slow down as quickly as possible. If running with your center of gravity high, you need to lower it before you can change direction. This takes time. A player with a high center of gravity who tries to change direction will take two to four steps to slow down and change direction. The player who runs with a low center of gravity can usually slow down and change direction in one or two steps. Obviously, this takes less time, and the player regains top speed in the new direction more quickly. For a low center of gravity, run with a good knee-bend. This goes back to the football stance.

Any drill in which players move in one direction and then stop and move in another should help develop agility. Different drills can work on different types of agility. You can work on shuffling sideways and stopping to move back in the opposite direction in a shuffle. You can run forward, stop, and run backward. You can work change of direction by having a coach (or friend) give a verbal or visual command to stop and change direction.

Change-of-direction drills can be combined with other skill-development drills. For example, a good agility drill for all players who handle the football involves a coach (or friend) throwing the ball to the player while he is running over bags on the ground. This is a great drill to help players focus on the eye–hand coordination needed to catch the ball. The coach can use his imagination on how players should run over the bags and when he will throw the ball. There are many variations.

Speed and change of direction are affected by overall lower-body flexibility. Other movements in football are also affected by flexibility. In general, the more flexible your body, especially the lower body, the better you can execute many of the core skills in football.

Change-of-Direction Running Drill 1
Short Shuttle

The most common measure of change of direction is called the short shuttle (figure 3.2). The short shuttle is a timed race in which players run a total of 20 yards, changing directions twice—once to the right and once to the left.

Players face the timer (coach). They run to one side for 5 yards and touch the line with a hand. They then run in the opposite direction for 10 yards and touch the line with the opposite hand. They finish by running back past the original start line.

Have players turn toward the timer (coach) each time. This ensures that they turn both to the right and the left during the run.

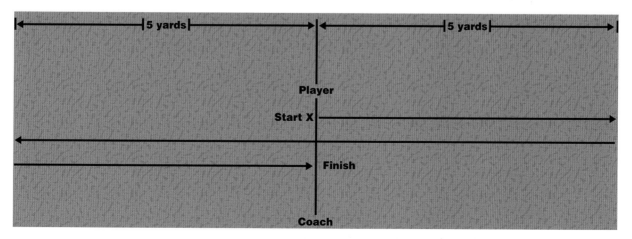

Figure 3.2 Short shuttle.

Success Check

- A good time in the short shuttle might be a better indicator of football success than a good time in the 40-yard dash. This is because success in football can require changing directions many times during a single play.

- As with time in the 40-yard dash, the relation of a short shuttle time to football success depends on the player's position and level of play.

Rate Your Success

Table 3.2 provides recommended short shuttle times with their relative values.

Table 3.2   Suggested Short Shuttle Times

Time (seconds)	Rating	Notes
Less than 4.0	Excellent	Very few players, even elite players, are in this range.
4.0 to 4.3	Very good	Successful defensive backs, running backs, and wide receivers are usually in this range.
4.3 to 4.5	Good	Successful linebackers, tight ends, and a few defensive linemen will be in this range.
4.5 to 4.8	Average	Most larger players will be in this range.
More than 4.8	Below average	A player in this range will struggle with moving quickly enough to be successful.

Change-of-Direction Running Drill 2   **W Drill**

Another drill that helps develop change-of-direction skills is the W drill.

Players start in a good football stance. On command, they backpedal at a 45-degree angle back and to the right (figure 3.3). At a point 5 yards back, which is designated by field lines or a cone, they plant their foot and push forward, changing their running direction from backward to forward. As they change direction, they angle forward at a 45-degree angle to the right. They should be facing the same direction throughout the drill. They continue changing direction six to eight times or for a designated distance, such as sideline to hash marks.

Success Check

- Begin in a good football stance.

- Focus on a strong change of direction, not necessarily speed.

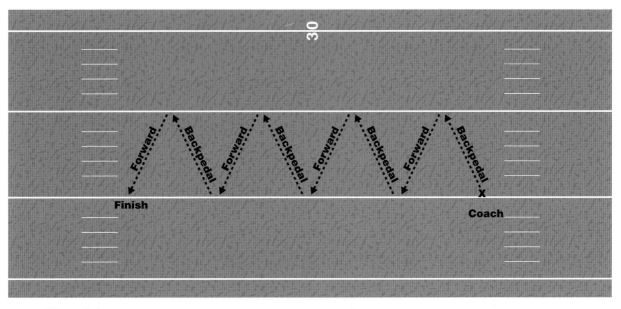

Figure 3.3 W drill.

Lower-Body Flexibility

Flexibility refers to the ability to move a joint in its full range of motion. Flexibility is controlled by the connective tissue of the joints, mainly muscle tendons and ligaments. We are all born with maximum flexibility in our joints. As we mature, we tend not to use our joints in their full maximum range motion, so we lose some of that flexibility.

A player who is not flexible in his ankles, legs, and hips will struggle with movements required in football. To be able to run or change direction quickly, you must have good range of motion in your joints, especially the ankles, knees, and hips.

Running speed is affected by stride length. The longer your stride, the faster you can run, assuming the turnover rate is the same. (Turnover rate is the number of strides per minute you take while running. The more strides per minute, the higher your turnover rate.) Tightness in the hamstrings (the muscles in the back of the upper leg) or quadriceps (the muscles in the front of the upper leg) will limit your ability to stride. The same is true of any of the other muscles of the hips.

We can all improve our flexibility. Doing regular lower-body stretching exercises can develop the flexibility needed for football. Yoga is also excellent for improving flexibility.

With good lower-body flexibility, players can maintain what we call the *football stance* throughout their movements. The football stance is the position you are in if you start to sit down in a chair but stop five or six inches short of the seat—hold that position, and you're in the football stance. With knees slightly bent, back slightly arched, chest out and head up, you are in the right position to start to run or to change direction quickly. Good flexibility allows involved muscles to fire quickly and powerfully in the desired direction to allow optimal movement. Players who are not flexible and can't bend their knees or hips to attain the football stance generally cannot move quickly and powerfully enough for success in football.

Flexibility Drill   Sumo Squat

This is a good drill to develop lower-body flexibility and to warm players up before practice. Players spread feet apart slightly wider than shoulder-width with toes pointed slightly out. They squat down as far as possible, keeping their feet flat on the ground. They try to get down far enough so that their hamstrings touch their calf muscles, like a catcher in baseball. They hold this position for 5 to 10 seconds before rising. Repeat four or five times.

Success Check

- Hold the down position; don't just jump back up.

- Feel the stretch in the legs.

Eye–Hand Coordination

All sports involving a ball require good eye–hand coordination. Football players need good eye–hand coordination to be able to catch, throw, punch (block), and react to blocks. Eye–hand coordination is a skill we begin to acquire as infants. The more work we get seeing objects and using our hands to catch, grab, push away, and so on, the better our eye–hand coordination becomes. Unfortunately, many young players don't get enough work on this critical skill. Many young players don't go out and simply play catch with any kind of ball. Practicing catching as you grow up develops spatial judgment, which develops eye–hand coordination. In my last 10 to 15 years of coaching, I've found I need to spend more and more time on this skill with my players.

Eye–hand coordination is critical to success in football. Aside from the obvious skills of throwing and catching passes, many other skills in football call for keen eye–hand coordination. In fact, nearly every football skill involves an element of eye–hand coordination.

When blocking, players must be able to judge where they need to place their hands to be most effective. When being blocked, they must be able to judge where the other player's hands are and react appropriately with their own hands to defeat the block.

Defensive players must be able to judge the flight path of a thrown ball in order to react in the best direction. To block passes, defensive linemen must be able to read when a quarterback is about to throw a pass and judge exactly where the quarterback's hand will be.

On special teams, one of the punt returners' most critical skills is catching the punt, which is related primarily to eye–hand coordination. The same is true to a lesser degree with catching a kickoff.

One of the keys to good eye–hand coordination is being able to track visually the object you intend to hit, catch, or block. For example, when catching a ball, you must see the ball clearly before you can catch it. You can't let surrounding objects divert your visual attention. This is called *focus*, a vital skill in football. In order to focus effectively and block out distractions, pick a small spot on the ball and concentrate on that spot, rather than trying to see the entire ball. On a spiraling pass, the best focal point is the point of the ball. It might appear to be darker than the rest of the ball. By focusing on this point and bringing your hands to it, you have a better chance of getting your hands exactly where they need to be to catch the ball.

One of the best ways to develop eye–hand coordination is to repeat a skill. If you're catching a pass, the more passes thrown to you, the better you will develop the skill. The more opportunities a blocker gets to hit a defender (or a bag that simulates the defender) with correct hand placement, the better he will be at it. This leads to a basic tenet of practice: repetition, repetition, repetition, repetition! The more times a skill is practiced correctly, the more the skill becomes automatic. This is why organizing practice time is so critical, along with identifying the skills that most need to be worked on. Practice time is usually at a premium. Coaches and players must always practice as efficiently as possible.

Eye–Hand Coordination Drill   Playing Catch

The easiest drill to develop eye–hand coordination is playing catch. You can use a football or another type of ball. Tennis balls are a good alternative, especially in the offseason when you have time to change up what you are doing. The tennis ball is smaller and requires more accurate hand placement while making the catch. The more players play catch, and the more they vary their types of throws, the more they will hone their eye–hand coordination skills.

Success Check

- Play catch with different kinds of balls: footballs, tennis balls, basketballs, softballs.
- Vary the type of throw. For example, catch balls thrown over your head, to the right or the left, or at knee level. You will need to accurately judge the flight and speed of the ball and make the right adjustments to successfully complete the catch.

POSITION-SPECIFIC CORE SKILLS

Figures 3.4 and 3.5 list the core skills required for each offensive and defensive position. Some of the skills overlap positions; some do not. In succeeding steps we'll look at each core skill along with ways to develop them as we address various aspects of playing the game of football.

Offensive Positions

Basic core skills for the offensive unit include some skills common to each position: movement ability (speed and change of direction), good knee-bend, and reaction to the opponent's movement. Those positions responsible for blocking on a run or pass play will have similar core skill requirements. For example, an offensive lineman and a receiver need to develop the same blocking skills to block on a run play. The players who may handle the ball will all have similar core skill requirements when it comes to handling the ball, catching the ball, and running with the ball and avoiding defensive players. Figure 3.4 lists the most important core skills necessary to play each offensive position effectively.

Figure 3.4 CORE SKILLS FOR THE OFFENSIVE UNIT

Offensive Lineman

1. Good knee-bend
2. Blow delivery on run blocks
3. Blow delivery on pass blocks
4. Ability to change direction
5. Good reaction to defensive player movement

Tight End

1. Good knee-bend
2. Blow delivery on run blocks
3. Blow delivery on pass blocks
4. Able to change direction
5. Pass-catching ability
6. Able to run with the ball

Wide Receiver

1. Route running, including overall running ability and ability to change direction
2. Blow delivery on run blocks
3. Pass-catching ability
4. Able to run with the ball

Quarterback

1. Good ball-handling skills
2. Passing ability
3. Able to run with the ball
4. Foot movement
5. Vision
6. Decision making

Running Back

1. Footwork
2. Good ball-handling skills
3. Pass-catching ability
4. Vision
5. Able to change direction, making cuts while carrying the ball
6. Blow delivery on run blocks
7. Blow delivery on pass blocks

Defensive Positions

Basic core skills for the defensive unit are similar to those for offense: movement ability (speed and change of direction), good knee bend, and sharp reaction to the opponent's movement. Those responsible for taking on blockers on run and pass plays have similar core skill requirements, such as using the hands to defend a block and disengage from the block. Linebackers and defensive backs require core skills in catching and handling the ball, including the proper way to catch the ball and the eye–hand coordination required to make a good catch (figure 3.5).

Figure 3.5   CORE SKILLS FOR THE DEFENSIVE UNIT

Defensive Lineman
1. Stance
2. Get off
3. Blow delivery
4. Escape blocker
5. Pursuit
6. Pass rush
7. Tackling

Linebacker
1. Stance
2. Initial step
3. Blow delivery
4. Escape blocker
5. Pursuit
6. Pass drop
7. Pass rush
8. Tackling

Defensive Back
1. Stance
2. Initial steps
3. Maintain cushion and position on pass receiver
4. Break on thrown pass
5. Pursuit
6. Tackling
7. Blow delivery
8. Escape blocker

Special Teams

The core skills required for specials teams have a lot of carryover from offense and defense. The difference is that a player on special teams can go from one emphasis (blocking) to the opposite emphasis (getting away from a blocker) on the same play.

Although the core skills needed for the blockers and returners on special teams are very similar to those needed on offense and defense, two positions unique to special teams are the punter and the placekicker (figure 3.6).

Figure 3.6 CORE SKILLS FOR THE PUNTER AND KICKER

Punter

1. Good eye–hand coordination for catching the snap
2. Leg strength and power
3. Ability to hold and drop the ball for the punt
4. Proper footwork leading up to the drop of the ball and the punt
5. Leg lock, the position of the leg at contact with the ball
6. Follow-through
7. Agility to adjust to a snap that is off target

Placekicker

1. Leg strength and power
2. Eye–foot coordination
3. Proper footwork to approach the ball
4. Leg lock at point of contact with the ball

SUCCESS SUMMARY

In step 3 we have looked at skills and abilities that help all players play the game of football successfully. All players require general movement skills such as running speed, change-of-direction speed, and joint flexibility as well as skills specific to their position. General movement skills are important for every position player. Position-specific skills may or may not be common among the many positions in football. Recognizing these skills will help players know what to work on to achieve success.

Step 4 is devoted to the skill of passing the football. Before moving ahead, answer the following questions to make sure you have a thorough understanding of football's fundamental skills.

Before Taking the Next Step

1. What are the two basic classifications of skills needed to play successful football?

2. What are the four basic movement skills important for all players in football?

3. What is a good test to measure change-of-direction speed (also called agility)?

4. Why is lower-body flexibility important for offensive linemen?

5. What is one position-specific skill common to many positions?

6. What common skill do both the punter and the placekicker require for success?

Passing

The American game of football evolved from rugby. In rugby, the forward pass is illegal. Early football was a game of running the ball with maximum effort in blocking for or tackling the runner. Because passes were not part of the game, every play resulted in a ball carrier being tackled, sometimes by many defenders. Football was an extremely physical game. In fact, in the early 1900s some people wanted the sport banned because it was considered so dangerous. Deaths during games were not unheard of. Because of the outcry about the danger of the game, in 1905 new rules were established to make football safer. One of the changes was to legalize the forward pass. The thinking was that passes would open the field and minimize masses of bodies colliding on every play.

In 1906, footballs were about the same shape and similar size as rugby balls. The ball was fatter than today's football, and the ends more rounded. Although the rugby ball is oblong, as is today's football, it was not an ideal shape and size to throw what we now consider a good forward pass. The ball's size and shape made it difficult to hold the ball in a manner that allowed a good spiral. Some players even threw the ball underhanded—a carryover from rugby. Over time, most players took to throwing overhead spirals, passes in which the ball rotates on its long axis. Players found that throwing spirals made the ball fly straighter and faster than if thrown end over end. As the game progressed, the shape of the ball was modified to its present size and shape. Whether these changes were mainly to improve the aerodynamics of the ball for the pass play is a point of debate. But we can safely say that the new shape did just that. In the years since 1906 the forward pass play has become an integral part of the game. At some levels and in some offensive schemes, the forward pass is the most common play.

FORWARD PASSES AND LATERAL PASSES

Technically, a forward pass is any ball thrown underhand or overhand by an offensive player toward the defensive team's goal. The pass does not have to pass the line of scrimmage to be considered a forward pass. If the ball is thrown horizontal to or backward from the defense's goal line, it is considered a lateral pass. The main difference between a forward pass and a lateral pass is the result when the ball is not caught in the air. A lateral pass not caught in the air that hits the ground is considered a loose ball that either team can recover. This is why players from both teams scramble to recover a ball that hits the ground when the pass appears to be sideways to the line of scrimmage. A forward pass that is not caught in the air and hits the ground is considered a dead ball and marks the end of the play. The offensive team retains possession of the ball, as long as the play was not fourth down.

An important coaching point for both the offense and defense is to try to recover any ball that appears to have been thrown horizontally to the line of scrimmage. There have been many cases in which players from both teams have let a ball go because they thought a pass was a forward pass, when in fact it was a lateral.

MISSTEP

Assuming a horizontal pass was a forward pass, a player gives up on the play once the ball hits the ground.

CORRECTION

Always try to recover any ball that hits the ground on a pass that might have been a lateral.

This happened once during a game I was coaching. My team threw a pass that was technically a lateral. A defensive player picked up the ball and tried to hand it to an official, thinking the lateral was an incomplete pass. When the official backed away, indicating the ball was still live, my players realized what had happened and immediately tackled the opponent. We lost the ball on the play, but had the defender known he had recovered a lateral, he could have easily scored an uncontested touchdown. We won the game by 3 points and went on to win the state high school championship that year, a feat we would not have accomplished had that defender known he had recovered a lateral.

In the rest of this step we cover the skill of passing. The skill progression includes the following:

1. Grip
2. Footwork and body position
3. Throwing with accuracy and velocity
4. Follow-through
5. Drop-back technique

GRIP

The grip on the football (figure 4.1) is critical to a well-thrown pass because the grip determines the quality of the spiral of the ball, as well as its velocity to some extent. It is important to throw a spiral because a spiraling football travels most efficiently with the least amount of wind resistance. The tighter the spiral, the better. The tightness of the spiral refers to the number of revolutions the ball spins as it travels. The more revolutions and the quicker they are, the tighter the spiral.

The passer grips the ball with his throwing hand so at least the first knuckles of his hand cross the threads. Some players prefer to have their second knuckles across the thread. Preferred grip is often based on comfort and hand size. If the ball is held with the forward tip pointing toward the ground, the hand should grip the ball on the top half.

Figure 4.1 **GRIP FOR PASSING THE BALL**

1. First knuckles cross the thread of the ball
2. Grip ball on the top half
3. Index finger angled toward the point, about 45 degrees from the threads

4. Thumb wrapped around ball
5. Slight space between palm and ball

MISSTEP

When thrown, the ball wobbles and lacks velocity.

CORRECTION

This is usually caused by failing to have the index finger come last off the ball. Make sure the index finger is separated from the second finger and pointing at a 45-degree angle. Also make sure when the ball is released that the end of the index finger rotates down and away from the ball.

The index finger should be angled up toward the point at about 45 degrees from the line formed by the threads. Again, the angle of the index finger can be slightly different for comfort. The thumb is wrapped around the ball to create a firm hold. You should be able to see a little daylight between the palm of the hand and the ball.

The pressure of the grip is important. Grip pressure should be sufficient to hold and control the ball, but not so much that the forearm becomes too tight. Gripping the ball too tightly will tighten up the passer's throwing muscles, interfering with a smooth throwing motion and impeding muscle contraction in his arm. Think of holding an egg. You want to hold it tightly enough so it doesn't slip from your hand, but not so tight that you break it.

FOOTWORK AND BODY POSITION

When throwing the football, the passer uses his body effectively to project the ball in the direction he intends, with sufficient velocity. As he prepares to throw the ball, he turns his hips so that the hip opposite his throwing arm points at his target (figure 4.2a). For a right-handed player, this is the left hip; for a left-handed player, this is the right hip. Likewise, the passer points the shoulder opposite his throwing arm at the target as well. His knees should be slightly bent in a comfortable position, with body weight on the balls of his feet.

Figure 4.2 THROWING FOOTWORK

Setup

1. Turn hips so hip opposite throwing arm points to target
2. Shoulder opposite throwing arm points to target
3. Keep knees slightly bent with weight on balls of feet

Step With Lead Foot

1. Shoulder and hip opposite throwing arm point to target
2. Front foot steps forward 1 to 2 feet
3. Toes of front foot point to target
4. Keep weight on back foot

Turn Toward Target

1. Rotate hips to point belly-button at target
2. Open shoulders to target
3. Drive elbow of nonthrowing arm toward target to extend nonthrowing arm and start shoulder rotation
4. Throwing arm begins forward motion
5. Weight shifts to front foot
6. Forearm of throwing arm stays upright to support ball

MISSTEP

Thrown balls tend to be off target to the right or left.

CORRECTION

Make sure the front foot is pointing directly at the target during the throw. The ball will usually travel in the same direction the lead foot is pointed.

MISSTEP

Thrown balls tend to be off target, either too high or to the right (for a right-handed quarterback).

CORRECTION

Ensure the elbow of the throwing arm is shoulder high as the arm comes forward. It's helpful to make sure the ball is above the head as the arm is brought forward. This keeps the elbow high.

Having feet and body in proper position is critical for several reasons. First, it allows the passer to initiate the throw as quickly as possible once he has decided to throw. Second, it allows him to transfer power from his lower body to his arms in a way that allows him to throw the ball with maximum velocity. Much of a quarterback's arm strength is really from his legs and hips.

The throwing motion begins with the feet. A right-handed quarterback will have his body turned so his left hip and shoulder point at the target. He begins the throw by stepping with his left foot at the target (figure 4.2b). This step is 1 to 2 feet in length (depending on the quarterback's size), with foot pointing at the target. Pointing the foot is critical to making a good throw. The ball tends to be thrown to where the front foot, the plant foot, is pointing.

Once the passer starts his first step, he rotates his hips to point his belly-button at his target (figure 4.2c). This movement rotates his shoulders open to his target, which pulls his throwing arm to start its path to the release. The motion should occur in sequence:

1. Step and point foot.

2. Rotate hips.

3. Rotate shoulders.

4. Bring throwing arm forward to release ball.

When the passing motion occurs in the correct sequence, the body acts like a rope whipping the ball with velocity.

The step with the front foot affects the aim to the target. If the passer points his front toe right of the target, he will tend to throw the ball right of the target. If he points the toe left of the target, the throw goes left. The length of the step also affects accuracy. The shorter the step, the more of a tendency to throw the ball too low. The longer the step, the more of a tendency to throw the ball too high. This is important to remember when trying to correct an inaccurate throw. If a passer is consistently throwing the ball higher than his target, he is probably taking too long a step with his plant foot (the foot opposite his throwing arm). If he is consistently throwing the ball low, his plant foot step is most likely too short.

MISSTEP

A passer consistently throws the ball too high to his target.

CORRECTION

He is likely taking too long a step with his plant foot. He must shorten his step.

MISSTEP

A passer consistently throws the ball too short to his target.

CORRECTION

He is likely taking too short a step with his plant foot. He must lengthen his step.

As you can see, passing accuracy is affected to a great extent by the step taken with the plant foot: left or right because of where the foot is pointed when it lands, and short or long because of the length of the stride.

THROWING WITH ACCURACY AND VELOCITY

Prior to releasing the ball, the passer's body must be in correct position to allow a fast and accurate throw. His body should be turned sideways, with the hip opposite his throwing arm pointed at the target. Shoulders should also be turned, with the shoulder opposite his throwing arm pointing at the target. This position allows a quick throwing motion. Turning the body any other way causes lost time in positioning the feet, hips, and shoulders perpendicular to the target before the pass can be initiated. The receiver might be open for only a brief time, so the ball must get to him quickly. Likewise, the passer might be getting pressured by pass rushers and be forced to release the ball quickly before being sacked. Turning the shoulders correctly might be the difference between a completion and an incompletion—or an interception.

The actual arm motion of the throw can vary from player to player, but the basic motion should follow a fairly consistent path. The motion starts with the position in which the passer holds the ball as he prepares to throw and begins to step toward his target. He holds the ball with both hands, in front of his chest (figure 4.3). This location puts the ball in a position that allows his arm action to proceed quickly and accurately once he begins his throwing motion. Holding the ball lower or with one hand will cause him to take more time to get the ball up to where it needs to be as he throws it, which makes it more difficult to get a quick release. A quick release is often critical to the success of a pass play.

Figure 4.3 **PREPARATION TO THROW**

1. Hold ball in both hands
2. Hold ball in front of chest

As he begins to throw the ball, the passer separates his hands and begins to pull his throwing arm back so that his hand is parallel to his shoulders, which are already pointing at his target. His arm should end up exactly opposite his target, with his elbow as high as his shoulders. This position allows him to move the ball through a maximum distance as he moves his throwing levers through their range of motion; this gives the ball maximum velocity. At the same time he begins to pull his throwing arm back, he should "throw" his nonthrowing arm and elbow at his target. This helps get his body moving in that direction, along with his feet and hips. At this point, he should be holding the ball in his throwing hand, with fingers on the side away from his body and elbow bent 90 degrees to his upper arm. The ball is supported by the forearm directly under it.

As he begins his initial step, the passer has more of his weight on his back foot, which enables him to push off with force as he begins his first step. This forceful step allows him to shift his weight forward during the throw to get more force on the throw. His initial weight distribution should be close to 60 percent on his back foot and 40 percent on his front foot before the start of his stride.

MISSTEP
The passer begins with too much weight on his front foot.

CORRECTION
Too much weight on the front foot won't allow a weight transfer during the throw, resulting in a slower pass. The passer should begin with 60 percent of his weight on his back foot.

The legs begin the throwing motion, with the hips and shoulders following in order. Last to come forward toward the target is the arm and the ball. The elbow of the throwing arm should proceed the hand and ball. The shoulder remains at shoulder height as its brought forward. The hand and ball follow. The ball is kept close to the head as it comes forward. It is much easier to throw the ball accurately if the forearm remains upright as the arm comes forward. This position puts the ball by the passer's helmet as he brings the ball forward.

Some people will tell a passer to throw the ball "from your ear," which is ineffective. Granted, by throwing the ball from his ear, the passer will have the ball elevated above his shoulder, where it should be, and he might even be able to release the ball quickly. But if he is not careful using this technique, he might not pull his elbow and arm back to a position directly opposite his target. This shortened position limits the velocity he can apply to the ball as he releases it. By bringing the elbow and ball to a position opposite his target (and keeping it above his shoulder), the passer can maximize velocity on the throw.

As the passer extends his throwing arm to release the ball toward his target, he flexes and rotates his throwing wrist down and to the outside (figure 4.4). As the ball is released from his hand and he rolls his wrist, his index finger should be the last part of his hand to touch the ball.

Figure 4.4 **RELEASE**

Release

1. Extend throwing arm
2. Rotate wrist down and outside
3. Release the ball
4. Index finger is last part of hand to touch the ball
5. Palm of throwing hand points down and outside

MISSTEP

A passer's throwing velocity is diminished, or his accuracy of throw is inconsistent.

CORRECTION

He might not be extending his throwing arm back far enough as he begins his throwing motion. He should point the elbow of his throwing arm directly opposite his target as he begins his throwing motion.

Once the ball has left his hand, the passer's palm should be pointing down and to the outside. This release imparts the spin he wants on the ball to make his throw more aerodynamic. The tighter the spin, the more velocity, especially in windy conditions.

FOLLOW-THROUGH

The follow-through (figure 4.5) is a continuation of the throwing motion. There should be no discernible break in the motion during the follow-through. In fact, if the throwing motion is executed correctly, most of the follow-through is automatic. As the passer releases the ball, his throwing arm should be coming down toward the ground and end up across his chest with his throwing hand next to his opposite hip and thigh. His body also follows through its forward motion by bending at the waist. This bend should be allowed, not forced. By that we mean the forward motion of the hips and arms should continue smoothly as the waist bends.

Figure 4.5   FOLLOW-THROUGH

1. Throwing arm comes across chest
2. Throwing hand ends up next to opposite hip
3. Allow bend at waist
4. Pivot foot comes off ground

MISSTEP

A passer throws consistently high or at consistently low velocity.

CORRECTION

This may be caused by the pivot foot not coming off the ground at the end of the throw. He should focus on transferring his weight to his front foot, allowing his back foot to come up on the toe and off the ground. These poor throws might also be caused by lack of proper waist bend. He must make sure he allows his weight to transfer to his front leg. He should consciously get his head over his front knee as his arm comes forward. This automatically causes the waist to bend.

As he releases the ball, the passer's plant foot (the foot opposite his throwing arm) needs to bend naturally to allow his upper body to follow through. If he lands with a stiff plant knee as he releases the ball, he forces the release point of the ball to be higher, which causes the pass to be high. His pivot foot (the foot on the same side as his throwing arm) should come off the ground immediately after he releases the ball and come forward naturally to a balanced position with the opposite foot.

DROP-BACK TECHNIQUE

Passers must use good technique to get to the correct spot on the field and in position to throw the ball. We'll discuss the drop-back technique both from under center and from the shotgun.

Under center means the quarterback starts the play with his hands under the center and receives the snap directly from him. The proper position and technique for taking this snap was covered in step 1. Taking the snap in the shotgun means the quarterback lines up several yards behind the center, and the center snaps the ball through the air to the quarterback. Each alignment has advantages and disadvantages, which were discussed in step 1.

When under center, the quarterback must take the snap and drop back away from the line of scrimmage to a position to throw the pass. The type of drop-back depends on the type of pass play. There are six types of drop-back a quarterback might use, depending on the offensive scheme:

- Three-step drop
- Five-step drop
- Seven-step drop
- Play-action drop (includes boot pass drops)
- Semisprint drop
- Sprint drop

We'll focus on the three-, five-, and seven-step drops. We'll discuss the play-action drop and semisprint and sprint-pass drop-backs as they relate to the throwing position.

The three-step, five-step, and seven-step drop techniques are usually used in some form of drop-back pass, in which the quarterback drops directly behind the center before he throws the ball. Whether he uses a three-, five-, or seven-step drop depends on the type of pass patterns being run. We'll go over pass patterns later in this step. In short, the time it takes to run a pass pattern determines which drop-back pass the quarterback chooses to use. The number of the drop (three, five, or seven) refers to the number of backsteps the quarterback takes after receiving the snap. In each case, the quarterback takes his first backstep with the same-side foot as his throwing arm.

Some coaches like the quarterback to take his initial stance under center with his feet parallel. From this stance, the quarterback must begin the drop-back by pivoting on the foot opposite the throwing arm and simultaneously stepping back on his throwing-side foot. Some coaches like the quarterback to have the foot opposite the throwing arm staggered back slightly in the stance. From this stance, once the quarterback takes the snap, he still steps with his throwing foot first. The staggered stance allows him to be farther from the center once he takes that first step, which can get him a little bit deeper on his drop-back. It also gets his feet away from the center, which prevents the center from stepping on the quarterback's pivot foot as he turns to drop. Whichever stance is used, the quarterback's first step is critical in a good drop-back. He must gain ground and point his foot in the direction he's going on that first step. Pointing the foot back helps him gain ground and get his hips turned so he can take a good second step.

The second step the quarterback takes depends on whether the pass is a three-step pass or a five- or seven-step pass. If it's a three-step pass, the quarterback begins to gather his momentum on the second step so he can plant his throwing foot on the third step. This stops his backward movement and gets him ready to throw the ball immediately. If the pass is a five- or seven-step pass, the quarterback needs to gain more ground with his second step. This requires a powerful crossover step, reaching as far as possible with that crossover foot. As in the three-step drop, on the next to last step in the drop, the quarterback gathers himself and prepares to plant his back foot and set his feet to prepare to throw the ball. Some pass patterns take longer than others for receivers to run, so the type of drop-back depends on the pattern called. After dropping back, the quarterback must plant his back foot and be ready to begin the throw on the correct step. One step too many or too few, and he won't be ready to throw the ball when he needs to.

After planting his back foot on his final step, the quarterback should be in the throwing position described earlier: a balanced stance with knees slightly bent, weight slightly on the balls of the feet and favoring the rear foot, near hip and shoulder pointing downfield at the target, and the ball held in both hands in front of the chest.

On a play-action pass or a semisprint pass, the quarterback's last two steps prior to getting ready to throw should be the same as they are for the three-, five-, and seven-step drops. The only difference is how he gets to those last two steps. If he's running a sprint pass, the throwing motion is different. On a sprint pass, he'll be running sideways toward one of the sidelines and will throw the ball on the run. This requires a slightly different position prior to the throw.

If sprinting toward his throwing-arm side, the quarterback will make his throw based on when he sees his receiver open. His makes his throw as he plants his throwing foot (right foot for a right-handed quarterback), which is the opposite of the normal drop-back throwing motion. When throwing the ball on the run to the side, if he throws the ball with his nonthrowing leg planted, he won't be able to rotate his hips and shoulders open toward the target. He's then forced to throw the ball across his body, which hampers accuracy and velocity. For this reason, when sprinting toward his throwing-arm side, he should throw the ball off his back foot (throwing foot). This allows him to open up his hips and shoulders toward the receiver, allowing his arm to move through its normal path.

Likewise, when sprinting away from his throwing-arm side, the quarterback should throw the ball when he plants his nonthrowing foot. Again, this is because he'll be able to open his shoulders and hips toward the receiver in this direction. If he attempts to throw the ball when he plants his throwing foot, he won't be able to open his shoulders and hips toward his receiver, hindering accuracy and velocity.

When sprinting to his nonthrowing-hand side, the quarterback must rotate his nonthrowing shoulder as close as possible to pointing at his receiver. Because that shoulder will be turned away from the receiver, it will take a conscious effort to get it turned properly.

When taking the snap from the shotgun position, the number of steps the quarterback takes for each type of pass will vary. Because he's already 4 to 5 yards behind the line of scrimmage, he doesn't need to drop back after he takes the ball. This of course is the main advantage of the shotgun—it gives the quarterback more time to find his receivers.

When throwing a three-step pattern from the shotgun, the quarterback needs only to turn his shoulders and feet in place after catching the snap. The timing of the snap allows him to make the throw with proper timing without dropping back any farther. Likewise, when throwing a normal five-step pattern, the shotgun quarterback will take three steps back once he catches the ball. The footwork is identical to the three-step drop from under center. The quarterback pivots on his nonthrowing foot while stepping back on his throwing foot, gathers on his second crossover step, and plants his throwing foot on his third step. He is now ready to throw the ball.

Throwing Drill 1   Shoulder Rotation Drill

The shoulder rotation drill develops upper-body flexibility and proper upper-body rotation to get the throwing shoulder directly opposite the target before the throw.

The passer stands 10 to 15 yards away from a partner, pointing his feet at the partner. He throws a pass to the partner while keeping his feet on the ground. Repeat 10 to 15 times. The passer rotates his shoulders so the shoulder opposite his throwing hand is pointing at his target before he throws the ball. The focus is on proper hand position on the ball, pointing the elbow of the throwing arm directly away from the target, and keeping the throwing elbow shoulder high as the arm comes forward. Stress proper follow-through mechanics on release of the ball.

Passers repeat the drill while pointing their feet 90 degrees to the right of their target. The focus is on upper-body rotation toward the target. Passers should follow through without moving their feet.

Passers repeat the drill while pointing their feet 90 degrees to the left of their target. The focus is on upper-body rotation to get the nonthrowing shoulder as close as possible to pointing at the target.

Success Check

- The ball has good spin and rotation.

- The ball is on target. Aim for the partner's chest.
- The ball has good velocity.

Throwing Drill 2   Knee Drill

The knee drill works the upper-body mechanics of the throw.

Passers face a partner about 10 yards away. They repeat the three phases of the shoulder rotation drill while kneeling on their right knee. This works the same upper-body mechanics and flexibility that the shoulder rotation drill works, with a focus on proper shoulder rotation.

Success Check

- The ball has good spin and rotation.

- The ball is on target. Aim for the partner's chest.
- The ball has good velocity.

Throwing Drill 3   Throwing on the Run

This drill works on making a pass while running to the right or left.

A passer runs a 10- to 15-yard circle around a partner standing in the middle of the circle. The partner should turn constantly to face the passer as he runs the circle. While running clockwise, the passer throws the ball to the stationary partner. He throws the ball as he steps with his left foot. The partner immediately throws the ball back to the passer as the passer continues to run. Repeat 10 to 15 times. The focus is on proper shoulder rotation. The passer attempts to point the shoulder of his nonthrowing arm at the target each time he throws.

Repeat the drill running in a counterclockwise direction. The passer now throws the ball as he steps with his right foot. The focus is on rotating the shoulders completely toward the target on the throw. The passer uses a proper follow-through with his throwing arm.

Success Check

- Ball has good spin.
- Ball is thrown accurately. Aim at partner's chest.

- Ball has good velocity.
- Maintain good balance during the throw.

SUCCESS SUMMARY

The forward pass has revolutionized the game of football since its inception. Throwing passes is a skill usually delegated to the quarterback, but other offensive players are allowed to pass the ball, including running backs, tight ends, and wide receivers. The ability to make a good throw is considered by some a skill players are born with. Although a strong arm and good eye–hand coordination are certainly important to passing effectively, the skill of passing can be developed and improved with proper practice. When done correctly, the forward pass is a potent weapon for the offense and an entertaining play for the fans.

In step 5 we look at the skill of catching the football. Before turning to step 5, answer the following questions to ensure complete understanding of step 4.

Before Taking the Next Step

1. When holding the ball and preparing to throw a pass, should the palm of the hand make contact with the ball?

2. How high should the elbow of the throwing arm be as a passer brings his arm forward to throw the ball?

3. What should a passer's target be when he throws the ball?

4. On the follow-through, should the passer step forward with his back foot?

5. On the follow-through, should the throwing hand rotate down and away from the ball or down and to the ball?

Receiving

Before we discuss the skill of catching the football, let's look at the four game situations when a catch is needed. First, there are passing plays in which an offensive player is intended to catch a thrown ball. Second, defensive players sometimes have a chance to intercept an offensive pass. Third, on a punt play, the punt returner often intends to catch the punted ball (sometimes he lets the ball drop and hopes for a good bounce). Fourth, on the kickoff, the kickoff returner usually intends to catch the kicked ball (again, balls at kickoffs are occasionally viewed as nonreturnable and allowed to drop in the end zone). These four situations have both similarities and distinct differences. We'll look closer at each situation in the context of catching the ball.

CATCHING AN OFFENSIVE PASS

The most common situation in which a player desires to catch the football is when a receiver is thrown a pass from the quarterback on an offensive play. In most games, this situation occurs far more often than the other three. When catching a pass on offense, the receiver must do the following:

1. Run a pass route to get to a designated point.

2. Get in position to make the catch.

3. Get body and arms in position to make the catch, including adjusting to the flight of the ball.

4. Make the catch.

5. Secure the ball and run.

Getting in position to catch a pass means arriving at the correct position on the field and having your body, arms, and hands in the position required to make the catch. To get to the correct position on the field, the receiver runs a pass route. There are many types of pass routes, including short out routes, deep out routes, shallow crossing routes, deep crossing routes, post routes, and more. We'll first discuss general principles that are important when executing any type of pass route.

Stance

Pass routes must be started in such a way to give receivers the best chance to run a good route and keep defenders off balance. This begins with the stance taken prior to the start of the play. A receiver lines up on the line of scrimmage in a two-point stance (upright stance, figure 5.1a) or a three-point stance (hand on the ground, figure 5.1b), like a lineman.

Figure 5.1 **RECEIVER STANCE ON LINE OF SCRIMMAGE**

Wide Receiver's Two-Point Stance

1. Balanced football stance
2. Feet one to two feet apart and staggered
3. Knees slightly bent
4. Elbows bent

Tight End's Three-Point Stance

1. Feet slightly staggered about shoulder-width apart
2. Hand on ground, slightly ahead of the head
3. Weight distributed about 60 percent on hand, 40 percent on feet
4. Head up, with hips and shoulders at about the same level

The tight end is typically the only receiver who starts in a three-point stance. Because the tight end might be required to block a defensive lineman, the three-point stance is his best option. Running backs and wide receivers, when running pass routes, usually start in two-point stances, which allows them to see the defensive alignment and initial defensive reaction at the start of the play. The defensive alignment and reaction may affect the pass route the receiver will run. We discuss this further in step 11.

In the two-point stance, the player must be in balanced football position. Feet are one to two feet apart. Knees are slightly bent, with a little more weight on the balls of the feet. Opinions differ on where the receiver should hold his hands prior to the snap. Some coaches have receivers hang their arms comfortably at their sides. Others have them hold their hands just in front of their chest. (This is more of a scheme philosophy.) For now, we'll tell receivers to keep their arms in a comfortable position, with elbows bent.

The feet should be staggered slightly. Which foot is forward, the inside or outside foot, depends on the offensive scheme or the pass pattern being run. For example, when running a short out route, the receiver needs to take three to five steps before making his out cut. He plants his inside foot as he makes the cut in order to push off to the outside effectively. With the outside foot up, this means an odd number of steps to plant the inside foot, assuming the receiver starts his steps with the back foot. With the inside foot up, this means an even number of steps to plant the inside foot.

Running the Pass Route

As the receiver starts to run his route, several factors come into play. First, the receiver should come off the line of scrimmage with the exact same body lean and speed no matter what the pattern is. This disguises the route from the defender. Second, if a pass defender in the receiver's immediate vicinity is lined up 5 to 7 yards off the line of scrimmage, the receiver must stem his initial route to end head-up on the defender. Most pass defenders try to favor one side or the other on a receiver because this makes it easier to defend a pass route to the side he is on. By favoring that side, the defender is already where the pass route may go, giving him a positional advantage. The defender can then focus on reacting to the receiver if the receiver makes a pass route cut either up the field or opposite the defender's alignment.

Stemming refers to the receiver starting his route running upfield and working to a head-up position on the defender. (Being in head-up position means being directly in front of the defender.) As the receiver starts to run, he runs or swerves to a head-up position as he approaches the defender. By getting head-up on the defender before making the pass route cut, the receiver puts the defender at a disadvantage. The defender can't defend both an inside cut and an outside cut as well as when he was aligned on one side.

Once the receiver is head-up to his defender, he can make his assigned pass cut. If the pass route is a three-step pass, the receiver makes the cut and turns his head immediately toward the quarterback to look for the ball. On these shorter pass patterns, the receiver must turn his head and focus his eyes as early as possible. The ball will be coming quickly. If he doesn't turn his head and focus quickly, he might have difficulty picking up the ball in flight and adjusting to make the catch.

A receiver running a route for a five-step pass has a little more time to get his eyes on the football. Often a five-step pass pattern involves the receiver changing his pattern on the fly based on what the defender does. This gets into reading defenses and running the offensive pass game philosophy, which we'll discuss in step 11.

Making the Catch

As the receiver watches the ball coming to him, he retains focus on the ball until he has secured it. A receiver who takes eyes off the ball prior to catching and securing it will likely drop the pass.

MISSTEP

The receiver looks away from the ball before he has caught it and secured it in his grasp.

CORRECTION

He should practice focusing on the point of the football during its flight toward him. He should use the triangle formed by both hands held close with thumbs and index fingers pointed toward each other. He needs to see the ball contact his hands. He must keep his eyes on the ball as he brings it down to a tuck position.

A good mental trick for the receiver to help retain focus on the pass is to look for the small dark spot formed by the seams at the tip of the ball as it spins. This gives a specific spot to focus on and blocks out distractions that might interfere.

Once he has made the catch, the receiver must keep his eyes on the ball until he has cradled it with his arm in a secure position. The receiver should point his nose at the ball as he catches it all the way until he secures it. The drill on seeing the ball is a good drill to do as a daily warm-up and to practice this skill.

On any pass pattern that ends with the receiver running close to parallel to the line of scrimmage, the receiver should turn his shoulders so that his chest faces the oncoming ball as much as possible. This allows the receiver to get his hands in the optimal position to make the catch. On any deep route (post, go, or corner), the receiver attempts to get as deep as possible as the ball is thrown. The idea is for the receiver to catch the ball while in midstride toward the opponent's goal line. The receiver catches the ball over his shoulder with his back to the line of scrimmage. The receiver retains eyes on the ball, just as on a shorter route.

When catching the ball on a shorter route, the receiver turns his shoulders and chest toward the oncoming ball. He catches the ball in one of two ways. If the ball arrives above or at the level of his abdomen, he catches the ball with his thumbs pointing in and fingers up and out (figure 5.2a). His thumbs are only an inch or two apart or are touching to avoid the ball passing through the hands. As he catches the ball with hands in this upright position, it is natural and effective to focus on the point of the ball, looking through the triangle shaped by his thumbs and fingers. Again, he retains focus on the ball as he makes the catch and secures the ball.

If the ball arrives below the abdomen, the receiver needs to catch it with his thumbs pointed out and his fingers in and down (figure 5.2b). He keeps eyes focused on the point of the ball but with this catch cannot use the triangle window.

Figure 5.2 HAND POSITION FOR MAKING THE CATCH

Pass Above Abdominal Level

1. Thumbs in
2. Fingers up and out
3. Thumbs and fingers create triangle

Pass Below Abdominal Level

1. Thumbs out
2. Fingers in and down

As the ball approaches, the receiver has his hands extended away from his body (figure 5.3a). Elbows are slightly bent. As the ball contacts his hands, he gives slightly with his arms, allowing his arms to bend as he catches the ball to provide a cushioning effect (figure 5.3b). He should also give with his hands. If his arms and hands don't give, it's like trying to catch the ball with a board. Giving with the catch creates a softer impact, and the ball won't bounce off.

Figure 5.3 **MAKING THE CATCH**

Prepare for the Catch

1. Turn shoulders and chest toward the ball
2. Get hands in proper position based on the ball's location
3. Extend arms

Catch the Pass

1. Focus on point of ball as it approaches
2. Give slightly with arms and hands as ball makes contact
3. Keep eyes on ball until it is secured

MISSTEP

The ball consistently bounces out of the receiver's hands. A loud slapping sound occurs as the ball contacts his hands.

CORRECTIONS

As the ball approaches, make sure arms are slightly bent. When the ball makes contact, allow the arms to give (bend slightly) on contact. Think about the hands giving on contact as well.

Some refer to this technique as catching with soft hands. Extending the arms prior to the arrival of the ball helps a receiver give as he catches the ball. If his hands are close to his body, the ball may hit his chest as his hands give. This is called catching with the body (rather than the hands), which can cause dropped passes.

MISSTEP

The receiver catches the ball with arms bent too much and hands too close to the body.

CORRECTION

This may prevent catching the ball with soft arms and hands because they don't have room to give. The ball may even strike the body first. Make sure that the arms are extended away from the body as the ball approaches.

INTERCEPTING

A second situation in which the ball is caught is when a defensive player intercepts an offensive pass. The skills of catching the ball—focus, hand and arm position, soft hands—are the same skills as for a receiver catching the ball. The difference for a defensive player attempting to intercept is in how he gets to where the ball is.

Defensive players face the line of scrimmage and the offense in most situations throughout most plays. So when a defender has an opportunity to make an interception, he will already have his shoulders and arms facing the oncoming ball. The major difference in receiving and intercepting is in how the defender moves to the reception point. When a pass is in an area where either the receiver or a defensive player has an opportunity to catch it, the player who gets to the ball first usually makes the reception. This being the case, the defender must assume the offensive player will move to the ball to get there first. This means the defender must attack the pass as it approaches.

If the ball is relatively level, the defender must move toward the line of scrimmage until he and the ball meet. If he stops and waits, the receiver will likely step in front and catch the ball first. If the ball is thrown high, the defender needs not only to move toward the pass but might also need to jump into the air to catch the ball before it comes down to the receiver. In this case he must time his jump to catch the ball as high in the air as he can. This gives him the best chance of beating the receiver to the ball. This principle, called catching the ball at its highest point, must be practiced by all defenders who want to increase their intercepting skills.

Defenders working on their interception skills should do the following ball-catching drills as they are described for receivers. When running these drills, defenders should also emphasize moving back to the ball for the catch. Catching the ball at the highest point involves the skill of judging the jump, which takes numerous repetitions. Players not great at judging thrown balls will need to drill this skill a great deal. Learning to judge distances and ball flight angle and speed can take time. This skill should be drilled in the off-season as well as during the season.

The other two situations that involve catching—catching a ball on a kickoff and on a punt—are discussed in step 13. The rest of step 5 is devoted to catching drills.

Catching Drill 1   Play Catch

Players play catch with a partner. This warm-up drill can easily be done prior to the start of practice. Players catch at least 10 passes prior to each practice.

Success Check

Emphasize correct technique:
- Focus on the ball.
- Use correct arm and hand position.
- Catch the ball with soft hands.
- Secure the ball.

Catching Drill 2   Seeing the Ball

Players stand 10 to 15 yards away from a partner and play catch. As the ball approaches, players hold their hands in front of their body with thumbs and index fingers pointed toward each other. They work on seeing the ball through the triangle formed by the thumbs and fingers. They should focus on the point of the ball as it strikes their hands. Once they have caught the ball, they move the ball down to a secure position against their body. They should point their nose at the ball from the time they catch it until the time it is secured. This emphasizes eyes on the ball.

Success Check

- Receivers see a dark spot on the end of the football as it approaches their hands.
- Receivers see the ball strike their hands.
- Receivers are bending their heads down with eyes looking at the ball as they secure it.

Catching Drill 3
Straight Line Perpendicular to Passer

Players line up in a single line. The coach stands 10 to 15 yards away on a perpendicular line to the running route. One player at a time runs straight across the field. The coach throws a pass to the running player (figure 5.4).

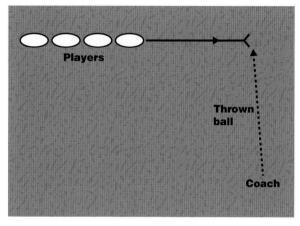

Figure 5.4   Straight line perpendicular to passer.

To Increase Difficulty

- On the ground, set up agility bags that are 3 to 4 feet long and 6 to 10 inches tall. The player must catch the ball as he runs over the agility bags. The addition of the agility bags makes concentration on catching the ball more difficult and more important.

Success Check

Emphasize correct technique:
- Focus on the ball.
- Use correct arm and hand position.
- Catch the ball with soft hands.
- Secure the ball.

Catching Drill 4   Distraction Drill

Players line up in a single line. The coach stands 10 to 15 yards away on a perpendicular line to the running route. A player stands 5 yards in front of and between the coach and the receiver's route. One player at a time runs straight across the field. The coach throws a pass to the running player (figure 5.5) as the player between the coach and receiver waves his arms to distract the receiver.

(continued)

Catching Drill 4 (continued)

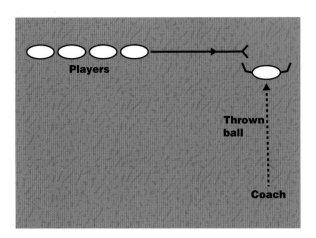

Figure 5.5 Distraction drill.

To Increase Difficulty

- On the ground, set up agility bags that are 3 to 4 feet long and 6 to 10 inches tall. The player must catch the ball as he runs over the agility bags. The addition of the agility bags makes concentration on catching the ball more difficult and more important.

Success Check

Emphasize correct technique:
- Focus on the ball.
- Use correct arm and hand position.
- Catch the ball with soft hands.
- Secure the ball.

Catching Drill 5   Running at the Passer

Players line up in a single line. The coach stands 15 yards away, directly in front of the first player in line. One player at a time runs toward the coach. The coach throws a pass to the running player (figure 5.6).

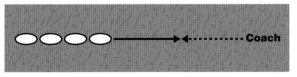

Figure 5.6 Running at the passer.

To Increase Difficulty

- On the ground, set up agility bags that are 3 to 4 feet long and 6 to 10 inches tall. The player must catch the ball as he runs over the agility bags. The addition of the agility bags makes concentration on catching the ball more difficult and more important.

Success Check

Emphasize correct technique:
- Focus on the ball.

- Use correct arm and hand position.
- Catch the ball with soft hands.
- Secure the ball.

Catching Drill 6   Running Routes

Players line up in a single line. The coach stands to the side of the line. One player at a time runs a set route, such as a quick out, out, slant, or post. The coach throws a pass to the running player.

Success Check

Emphasize correct technique:
- Focus on the ball.

- Use correct arm and hand position.
- Catch the ball with soft hands.
- Secure the ball.

Catching Drill 7   Head Turn

Players stand in a straight line about 10 yards from the coach with backs turned to the coach. As the coach begins to make the throw, he yells "ball," signaling the first player to quickly turn around, find the ball, and make a proper catch.

Success Check

- Get the head around first and find the ball.
- Focus on the ball as the pass arrives.

- Get hands and arms in correct position.
- Catch the ball with soft hands.
- Secure the ball.

SUCCESS SUMMARY

In step 5 we have focused on catching, covering all the important elements that go into catching a thrown ball:

- Getting into proper body position
- Running routes
- Getting arms and body ready to make the catch
- Adjusting to the ball's flight
- Making the catch
- Securing the ball after the catch

As is true of most football skills, catching can be improved with practice. We have presented several drills that run on a daily basis will yield positive results.

In step 6 we move to the skills of tackling and blocking. Before turning to that step, check your understanding of step 5 by answering the questions that follow.

Before Taking the Next Step

1. When catching a ball from the front and above the waist, in what position should you hold your hands prior to the ball arriving?

2. What does catching with soft hands mean?

3. When do you take your eyes off the ball during a pass reception?

4. When on defense and attempting to intercept a thrown pass, should you move toward the ball or away from the ball during its flight?

Tackling and Blocking

The sport of football has many elements. If you sat in on any college or professional football staff meeting, you might find the game too complicated for a mere mortal to comprehend. What football really comes down to, though, are two skills at the foundation of the game: tackling and blocking. Take these aspects of the game away, and football might be unrecognizable. The whole point of the game is to move the ball into the opponent's end zone without getting tackled. To do so, the offensive team must block potential tacklers. That's as simple an explanation of the game as there is. If it sounds too simple, well, it is. The point is that tackling and blocking are at the very heart of the game. For your team to succeed, your players must be well skilled in both. In this step, we'll cover the concepts of tackling first, and then move to blocking. If you study only one step in this book, this is the one.

TACKLING

Tackling sounds simple: You grab the man carrying the football and throw him (or knock him, or drag him) to the ground. Easy, right? Not so fast. First, that man is not going to just let you take him down. Second, you might meet the ball carrier from the front, back, or side, with fellow defenders around or all by yourself. Each situation creates a different set of difficulties that must be addressed.

Fundamentally, tackling can be broken down into four basic elements: approach, settle, contact, and follow-through. Each element varies slightly depending on the type of tackle required. Let's begin with the basic straight-on tackle.

Straight-On Tackle

As the tackler approaches the ball carrier from the front, he closes the distance between them as quickly as possible until he is 5 to 7 yards away. At this point, the tackler settles (figure 6.1), which means he gets his body in correct position to contact the ball carrier while he's still closing in on him.

Figure 6.1 STRAIGHT-ON TACKLE: APPROACH AND SETTLE

1. Close the distance to the ball carrier
2. At 5 to 7 yards, begin your settle
3. Get into football position
4. Slow forward progress under control
5. Be ready to react to any change of direction

The settle involves slightly slowing down forward progress, maintaining control, and getting into good football position: knees slightly bent, weight on the balls of the feet, chest out, and back slightly arched. This position allows the tackler to be ready to move in any direction quickly and efficiently. As he approaches the ball carrier, the tackler must to be ready to react to any possible change of direction as the ball carrier attempts to avoid the tackle.

As he settles into good football position, the tackler continues to move forward to reduce the distance between himself and the ball carrier. This gives the ball carrier less space and time to make a cut to avoid the tackle. To move forward in a football position, the tackler takes quick, short steps, keeping feet shoulder-width apart. Keeping feet apart is important; if the tackler allows his feet to get close to each other, he won't be able to react and push off in either direction if the ball carrier makes a cut.

MISSTEP

The tackler gets too close to the runner before slowing down and settling his hips into a good football stance.

CORRECTION

The tackler should begin to come under control 5 to 7 yards from the runner. Getting too close earlier makes it more difficult to react to the runner's sudden change of direction. Settling the hips also aids in reacting to the runner's cut. If the tackler's weight is too high, he'll need a step or two more to stop and change direction, allowing the runner space to get by.

As he gets within 1 yard of the ball carrier, the tackler prepares for contact. For straight-on contact, the tackler keeps his head up and aims his head slightly to one side of the ball carrier (figure 6.2). He must avoid making contact with his head first, which invites a head or neck injury. Turning his head to the side on the tackle also risks a neck injury. Whenever possible, first contact on the tackle should be with the chest. If the head and eyes are up, not looking at the ground, injury is less likely.

MISSTEP

When making a tackle, the tackler's head is down, exposing him to a head or neck injury.

CORRECTION

When making contact with the ball carrier, the tackler's head must be up. Contact should be with the chest, not the head. As contact is made, the tackler swings both arms forward and up to grab the ball carrier in a lifting motion. This puts the tackler in a good position to avoid head-first contact.

When tackling, the best way to aim is to point your nose at the ball carrier's armpit. Another possible aiming point is the ball. Because the ball carrier will hold the ball in one hand against his body, this aiming point will naturally move the tackler to the side. If the tackler can hit the ball with force, there's also a chance of knocking the ball out of the ball carrier's hands.

Figure 6.2 STRAIGHT-ON TACKLE: CONTACT

Contact

1. Aim head slightly to one side of ball carrier
2. Aim at ball carrier's armpit or the football
3. Hit ball carrier with chest first
4. Maintain good knee-bend
5. Club both arms up on either side of ball carrier
6. Roll the hips and come out of football stance
7. Keep moving feet in short, choppy steps
8. Finish tackle by grabbing ball carrier around the back and driving him to the ground

If the tackler can hit the ball carrier chest first, this keeps the tackler's body square to the ball carrier and keeps his head up and out of the way of the initial contact. As the chest makes contact, the tackler maintains a good bend in the knees. If he rises too soon, he won't have any force behind his tackle and might get knocked back himself.

MISSTEP

When attempting to make a tackle, the tackler rises up too soon prior to contact with the ball carrier.

CORRECTION

The tackler must maintain a good knee-bend until contact. On contact, he swings both arms forward and up. This creates a rising motion of the tackler's body at the right time.

As he makes contact, the tackler clubs both arms up on either side of the ball carrier, ending with both hands pointing to the sky behind each of the ball carrier's arms. This clubbing motion of the arms does two things: First, it creates a striking force from the tackler to the ball carrier, knocking the ball carrier back. Second, it enhances what we call rolling the hips, another important movement that helps deliver a blow to the ball carrier. As the tackler makes contact, he begins to come out of his football stance by pushing his pelvis forward and straightening up into the contact. The combined arm club and hip roll imparts maximum force into the ball carrier to stop his momentum.

As he makes contact and begins his arm club and hip roll, the tackler continues to move his feet to finish the tackle. Think of running through the ball carrier with quick, choppy, powerful steps. Once the tackler stops the ball carrier's forward motion with the initial contact and hip roll, he follows through by driving the ball carrier back and toward the ground with the leg drive. At the same time, the tackler grabs the ball carrier around the back with his arms as forcefully as possible. Done properly, this ends with a good solid tackle.

Approach, settle, contact, and follow-through. Nearly all straight-on tackles include these four fundamentals, sometimes with slight variations. Three other basic types of tackles are the angle tackle, the open-field tackle (which is a type of angle tackle), and the tackle from behind.

Angle Tackle

The angle tackle is almost identical to the straight-on tackle. The difference is as the tackler approaches the ball carrier he needs to aim slightly ahead of him to cut him off. His aiming point as he approaches the ball carrier and settles should be the ball carrier's far arm pit (figure 6.3). This results in having his head in front of the ball carrier on contact. If he makes contact with his head behind the ball carrier, the tackler might miss the tackle entirely, or the ball carrier might run through the tackle because the would-be tackler has only one arm in front to stop the ball carrier's forward motion.

Figure 6.3 **ANGLE TACKLE**

1. Aim slightly ahead of ball carrier to cut him off

2. Aim for the ball carrier's far armpit

3. Have head in front of ball carrier at contact

4. Finish the tackle

MISSTEP

When making an angle tackle, the tackler places his head behind the runner, thus attempting the tackle with only his arms. This usually results in a missed tackle.

CORRECTION

As the tackler approaches the ball carrier from a side angle, he must aim his nose at the far arm pit of the ball carrier. He must also keep his feet moving as contact is made to ensure that his body stays in front of the ball carrier.

Maintaining the body in front during the tackle allows the tackler to stop the ball carrier's forward motion and keep him from running through the tackle. Once the tackler has made contact, the finish is the same as for a straight-on tackle.

Open-Field Tackle

The open-field tackle is a form of angle tackle, but here the tackler approaches the ball carrier from the front with no other defenders around to help. If the ball carrier can make a cut in either direction, the tackler must be in position to react to the cut and then execute an angle tackle. As the tackler gets within 5 to 7 yards of the ball carrier and settles, as in a straight-on tackle, he must be ready to move either right or left based on the ball carrier's cut. Once the ball carrier makes his cut, the tackler takes one shuffle step with his near foot in the same direction as the cut and follows with an angle tackle. The shuffle step prevents the ball carrier from making a second cut back into the tackler. The shuffle step allows the tackler to get slightly to the side, so that if the ball carrier tries to make a second cut back toward the tackler, the tackler will not overrun him. The shuffle step also keeps the tackler's feet apart, which allows him to react in case the ball carrier makes a second cut.

Tackle From Behind

When tackling from behind, the settle and arm club are not as important as in the straight-on tackle. The critical part here is to tackle the ball carrier high enough so that the tackler does not slip off the ball carrier as he tries to escape. This requires getting as close as possible from behind before committing to the tackle. It also means the tackler will need to strongly wrap his arms around the ball carrier to prevent him from escaping—because the tackler's body won't be out in front to prevent the escape. The follow-through is slightly different as well. If the tackler drives his legs on contact, he might push the ball carrier a few yards forward. After getting a good hold, the tackler should pull the ball carrier down by falling down himself.

Tackling Practice

Tackling requires a lot of practice to master. But the collisions that occur when tackling can be an issue during practice sessions. It's simply impossible to practice a full-out tackle enough to become proficient without a risk of injury.

To practice tackling, break the skill down to its components and work on those components individually in controlled drills. Also, execute proper tackling technique up to but just short of taking the ball carrier to the ground. We call this type of tackle a thud. The thud is more difficult than an actual tackle because the "tackler" must be in perfect position and execute the elements of a successful tackle correctly to be able to avoid knocking the ball carrier to the ground at the end of the thud. Thus, by using the thud technique, tacklers can become even more proficient at tackling. Note that, when thudding, the tackler must emphasize his leg drive because he won't be using it to bring the ball carrier down.

The first four tackling drills—the fit drills—work basic tackling fundamentals. Once the fundamentals are learned, the drills can be expanded to cover actual game conditions. For example, most tackles are angle tackles in which the tackler comes from the side and in front of the ball carrier. A simple drill to work this is drill 5, the angle tackle drill.

Many variations of tackling drills can be done. When designing your own, try to create drills that mimic game situations and produce multiple repetitions in a short time.

Tackling Drill 1   Fit

The tackler gets into position in contact with the ball carrier, as if he has already made contact. Emphasize proper body position in relation to the ball carrier: head up, knees bent, chest in contact with the ball carrier's upper abdomen, head to one side with eyes up, near leg between the ball carrier's legs, outside leg behind and near leg forward. Once the tackler is in this starting position, the coach whistles or gives a "hit"

command. The tackler clubs his arms up and around the ball carrier while simultaneously stepping forward with his outside leg.

Adjust the drill slightly by having the tackler take a step back with the leg closest to the ball carrier. On command, the tackler takes one step with the near leg and clubs up at the same time.

To Increase Difficulty

- Add a drive to the end of the drill. The tackler finishes by driving the ball carrier back three or four steps using quick, choppy steps and rolling his hips forward as he attempts to lift the ball carrier off the ground.

Success Check

Check for proper body position in relation to the ball carrier:
- Head up.
- Knees bent.
- Chest in contact with the ball carrier's upper abdomen.
- Head to one side.
- Near leg between the ball carrier's legs.
- Outside leg behind and near leg forward.

Tackling Drill 2   Two-Step Fit

The tackler starts in a fit position on the ball carrier, then takes two steps back, starting with the near foot first. The tackler should end up with the near

foot forward in a ready stance. On command, the tackler takes two quick steps to the fit position and clubs up.

To Increase Difficulty

- Add a drive to the end of the drill. The tackler finishes by driving the ball carrier back three or four steps using quick, choppy steps and rolling his hips forward as he attempts to lift the ball carrier off the ground.

Success Check

Check for proper body position in relation to the ball carrier:
- Head up.
- Knees bent.
- Chest in contact with the ball carrier's upper abdomen.
- Head to one side.
- Near leg between the ball carrier's legs.

Tackling Drill 3   5-Yard Fit

The tackler starts 5 yards from the ball carrier. On command, the tackler runs to the ball carrier and executes a fit tackle. The tackler must time his steps to make contact with the ball carrier as the tackler's inside foot hits the ground between the ball carrier's legs.

To Increase Difficulty

- Add a drive to the end of the drill. The tackler finishes by driving the ball carrier back three or four steps using quick, choppy steps and rolling his hips forward as he attempts to lift the ball carrier off the ground.

Success Check

Check for proper body position in relation to the ball carrier:
- Head up.
- Knees bent.
- Chest in contact with the ball carrier's upper abdomen.
- Head to one side.
- Near leg between the ball carrier's legs.

Tackling Drill 4   Fit and Drive

The tackler starts 5 yards from the ball carrier. On command, the tackler runs to the ball carrier and executes a fit tackle. The tackler finishes by driving the ball carrier back three or four steps by using quick, choppy steps with his feet apart and rolling his hips forward as he attempts to lift the ball carrier off the ground.

Success Check

Check for proper body position in relation to the ball carrier:
- Head up.
- Knees bent.
- Chest in contact with the ball carrier's upper abdomen.
- Head to one side.
- Near leg between the ball carrier's legs.
- Legs driving with short choppy steps.

Tackling Drill 5   Angle Tackle

The ball carrier and tackler begin 5 yards apart, facing each other. On command, the ball carrier runs at a 45-degree angle to the tackler's right or left. The tackler runs at the same angle and executes a thud tackle or full tackle on the ball carrier. After the initial fit contact, the tackle is the same as the fit-and-drive drill.

To Increase Difficulty

- The ball carrier tries to cut back behind the tackler to force the tackler to stay in the correct position.

Success Check

- The tackler should stay slightly behind the ball carrier as he approaches him from inside out. This prevents the ball carrier from cutting back behind. Starting with a shuffle step helps maintain this position.
- As the tackler makes contact, his head must be in front of the ball carrier. He steps with his foot in front of the ball carrier on the fit.

Tackling Drill 6   Cutback Drill

This drill is good for working on redirecting and getting into good tackling position. The ball carrier begins 5 yards from the tackler in the opposite corner of an imaginary 5-yard box. The tackler runs straight ahead for 5 yards. At this point, the ball carrier waits and does not move. As the tackler reaches a point directly across from the ball carrier, the tackler plants and redirects at a 45-degree angle. At the same time, the ball carrier takes off just as he would in the angle tackle drill.

Success Check

Check for proper body position in relation to the ball carrier:

- Head up.
- Knees bent.
- Body slightly behind ball carrier prior to contact.
- Chest in contact with the ball carrier's upper abdomen.
- Head in front of ball carrier at contact.
- Legs driving with short choppy steps.

Tackling Drill 7   Open-Field Tackle

An open-field tackle is one of the most difficult tackles to execute. It entails making the tackle out in the open, away from any help, where the ball carrier has room to go in any direction he likes, often at full speed. The tackler must work several skills to be able to make the open-field tackle. He must get into position to make the tackle, be ready to react to the ball carrier's cuts, make solid contact, and finish the tackle.

A good drill to work the open-field tackle comes in two phases. The first phase works on closing the gap to the ball carrier while getting in proper position to tackle.

The tackler stands on the sideline lined up on a yard line, facing a coach positioned on a hash mark. On command, the tackler runs down the line at the coach. After the tackler gets to the bottom of the numbers, the coach calls

(continued)

Tackling Drill 7 (continued)

"settle." The tackler lowers his hips and center of gravity while continuing to run at the coach. At this point, the tackler is running with bent knees and feet about shoulder-width apart, using short, choppy steps. Once the tackler is in the settle position, the coach points either left or right. The tackler changes direction according to the coach's instruction. Once the tackler moves three or four steps in the new direction, the coach points in the opposite direction, and the tackler changes direction again. The tackler should not allow his feet to come together while changing direction. As the tackler approaches the coach, he finishes with an arm club on air as if making the tackle, or he just runs past the coach. Several players can run the drill at once on parallel yard lines to get more repetitions in a short period of time (figure 6.4).

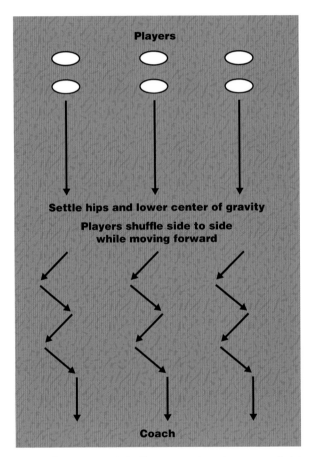

Figure 6.4   Multiple lines running the open-field tackle drill, phase 1.

The next phase of the drill adds a ball carrier (figure 6.5). The ball carrier lines up on the hash marks and starts running at the same time as the tackler. The ball carrier should make at least two cuts left and right, two or three steps each, to force the tackler to change direction. The tackler finishes with a thud angle tackle on the ball carrier. The key to this drill is for the tackler to continue to close the distance to the ball carrier as he maintains bent knees and feet apart, using quick, choppy steps. The tackler should settle into this position 5 to 7 yards from the ball carrier, depending on how fast the ball carrier is coming.

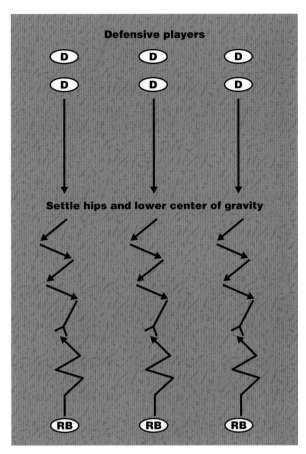

Figure 6.5 Multiple lines running the open-field tackle drill, phase 2.

Success Check

- On the "settle" command, the tackler lowers his hips as he continues to close the gap.
- The tackler runs with short, choppy steps in good football position as he approaches the coach or ball carrier.
- The tackler's feet stay about shoulder-width apart as he changes direction. The feet do not cross over.

BLOCKING

Blocking is the act of using the body to stop the defensive man from getting close enough to the ball carrier to tackle him. Any offensive player might need to block at some point during a game, but blocking is most often required of offensive linemen. A blocker may not hold the defensive player during the block; nor, in most cases, may he block below the waist.

There are several types of blocks:

- Drive block
- Stalk block
- Cut block
- Trap block

- Reach block
- Scoop block
- Pass-protection block

Some basic concepts are common to all blocks (figure 6.6). One of the most important aspects of blocking involves the use of the blocker's hands and arms. To effectively block a man, you must have your hands on the defender's chest, inside his arms. Use the hands to grab the defender and control him. Grabbing the defender is legal as long as the blocker's hands are inside the defender's arms, and as long as the blocker lets go when the defender pulls away from the block.

Figure 6.6 BLOCKING

Approach

1. Come out of stance low
2. Lean body toward defender
3. Maintain knee-bend
4. Head up
5. Feet below center of gravity

Contact

1. Hands on defender's chest, inside defender's arms
2. Grab defender and control him
3. Maintain knee-bend
4. Head below defender's head

Follow-Through

1. Move feet to stay with defender
2. Maintain knee-bend
3. Feet shoulder-width apart
4. Good balance

Another important aspect of blocking is body position. It's vital to have good leverage on the defender. First, the blocker comes out of his stance low with good body lean toward the defender. As he approaches the defender, he maintains a good knee-bend with his head up and his feet below his center of gravity. On contact, he maintains the knee-bend and head position, which should result in his head being below the defender's head. If he stands up straight, he won't have good balance or be able to use the power in his legs and hips to control the defender.

MISSTEP

Just prior to contact, the blocker raises up too high, reducing his ability to change direction with the defender.

CORRECTION

As he approaches the defender, the blocker settles his hips, bending his knees slightly, and maintains until contact. His eyes should be level with the defender's chest.

The third important aspect of blocking is being able to move your feet to stay with the moving defender. Usually a defender won't just stand still and let himself be blocked. Once the blocker makes contact on the block, he needs a good knee-bend, keeping his feet shoulder-width apart to maintain good balance. In other words, he needs a good football stance.

Drive Block

The drive block is used most often by offensive linemen and tight ends on running plays. It involves coming out of a three-point stance and making immediate contact with a defender, attempting to drive or push him in a direction away from the runner's path. A double-team block is a combination of two players executing drive blocks on a single defender.

The first important element of the drive block is the first step. In most cases, the blocker needs to take a positive step, one that gains ground from the stance, in a specific direction. The direction depends on where the defender is lined up in relation to where the runner is going. In general, the step needs to be in a direction that allows the blocker to get between the defender and the runner. This first step should be 6 to 10 inches long. The blocker must point his foot in the direction he wants to go. This sounds simplistic, but it's a common fault.

MISSTEP

On his first step from the stance, the blocker points his lead foot too far to the right or left of the defender he's going to block, causing him to be off target on the man and missing the block.

CORRECTION

Prior to the snap, the blocker should visualize his aiming point and make sure his first step is at that point, with the toe of his lead foot pointing in that direction.

As he takes the first step and comes up out of his stance, he keeps his body bent so that his back is flat, head is up, and arms are working as if he is running.

The second step must also be positive in the intended direction and 6 to 10 inches long. The step must not be too long. A long step causes the blocker to rise too high and may bring his feet too close together, creating improper balance.

MISSTEP

The blocker's first step out of his stance is too long, causing him to lose balance on contact with the defender.

CORRECTION

On his first step, the blocker must make sure his foot lands either flat footed or on the ball of the foot. The heel should not land first, which can only happen when he has taken too long a step. Landing on the ball of the foot or flat footed automatically forces a shorter step. If the defender is on the line of scrimmage, contact is usually made by the second step. As the blocker nears contact, he prepares his arms and hands. He attempts to strike the defender with both hands on his chest, inside his armpits. His hands should be open, with thumbs pointed up and fingers out. This position makes it easier to grab the defender's jersey or shoulder pads on contact. Remember that the blocker can't grab the defender if his hands are on or outside the defender's arms.

MISSTEP

On contact with a defender, the blocker's hands are turned so that his thumbs are pointing at each other, making it hard to grab the defender's chest.

CORRECTION

Visualize the defender's shoulder pad front. On contact, the blocker tries to wrap his fingers outside and around the side edge of the front of the defender's pads. This puts the blocker's fingers, and subsequently his thumbs, in proper position. As he makes contact with his hands, he must keep his head up. He should be able to see his hands make contact. Dropping his head creates poor body balance and usually results in a poor block. Keeping the head up is also a safety measure. The major part of the contact should be with the hands. Sometimes the helmet may also make contact. If the blocker's head is down, his head or neck could be injured. The head should stay up throughout the block.

As he makes contact with the defender, the blocker stays in good football position—knees bent, back slightly arched, head up—allowing him to get leverage on the defender. The lower player with good position usually wins the blocking battle.

After contact, the blocker follows through by moving his feet in quick, short steps, maintaining feet shoulder-width apart. Again, large steps create imbalance. Shorter steps keep both feet on the ground and allow a transfer of power to the block. When the blocker has one foot on the ground and one foot in the air, he has no power at all. Feet must stay shoulder-width apart. When the defender attempts to get off the block, he will move left or right. If the blocker's feet are close together, he will lose balance and maybe fall off the block. Keeping his feet apart enables him to take quick lateral steps to avoid being thrown to either side, allowing him to stay with the block a little longer.

Finishing the block involves keeping the feet driving and maintaining contact with the defender until the whistle blows. If the defender attempts to get off the block, the blocker tries to maintain contact as long as possible, remembering that he must not grab the defender as he attempts to disengage from the block. If he has grabbed the defender in any way, he must now let go.

Drive Block Drill 1   Drive Block on Air

The blocker comes out of his stance and takes two or three quick, choppy steps at a 45-degree angle to the right, at a 45-degree angle to the left, or straight ahead. This block is done against air, not against a defender. The focus is on getting a good knee-bend, good hand position (up and ready to engage the defender), upright head position, and straight back. The blocker takes short, choppy steps with feet shoulder-width apart.

Success Check

- Good knee-bend.
- Hands up and ready to make contact with the defender.
- Head up.
- Back straight.
- Short, choppy steps with feet shoulder-width apart.

Drive Block Drill 2   Drive Block With Sled

A second good drill involves using a blocking sled, ideally a five- or six-man sled that can accommodate the entire offensive line or the offensive line plus the tight end. Each man lines up directly across from one of the blocking pads. On the snap, the entire group comes out of the stance and drives the sled straight ahead until the coach blows the whistle to simulate the end of the play. Each player must take short, choppy steps with feet shoulder-width apart, have their hands in proper position on the pads, and their heads up. The great thing about a blocking sled is that it forces players to keep driving their feet or the sled won't move. This is also an excellent conditioning drill.

Success Check

- Use short, choppy steps with feet shoulder-width apart.
- Hands in correct position on the pads.
- Head up.
- Keep the sled moving until the whistle.

Stalk Block

The stalk block is used by wide receivers and backs away from the line of scrimmage. This block usually entails blocking a defender who's off the line of scrimmage. It starts with the blocker getting between the defender and the runner and working to stay there. For a successful stalk block, the blocker doesn't necessarily have to drive the defender back, as in the drive block. The mere act of shielding the runner from the defender is usually enough to allow the runner to get by.

The basics of the stalk block are the same as for the drive block. As the blocker approaches the defender, he settles his hips to get into good football position. His hands need to strike the defender in the chest, with thumbs up and inside the defender's arms. On contact, he moves his feet in quick, choppy steps with feet shoulder-width apart. He wants to move his feet side to side to react to the defender's movement, which is more important here than driving the defender back. Sometimes we use the phrase "block him with your feet," which means to maintain the block by moving the feet as quickly as possible to keep the body between the defender and the ball carrier.

Stalk Block Drill   Perimeter Drill

The perimeter drill is a favorite drill for the stalk block. An offensive blocker lines up wide, with a defender 5 to 7 yards off him. On the snap, the quarterback drops back and throws a swing pass to a receiver. After catching the pass, the receiver turns upfield toward the blocker and defender. On the snap, the defender drops back to defend a pass play, reacting back up to make the tackle once the ball is passed. The blocker runs downfield and stalk blocks the defender, attempting to keep him from getting to the receiver.

We usually have two lines on each side of the quarterback (figure 6.7). Two blockers and defenders go at a time on one side, followed by the two blockers and defenders on the opposite side. This way, the drill goes back and forth, giving each side a chance to get ready while the other side is going. This also gives the coach a chance to watch and correct one side at a time without slowing the drill. Players get a lot of repetitions in a short amount of time. Once the drill is set up, we can normally get 20 repetitions in 2 minutes.

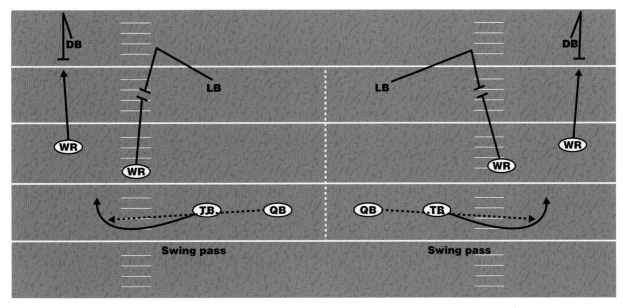

Figure 6.7 Perimeter drill with two lines.

Success Check: Defenders

- Take proper angles on pass drops at snap.
- When the ball is thrown to the tailback, redirect and attack the blocker (the wide receiver).
- Take on the blocker with good knee-bend and hand placement.
- When the tailback commits to a direction, the defender gets off the blocker cleanly in the proper direction.

Success Check: Blockers (Wide Receivers)

- Attack the defender with the proper angle.
- Make contact with hands extended, elbows bent slightly, and hands in proper position.
- Move feet to maintain position between the defender and tailback as long as possible.

Cut Block

The cut block is a block any player can use, but it has strict guidelines. Offensive linemen may use the cut block against any defender within 3 yards of the line of scrimmage. Backs may use the cut block if the back lines up behind the line of scrimmage and within the tackle box, the area from just outside each offensive tackle that extends behind the line of scrimmage. In college and professional football, anyone lined up outside the tackle box may cut block only if the defender is in a position directly opposite or outside the offensive player at the time of the block.

In the cut block, the blocker approaches a standing defender and blocks him below the waist to try to knock him down. The idea is to hit the defender's legs with the body to knock them out from under him. To execute an effective cut block, the blocker must approach the defender with good speed. When he is about 2 yards away, he dips his shoulder and body and attempts to drive his shoulder through the defender's thigh board. On contact, he finishes the block by driving his legs and attempting to run through the defender's legs as the blocker goes down to the ground. If the block is done correctly, the defender should end up on the ground along with the blocker.

The cut block is an effective tool when the defender is bigger than the blocker and a regular drive or stalk block is difficult. It's also a good surprise block. When the defender is expecting the blocker to use either a drive or stalk block, he might not be prepared to defend the cut block. The cut block can also be effective in the passing game when the blocker wants to keep the pass rusher from reaching his hands up to block a pass. To defend a cut block, the defender must keep his hands down to protect his legs, so he can't reach up to block the pass.

The cut block has two disadvantages. First, if the blocker misses his initial aiming point, he might simply fall to the ground without making any block, allowing the defender to get to the ball carrier quickly. Second, once the cut block has been made, the blocker is on the ground and cannot continue to block, which might allow the defender to get up and finish the play unblocked. To avoid these two situations, the blocker must work on good execution of the block and be selective about when to use it. This block works best when the defender doesn't have time to get knocked to the ground and still get back up to make the tackle.

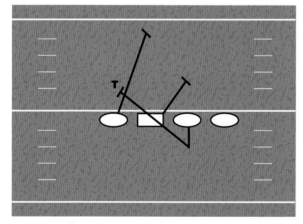

Figure 6.8   Trap block.

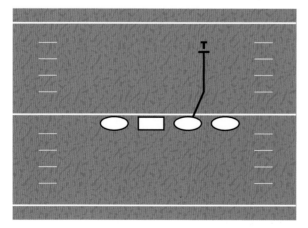

Figure 6.9   Reach block.

Trap Block

A trap block is a drive block performed on a defender who's aligned several men away. The blocker pulls toward the defender, runs down the line, and executes a drive block from the inside out (figure 6.8).

Reach and Scoop Blocks

A reach block is a drive block in which the blocker steps laterally down the line to get in front of a defender who's not directly on him (figure 6.9). The object is for the blocker to get in front of the defender so he can drive block him.

A scoop block is the same as a reach block but is normally to the inside of the blocker.

THE ILLEGAL CHOP BLOCK

A chop block is a two-on-one block in which the first blocker makes contact high on the defender followed by a second blocker making contact below the defender's waist from the side. This is an illegal block because it can easily cause a knee injury to the defender.

Pass-Protection Block

Pass-protection blocks are designed to stop the pass rush of a defender by getting between the quarterback and the rusher. There are several types of pass blocks, including the drop-back, sprint-out, and turn-protection block. All have common traits that occur once the blocker is in position to make the block.

The blocker must have a balanced stance, with one foot back at about a heel-to-toe relationship with his other foot. He needs to be in a good football stance with his knees bent. The blocker must keep his head up and back slightly arched forward with his weight over his toes. Probably the most important part of the stance is the head position and *not* being bent at the waist with the chest tilted toward the ground, which negatively affects balance.

MISSTEP

On a pass play, the offensive blocker bends at the waist or has his head down, causing him to lose his balance forward as the defender rushes.

CORRECTION

On the snap, the blocker must focus on keeping his head up, his back slightly arched, and his shoulders held back.

The blocker must maintain balance and be able to move his feet quickly to stay between the rusher and the quarterback.

The actual block is with the hands. The blocker uses a punching action aimed at the pass rusher's chest. His hands should be held close so they make contact inside the rusher's shoulders. After each punch, the blocker slightly gives ground, which allows him to reestablish proper body balance between contact. When the rusher approaches again, the blocker repeats the punch and give of ground. In effect, the blocker is buying time for the quarterback by slowing the rusher down long enough for the quarterback to release the pass. During this punch and give sequence, the blocker must keep his back turned to the quarterback.

DROP-BACK PASS BLOCK

Part of the drop-back pass block involves the initial footwork to get in position. On the snap, the blocker quickly shuffles back several steps to establish his balanced position and prepare for contact with the pass rusher. By giving ground, the blocker gives himself time to get balanced and see what the rusher is attempting to do.

Another key element in the blocker's initial movement is that he should never shuffle to the outside as he gives ground. This opens up an inside rushing lane for the defender, which is more direct to the quarterback. The blocker should always attempt to make the rusher go around to the outside in his path to the quarterback.

SPRINT-OUT AND TURN-PROTECTION BLOCKS

In the sprint-out and turn-protection pass blocks, the difference is in the initial setup and body position in relation to the defender. In the sprint-out pass, the quarterback runs to a throwing position outside the offensive blocker. Thus the blocker must first shuffle a step or two in that direction to get an angle on the rusher. The blocker then keeps his back to the quarterback and stays in his position between the quarterback and rusher.

In turn protection, the offensive blocker usually pivots his body in place at about a 45-degree angle to turn and pass-block the gap to the side he's now facing. The main difference in the two blocks is in the blocker's initial steps. The final part of both blocks is identical.

Blocking Drill 1   Six-Point Explosion

The blocker starts on his knees with his hands on the ground directly in front of his knees. His feet should be on the ground with his toes pulled up under his feet. On the coach's command, the blocker forcefully brings his hands up to a blocking position while rolling his hips forward. He should end up with his body extended forward at a 45-degree angle to the ground. He pushes off with his feet and keeps his knees in contact with the ground.

The blocker can strike a sled pad, block another player lined up across from him, or simply extend forward as if blocking air.

The blocker should follow through by fully extending his body and landing on the ground on his abdomen and chest.

Success Check

- Head and eyes are up throughout the drill.
- The arms are extended on contact with thumbs up and fingers to the side.

- Hips roll forward as contact is made.
- The body is fully extended and flat on the ground at the end.

Blocking Drill 2   Four-Point Explosion

The four-point explosion drill is very similar to the six-point explosion drill, but here the blocker starts with knees on the ground and hands resting on his thighs. His toes are up under his feet as in the six-point drill. On the coach's command, the blocker brings his hands up to strike his target (a sled, another man, or a pad). As he strikes the target, the blocker rolls his hips forward, extends his upper body, and pushes off with his feet, keeping his knees on the ground. This works the same fundamentals as the six-point drill but emphasizes rolling the hips forward without the help of the body lean to begin with.

Success Check

- Head and eyes are up throughout the drill.
- Arms are extended on contact with thumbs up and fingers to the side.
- Hips roll forward as contact is made.
- Body is fully extended and flat on the ground after contact.

Blocking Drill 3   Three-Point Explosion

This is a continuation of the six- and four-point drills. The blocker begins in a three-point stance. On the coach's command, he explodes out of his stance, bringing his hands up to strike the target in front of him, which is a sled, another man, or a pad. As he strikes the target, the blocker rolls his hips forward, extending his upper body as he pushes off with his feet. His feet should remain in place, and he should end up flat on his abdomen on the ground after striking his target. This continuation drill focuses on even more realistic body angles as the blocker works to roll his hips and strike with his arms.

Success Check

- Head and eyes are up throughout drill.
- Arms are extended on contact with thumbs up and fingers to the side.
- Hips roll forward as contact is made.
- Body is fully extended and flat on the ground after contact.

Blocking Drill 4   Drive Block on the Sled

This drill can be done on a two-man sled, a five-man sled, or a seven-man sled. The blockers line up directly in front of the sled in a three-point stance. On command, the blockers come out of their stances and strike the sled with their hands, rolling their hips and driving their feet. They should drive the sled straight back until they hear a whistle to stop them. The coach can emphasize various parts of the block by blowing the whistle at various points. If he wants to focus on coming out of the stance and the initial strike, he can blow the whistle to stop the drill after the players take three or four steps. If he wants to focus on the post contact drive of the block, he can blow the whistle after 8 to 10 steps. If he wants to use this drill for conditioning, he can keep the players driving the sled for extended distances (15 to 30 yards).

(continued)

Blocking Drill 4 (continued)

Success Check

- Head and eyes are up. (The coach can stand in front of the sled and players and look for eyes up. Or he can hold up fingers, and after the drill ask the blockers how many he had up. This encourages the players to look up.)

- Arms are extended on contact with thumbs up and fingers to side.
- Hips roll forward as contact is made.
- Legs and feet keep driving with short, choppy steps.
- Feet stay about shoulder-width apart as legs drive.

Blocking Drill 5   Reach Block on Sled

This is the same drill as the drive block drill on the sled but with a different alignment and starting point. The blocker aligns in a three-point stance offset to the right or left from the sled pad he'll be blocking. On the coach's command, the blocker comes out of his stance, taking a 45-degree step to the pad he is to block. On the second step, he should square up and block the pad straight ahead, just as in a drive block.

Success Check

- Head and eyes are up. (The coach can stand in front of the sled and players and look for eyes up. Or he can hold up fingers, and after the drill ask the blockers how many he had up. This encourages the players to look up.)
- The first step is at a 45-degree angle and 6 inches long.

- Arms are extended on contact with thumbs up and fingers to side.
- Hips roll forward as contact is made.
- Legs and feet keep driving with short, choppy steps.
- Feet stay about shoulder-width apart as legs drive.

SUCCESS SUMMARY

In step 6 we have discussed what many coaches believe are the two most important fundamentals of football: blocking and tackling. We have covered the basics of each skill and described the various types of tackles and blocks. Scattered throughout the step are basic drills to help players gain proficiency.

In step 7 we look at running the ball on offense. Before moving to that step, answer the following questions to review the important elements of blocking and tackling.

Before Taking the Next Step

1. When blocking, how should your hands be positioned when they make contact with the defender?

2. Should your head be up or down when executing any type of block?

3. After making contact on a block, how far apart should your feet be as you drive your legs?

4. What are the four elements of a tackle?

5. Why is it important to keep your head and eyes up when making a tackle?

6. What part of the blocker's body should contact the ball carrier first whenever possible?

Running the Ball

In this step we cover the Xs and Os of football—how to run the ball. We can divide our discussion into two parts: the skill of running the ball, and the offensive scheme used to design the run and execute the running play. We'll start with the skill of running the ball.

BALL-RUNNING SKILL

When running with the football, a few basics are critical, mainly to maintain ball security. (No fumbling the ball!) First is the way the runner holds the ball. In general, hold the ball in one hand, with the hand over one end of the ball and the forearm covering the remainder of the ball (figure 7.1). The hand should be wrapped around the narrow point of the ball with the thumb and little fingers on or very near the white strip. The index finger should extend up toward the point of the ball. As the ball is held against the runner's chest, the point of the ball with the hand should be angled up toward the runner's sternum. This positions the ball at about a 45-degree angle going from the runner's elbow up to his sternum. Pressure should be applied with the hand and forearm pressing the entire length of the ball against the runner's body.

In most cases, the football is held in only one hand: your outside hand. Which hand is your outside hand depends on the direction you're running. If running to the right, with most defenders coming from the left, your outside hand is your right hand. Holding the ball in your right hand keeps the ball away from defenders so they can't knock it out of your grasp. If running to the left, your outside hand is your left hand. Hold the ball in your left hand to protect it from defenders coming from the right.

MISSTEP

The player runs while holding the ball in his inside hand, allowing a defender to dislodge the ball.

CORRECTION

When receiving the handoff or pass from the quarterback, always place the ball immediately in the outside hand. Make this part of every ball-handling drill you do so the skill becomes automatic.

Figure 7.1   **GRIP ON BALL**

1. Hold ball in one hand
2. Wrap hand around narrow end of ball
3. Hold ball against chest at 45-degree angle

4. Apply pressure by hand and forearm, pressing ball against body

As a rule, once the runner secures the ball in one hand, he should not switch it to the other side. If there is a compelling reason to switch, such as a defender approaching on the same side as the ball, and if the runner is not near another defender, he may choose to switch sides. In this case, the ball must be switched while retaining contact with the runner's body. This is done by bringing the ball down to a position parallel to the ground, still holding it against the body. The runner reaches over the top of the ball with his free hand and places that hand on the free point of the ball. For a moment, he'll hold the ball with both hands on opposite ends and both forearms pressing on the ball. Once the free hand is secured, he releases the original hand and slides the ball to the new side, keeping the ball pressed against his body the entire time. He ends with the ball back up in the 45-degree angle position in the new arm.

Sometimes the ball should be held with both hands (figure 7.2). When running in a crowd and you anticipate being tackled by several defensive players, keep both hands on the ball to prevent it from being dislodged by the multiple hits. Defenders are taught to grab at the ball to cause a fumble, so you must always protect the ball. But use the two-hand grip only when in a crowd because not swinging your free arm tends to slow you down.

MISSTEP

The runner holds the ball with both hands wrapped around it when no defenders are near, slowing the pace of his run.

CORRECTION

Stay aware of your surroundings when running the ball. If a tackle is imminent, put both hands on the ball. If not, keep only one hand on the ball so the free arm can swing naturally, which promotes speed.

Figure 7.2 **TWO-HANDED GRIP IN TRAFFIC**

1. Runner anticipates multiple defenders
2. Hands grip narrow ends of ball
3. Forearms cover ball
4. Ball is held tight to the torso

Another important factor in running the ball is the runner's body position and running style. When running the ball, the runner should generally maintain a good body lean and low center of gravity. In the open field, he can run at a normal gait in relation to his foot position and body lean. In a crowd, he should run with a slightly wider base to allow him to make quick cuts left or right as needed. He should also have a little more body lean while in a crowd to prepare for contact that may occur.

VISION AND ADJUSTMENTS

Vision is critical for a good running back. Most running plays are designed to go through a specific hole or gap between two offensive linemen. The designation of this gap allows blockers to work to block their assigned defenders away from that spot. The gap also gives the runner a set place to run, knowing his blockers are working to open this space for him. However, even the best plans don't always work out. If blockers can't clear their assigned defenders from the gap, the runner must adjust and get as much yardage as possible. This is when vision becomes key. The runner keeps his eyes on the designated gap but remains ready to cut to another gap if the original one closes.

A popular running play, the zone play, is designed so the runner can cut into whatever gap is open. The offensive line blocks whoever is aligned to the right or the left, depending on where the play is going. The runner starts in that direction, looking for daylight. When he sees an opening, he makes his cut. This allows for plus yardage when one blocker doesn't do a great job but another does. In essence, the runner can't be wrong about making his cut as long as there's an opening. We'll revisit the zone play later in the chapter.

HANDOFFS

A critical part of running the ball is the exchange between the quarterback and the running back. The quarterback must hand the ball off to the running back quickly with minimal chance for a fumble. It's the quarterback's primary responsibility to ensure the ball is placed in the correct spot for the running back.

If the play is a straight run by the running back with no additional read by the quarterback required, the quarterback must focus on the handoff as he delivers the ball. As the quarterback comes away from the offensive center with the snap, his eyes go to the running back, specifically to his abdomen. The quarterback holds the ball with one hand on either side of the ball as he prepares to hand the ball off. As he reaches to place the ball in the runner's "pocket" (his abdomen), the quarterback slips his near hand off the ball and places the ball with his far hand (the hand away from the runner; see figure 7.3). The quarterback firmly places the ball on the running back's abdomen. The handoff must be firm and precise so the runner knows the ball is there when he clamps his arms down on it.

The role of the runner is to receive the ball, providing a good pocket for the quarterback, and to secure the ball as he starts to run to the called gap. The pocket is formed by the runner's arms and hands. As the runner approaches the quarterback for the handoff, he forms the pocket by holding the arm closest to the quarterback up with the forearm across the chest and parallel to the ground with the palm of the hand turned down. The arm away from the quarterback should be held across the abdomen with the forearm parallel to the ground and palm of the hand turned up. The arms should be 10 to 12 inches apart, open enough to allow the ball to move into the space.

Once the quarterback has placed the ball in the pocket, the runner clamps both arms down on the ball, placing hands on either end of the ball to secure it. From here, he can slide the ball to the proper side, depending on which way he's running.

In some plays, the quarterback will read a defensive player and then decide either to hand the ball to the running back or keep it himself, depending on what

Figure 7.3   HANDOFF FROM QUARTERBACK TO RUNNING BACK

1. Quarterback places ball with his far hand
2. Quarterback puts ball on running back's abdomen
3. Running back creates a good pocket for the ball
4. Running back secures the ball

the defender does. With this kind of handoff, the quarterback makes the decision to hand off as the ball is put in the pocket and not before. In this case the quarterback must keep both hands on the ball until he makes his decision. If he decides to keep the ball himself, he firmly pulls it back out with both hands. If he decides to hand it to the runner, he pulls out his near hand (the hand closest to the runner's body), simultaneously pressing the ball into the runner's belly with his outside hand. This pressure from the outside hand is critical so the runner knows he's being given the ball. The runner must take the ball the same way whether he is given the ball or not. He clamps down assuming he has it. It is up to the quarterback to pull it out or not.

TOSS AND OPTION PITCH

There are two basic kinds of laterals from the quarterback to the running back: the toss and the option pitch. These plays involve the quarterback tossing the ball underhand or flipping the ball with an end-over-end spin to a running back who is 4 to 5 yards away.

The toss (figure 7.4) is usually used on the toss play. The running back aligns behind the quarterback who is taking the snap from under center. On the snap, the running back turns and sprints to the side in an attempt to get outside the defender's position as quickly as possible. To get the ball to the running back, the quarterback takes the snap, steps toward the running back, and tosses the ball underhand with both hands. This toss will usually be 5 to 7 yards in length. The quarterback aims the toss in front of the running back so the running back need not slow down to catch it.

The quarterback will use one of two accepted toss techniques: the spin or the dead toss. With the spin technique, the quarterback spins the ball as he tosses it with the point of the ball directed at the running back. This technique causes the ball to travel to the running back a little faster, but it might be a little more difficult to catch. With the dead toss technique, the quarterback tosses the ball with no spin at any axis on the ball. This toss is easier to catch, but it travels slower, so the quarterback must put more effort into the toss to get the ball to the running back.

Figure 7.4 QUARTERBACK TOSS TO RUNNING BACK

1. Quarterback tosses ball underhand
2. Quarterback either puts spin on ball with point at running back or tosses ball with no spin

3. Quarterback steps toward running back as he makes the toss

MISSTEP
When the quarterback tosses the ball with spin, the ball is off target and tough for the running back to catch.

CORRECTION
Try the dead toss technique. A dead tossed ball is softer to catch and might be easier to aim.

MISSTEP
When tossing the ball using the dead toss technique, the quarterback has trouble leading the running back, so the running back must slow down to catch the ball.

CORRECTION
Try the spin technique, which gets the ball quicker to the running back.

The option pitch is used on a play in which either the quarterback or the tailback will carry the ball, depending on what the defense does. The quarterback and tailback run to the outside with the tailback behind and slightly outside the quarterback. The tailback is about 3 yards outside and 5 yards behind the quarterback. The quarterback runs toward his pitch key, usually the defender at the end of the line. If the defender turns to take the tailback, the quarterback keeps the ball. If the defender turns to take the quarterback, the quarterback pitches the ball to the tailback. The tailback maintains his position relative to the quarterback (3 yards outside, 5 yards behind) until he receives the ball or until the quarterback tucks the ball to run himself.

To execute the option pitch (figure 7.5), the quarterback holds the ball in both hands, with ball positioned the same as for a pass—first knuckles across the ball thread, gripping the upper half of the ball. He carries the ball in both hands in front of his abdomen with the point of the ball up. To make the pitch, he flips the ball with the hand nearest the tailback. The flip should be end over end, with the bottom of the ball rotating toward the running back first.

Figure 7.5 **OPTION PITCH**

1. Quarterback holds the ball in both hands in front of his abdomen

2. Quarterback flips ball to the tailback with his near hand

3. The ball is flipped by rotating it end over end, bottom first

MISSTEP

The quarterback doesn't put enough velocity on his pitch, causing the ball to be off target to the tailback.

CORRECTION

Always flip the ball with a quick arm extension, pushing the bottom of the ball with the thumb of the near hand. Step toward the target with the near foot as the ball is pitched.

Handoff Drill   Handoff Repetition

Two lines of players face each other about 5 yards apart. The first player in the first line has a ball. On command, the first player in each line runs toward the other, staying to a designated side (right or left). The player in line 1 with the ball hands off to the player in line 2.

As the handoff occurs, the next player in line 1 starts running and receives a handoff from the player from line 2. Continue the drill, with each man handing off to the player in the opposite line. Repeat three or four times for each player.

Success Check

- The player handing off the ball places it firmly on the running back's abdomen.
- The player receiving the handoff has his near arm up across the bottom of his upper abdomen with forearm parallel to the ground.
- The player receiving the handoff has his far arm parallel to the ground and across the bottom of the abdomen.
- The player receiving the handoff has both hands open with palms facing each other.
- When receiving the handoff, the player clamps both forearms down on the ball.
- After receiving the handoff, the player grasps both ends of the ball with his hands.

Run-and-Cut Drill 1   Sideways Cuts

This drill develops a running back's ability to make a cut when running the ball.

Set up cones or agility bags on the ground, as shown in figure 7.6. On the coach's command, the ball carrier runs to the first barrier and makes a sideways cut, and then runs to the second barrier and makes another sideways cut in the opposite direction. He continues and finishes after the last cut. The ball carrier should keep his shoulders pointing toward the finish all the way through the drill. He can execute one of two possible types of cuts. First is the jump cut, in which the ball carrier plants the foot opposite of the direction he is cutting to and jumps with both feet sideways. He should not cross his feet during a jump cut. As he lands, the ball carrier plants his other foot and redirects to the next barrier. The second cut is the crossover cut. In this technique, the ball carrier plants the foot opposite of where he is moving to, and then takes three quick steps to plant his opposite foot and redirect toward the ball. You can work one type of cut throughout the drill or change up the cut on each barrier.

Success Check

- The runner maintains a good knee-bend on the cut.
- The runner keeps his shoulders pointing toward the barriers throughout the drill.
- The runner changes direction sharply and doesn't round off his path on the cut.

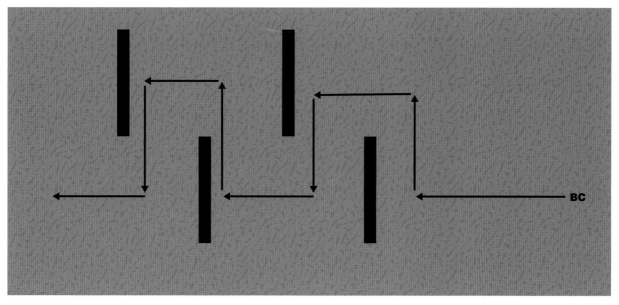

Figure 7.6 Setup for sideways cuts drill.

Run-and-Cut Drill 2   Cut on Defender

In this drill, the ball carrier works on making a cut around a defender by reacting to the defender's movement.

A defender stands 5 yards away from the ball carrier, facing each other. On the coach's command, the ball carrier runs toward the defender. When the ball carrier is 2 to 3 yards from the defender, the defender takes one step to the side. The ball carrier makes a cut opposite the defender, and then continues upfield.

Success Check

- The runner makes each cut with only one step.
- The runner keeps his knees bent and center of gravity low.

- The runner keeps his feet slightly apart as he starts to make each cut.
- The runner accelerates out of the second cut as he continues upfield.

RUNNING SCHEMES

In the Xs and Os of running the ball, there are a multitude of possible formation alignments and play designs. The formation can vary from three running backs and two tight ends to no running backs and five wide receivers. What you do will depend on your team's basic offensive philosophy and player strengths.

Running the ball means dealing with offensive plays and schemes designed to take the ball and move it as far downfield as possible. Over the years, many running plays have been designed to do this effectively. Each has strengths and weaknesses.

When designing running plays, try to answer the following questions.

1. What do you want the play to accomplish? Will the play be used when you need only a few yards to get a first down or a touchdown? Will the play be used when you need a big chunk of yardage?

2. What kind of defense is the play designed to attack? What are the strengths and weaknesses of the defense?

3. What kind of runner will carry the ball? Is he a fleet-footed player with good speed who isn't as strong a runner in a crowd? Is he a big player who can pound out tough yards on the inside?

4. What kind of blockers do you have? Are they big, strong guys who can come out of their stances and physically drive defenders back? Are they smaller, quicker players who can run well but aren't as physically strong?

Once you determine the types of runners you have and the kind of running plays you need, you can begin to design your plays. Keep some basic principles in mind when designing each play. First, the play must be simple enough for your team to execute. Don't ask players to try to execute complex moves that take a long time to learn. The more complex the play, the more chances for mistakes. Keeping the design simple improves the chances for good execution.

Second, the play should develop in a reasonable amount of time. A play that takes more than a few seconds to develop and attack the defense has a much greater chance of being identified and defended. This isn't to say that a play that tricks the defense into doing something that helps the play succeed is not a good idea. For example, one of the better trick plays is the reverse play. In the reverse play, the offense fakes a particular running or passing play in one direction, baiting the defense to pursue to one side of the field, and then has a player reverse field and take the ball in the opposite direction. This type of play works especially well against fast defenses that react quickly in a particular direction to the initial play. In general, though, the simpler the play, the greater chance for success.

Let's look at several types of plays, starting with the most simple and moving to the most complex.

Quarterback Sneak

One of the simplest running plays is the quarterback sneak (figure 7.7). In this play, the quarterback takes the center's snap and immediately runs forward behind the offensive line's blocking. The offensive linemen come out of their stances and block the gap to their inside as they drive the defenders back. The quarterback can run to either side of the center and may sometimes slip farther outside if a gap opens in the defense.

This play is simple, quick, and easy to execute. There is no handoff, so the chance of a fumble is reduced. The quarterback is already close to the line of scrimmage, which reduces the time the defense has to react once they see the play start. The sneak is designed to gain only a yard or two but can gain more if the defense doesn't react quickly.

Fullback Dive

Another simple running play is the fullback dive (figure 7.8), which is similar to the quarterback sneak in that it's an inside play that develops fast. The fullback quickly reaches the line of scrimmage. The play involves a handoff from the quarterback to

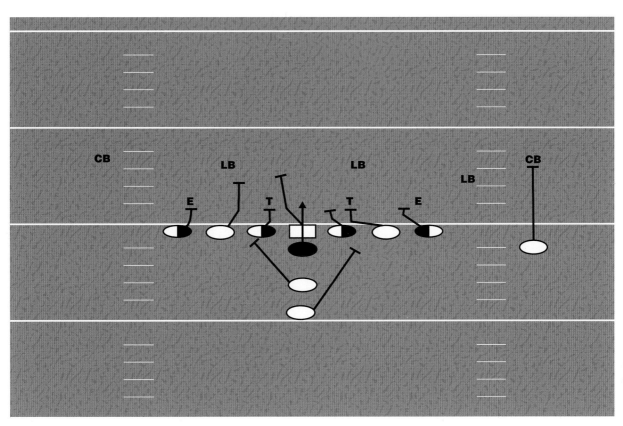

Figure 7.7 Quarterback sneak.

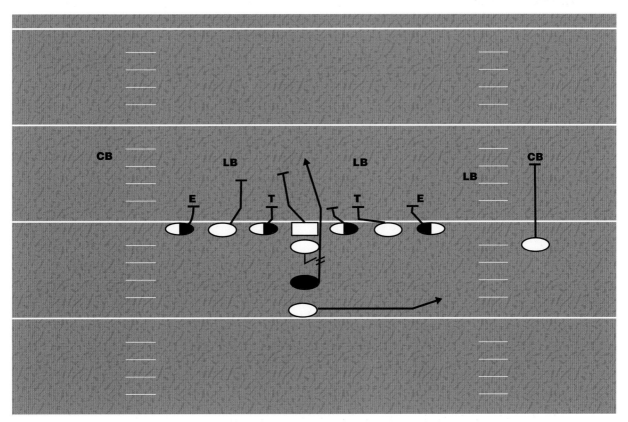

Figure 7.8 Fullback dive.

the fullback. The line blocking can be the same as shown in the quarterback sneak (wedge blocking) or can be designed to lead into the next logical play off the fullback dive.

Dive plays to the fullback, halfback, or running back are popular plays that all coaches include in their arsenal. These plays can be run from several positions in the backfield. The downside to dive plays is that they are designed to go in one particular gap between offensive linemen. If that hole is filled by a defender, the dive play might fail to make yardage.

Zone Play

A dive play that compensates for the defensive line's movement is the zone play (figure 7.9). The zone running play is a dive play that can hit any of several possible holes as the play develops. In general, the offensive line blocks an area to the side to which the play is designed to go. Whoever shows up in that area is who the lineman will block. The running back also runs to an area, but then chooses whether to run to the designed hole or change to another hole based on if the hole is filled or not. This gives the running back the option to change holes on the run and, theoretically, run to the open hole every time.

A zone play can be run either inside or outside and from just about any position in the backfield. The blocking technique and assignment for the offensive line is consistent. A zone play can account for unforeseen defensive movements. It can

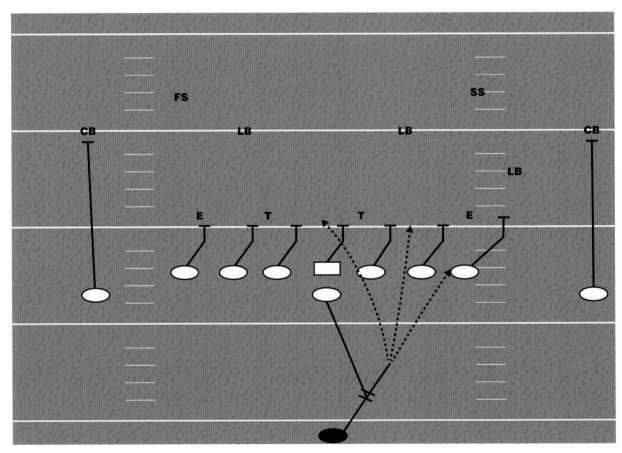

Figure 7.9 Zone play.

also compensate for a mismatch in personnel between the offensive lineman and the defensive lineman. If the defender defeats the offensive lineman's block on one side, the runner simply cuts to the other side. The same thing applies to a blitzing linebacker. If he plugs the designated hole, the runner moves to the next open hole. In this way, the offensive play has a greater chance of success than when the runner is told to hit a specific hole no matter what.

Gap Schemes

Some plays are designed to help the blocker create a better angle to block his defender. These plays are typically designed to go to a specific hole, with little deviation. They are called gap scheme plays because the blocking scheme is designed to go to a specific gap. The power play (figure 7.10) is a common example of a gap scheme play. The linemen to the side of the play block at an angle away from the play while blockers from the backfield and the other side of the offensive line block in the opposite direction at the point of attack.

The advantage of the gap scheme play is that the offensive blocker knows where he's going before the ball is snapped and usually has a good angle from which to block the defender. The disadvantage is that the runner is confined to a relatively small area in which to run the ball. If the designated hole is not there or a defender is waiting, the runner has few alternatives.

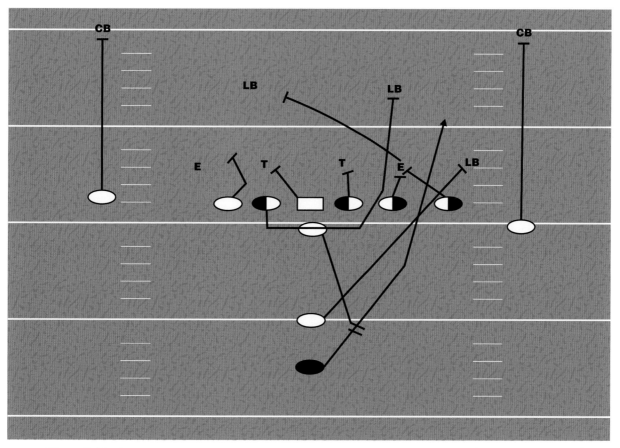

Figure 7.10 Power play gap scheme.

SUCCESS SUMMARY

In step 7 we have covered basic information on the running game. We have discussed how to hand off to a running back and how to receive the handoff. We covered how running backs should handle the ball to keep it secure while running. Several types of handoffs for the quarterback to use on various types of plays have been described. Finally, we have outlined some basic running plays, from the quarterback sneak to the gap blocking scheme.

Now that we've covered the basics of the offensive running game, in step 8 we look at ways of stopping the run on defense. Before moving to that step, answer the questions that follow to ensure you have absorbed the important points in step 7.

Before Taking the Next Step

1. What is the most important aspect of running the ball on offense?

2. How should the ball carrier hold the ball when running in the open field?

3. When should the ball carrier hold the ball with two hands while running the ball?

4. On a toss play, what technique should the quarterback use to toss the ball to the running back?

5. On an option play, how does the quarterback decide whether to pitch the ball to the tailback?

6. What is the advantage of a zone play over a regular dive play?

Stopping the Run

Stopping the run sounds simple: You find the player carrying the ball on the running play, get to where that player is running, and you tackle him. Simple! Well, at least the concept is simple. The problem is that the offense is doing everything it can to prevent defenders from making the tackle, including blocking defenders so they can't get to the runner, and using deception to try to lure defenders into the wrong position. Of course the runner himself usually has a move or two meant to avoid tacklers.

The first thing defenders must do is determine where the ball is going. Each player on defense should have a designated gap or area of the field that he is responsible for defending. The defensive linemen and linebackers are usually responsible for defending the gaps on either side of the offensive linemen. The defensive backs may also be assigned a gap or area outside the offensive linemen in which to defend the run. The safeties are typically given this responsibility. Depending on the defensive coverage scheme, however, the cornerbacks may also have a primary run responsibility.

Once the defender knows his primary run responsibility, he must read his run-pass key to determine if the play is a run. If it is a run, he must quickly figure out which gap or area the ball is being run to. Sometimes the defender is told to read someone in the offensive backfield. Sometimes he's told to read one of the offensive linemen to determine run or pass and, then, where the ball is going. We'll discuss these possible keys and reads starting with the defensive linemen.

DEFENSIVE LINEMEN AGAINST THE RUN

Defensive linemen are almost always told to read the offensive lineman or tight end they are lined up on to determine run or pass and direction.

For the defensive lineman to read run or pass, he must read how the offensive lineman is coming out of his stance. If the offensive lineman crosses the line of scrimmage and initiates contact on the defensive lineman, the play is a running play.

At times, the offense will try to fool the defense by running a play-action pass—faking a run, and throwing a pass. On these plays, the offensive linemen usually try to come out of their stances looking as if they plan to block for a run. They attempt to be aggressive, stay on the line of scrimmage instead of dropping back off it, and even keep their heads down to look as if they are run blocking.

A defensive lineman has several keys to read to discern a run play from a pass play. First, the offensive man cannot cross the line of scrimmage on a passing play. If he does cross the line, the defensive lineman plays the run. Second, the offensive player will usually have his upper body and head more upright to keep balance on the passing block. This upright position is a giveaway that the play is a pass and not a run.

Once the defensive lineman is confident the offensive lineman is blocking for a run, he reacts accordingly. A key element is how the defensive lineman initially moves and reacts while determining whether the play is a run or pass. In most cases, he must assume the play will be a run and come out of his stance aggressively to meet the blocker as forcefully as possible. If he fails to do so, he will be soft and give the blocker an advantage.

As the defender comes off aggressively, looking for a run, he reads the release and intentions of the offensive lineman and confirms the play is a run. Once he does this, he then watches the offensive blocker's head and body position to determine which direction the ball is going. The blocker will attempt to put both his head and body between the defender and the direction the ball is going. In other words, where the blocker's head is going, the ball is going. This is true in almost every block the offensive man will use. One partial exception is in the back block (figure 8.1). In a back block, the man the defender is lined up on (blocker 1) pulls around the offensive man next to him (blocker 2), allowing blocker 2 to turn back and block the defender away from the play.

In the back block, blocker 2 will have his head between the runner's direction and the defender, but his body will be working back away from the runner. For the defender, this is not a difficult read. Blocker 1 pulling in one direction is the first indication where the ball is going, whereas blocker 2's aggressive block confirms that the play is a run.

There is a type of offensive block that's more difficult for the defensive lineman to read and which takes practice to overcome. This is the influence trap block (figure 8.2). In the influence trap, the offensive blocker (blocker 1) again pulls away from the defender, but he pulls away from where the

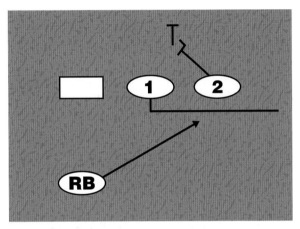

Figure 8.1 Back block.

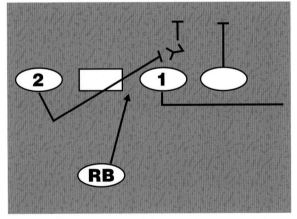

Figure 8.2 Influence trap.

ball is being run. This is followed by another lineman blocking back on the defender from the direction of the play. The difficulty is in knowing the ball is actually being run away from the initial blocker's pulling direction. The key is for the defender to realize within one step that as blocker 1 pulls, the offensive man directly next to him in that direction is not blocking him. Once the defender realizes this, he must immediately turn back to the opposite side to take on the lineman who is blocking him (blocker 2). This takes a moment to recognize and react to. This block requires a lot of practice for the correct reaction to be learned.

MISSTEP

When the man over the defensive lineman pulls to the outside, the defensive lineman either runs upfield or reacts to the outside in response to the offensive lineman's pull. Doing this allows the opposing offensive guard to pull and trap the defensive lineman out.

CORRECTION

When the offensive lineman pulls to the outside, the defensive lineman should be aware of the block of the next offensive lineman in that direction. If the blocker comes down to block the defensive lineman, the play is going to the outside. The defender can then work to the outside to help defend that play. If the blocker does not come to block the defensive lineman, the play is going inside. The defensive lineman must then react back inside to defend the trap block coming from that direction.

Once the defensive lineman reads the initial run block and knows the direction the ball is going, he gets into position to defend his designated gap. In doing so, he positions to escape the blocker and make the tackle. If the play is not coming to his gap of responsibility, he gets off the block and pursues the runner.

The success of these defensive plays depends on the defensive lineman being able to escape the blocker. To do this, the defender must use his hands, which means the defender must make initial contact on the blocker with his hands (figure 8.3a). In the past, many defenders used their forearms on the blocker, allowing more violent contact to stop the blocker's charge. With modern rules allowing blockers to use their hands, defenders are forced to use their hands as well. If the defenders use their forearms, they give blockers more surface area to grab. Because it's legal for blockers to grab defenders as long as the blocker's hands are inside the framework of his shoulders and body, the defender's forearm becomes a great place to grab. By using his hands to make contact with the blocker, the defender does two things: He removes his arm and body from the blocker, making it difficult to grab him, and he creates space for himself, which makes it easier to escape the blocker.

Figure 8.3 DEFENSIVE LINEMAN MAKING CONTACT ON THE BLOCK

Initial Contact

1. Defensive lineman makes contact with both hands
2. Fingers are out and thumbs up
3. Defensive lineman aims for blocker's chest

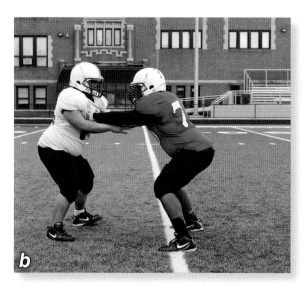

Extension

1. Defensive lineman locks out arms to full extension
2. Shoulders are parallel to the line of scrimmage
3. Feet stay apart
4. Knees are bent

As he comes off the line of scrimmage to attack the blocker, the defender strikes the blocker with both hands, with fingers turned out slightly and thumbs up, aiming at the blocker's chest. The defender should shoot his hands up from a lower position, without winding up to do so. Think of a gunslinger drawing both guns from their holsters at the same time and pointing them at the other man. As he makes contact, the defender keeps his hands inside the blocker's shoulders, preferably inside the blocker's own hands. The defender takes care not to make contact too high on the blocker's shoulder pads because his hands might slip off the top.

On contact, the defender locks out his arms to nearly full extension (figure 8.3b). At the same time, he ensures that his shoulders are parallel to the line of scrimmage. Allowing his shoulders to turn from this position puts him in a weaker position and allows the blocker to cut off his angle of pursuit. The defender immediately works to prevent the blocker to get between him and the ball carrier.

If the blocker is trying to get his head outside the defender, the defender should shuffle his feet quickly outside while maintaining his locked-arm position. When he shuffles, he must make sure not to allow his feet to come together because this puts him in a weak position, with little balance or power. Keeping his feet apart as he shuffles allows him to stay lower with bent knees and use the strength of his legs to ward off the blocker.

MISSTEP

When taking on a blocker, the defender has his feet close together, making him off balance and unable to fight against the blocker's push.

CORRECTION

Work constantly on playing with feet at least shoulder-width apart when taking on a blocker. Keep knees bent for a lower and wider center of gravity.

If the blocker is already between the defensive lineman and the ball, the defender must try to force the blocker in that direction. To do this, the defender maintains his locked-out arms while shuffling his feet toward the blocker, forcing him toward the runner. The defender uses his leg strength to do this. The defender keeps his feet apart as he shuffles and forces his near hip (nearest to where the ball is going) toward the ball, keeping his shoulders parallel to the line of scrimmage.

Once the defender knows the ball will not cut back to his gap of responsibility, he must get past the blocker and pursue to the ball. To do this, he needs to cross the face of the blocker and then turn and run to the ball carrier (figure 8.4).

The defender must not run behind the blocker, which is the way the blocker wants him to go. That way is longer, and the delay usually means the defender won't be able to get to the runner. Instead, the defender should cross in front of the blocker and then turn and pursue. When crossing the face of the blocker, the defender puts himself in position

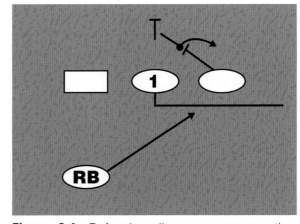

Figure 8.4 Defensive lineman crosses the blocker and turns to run toward the ball carrier.

for the blocker to grab him and prevent him from pursuing or to simply knock him down. Thus the defender must cross the face of the blocker in a certain way.

As the defender crosses the blocker's face, he keep his arms extended as much as possible. He maintains a power position with good balance so the blocker can't knock him down. A common mistake is for the defender to turn his shoulders and cross his back foot over his front foot as he turns to run. If the defender does this in front of the blocker, he's vulnerable to a punch by the blocker and will usually go down because he has no balance or power. Instead, he should pull himself across the blocker's front with his arms still extended. He should use quick shuffle steps as he crosses in front with his feet apart. This allows him to maintain balance and power when he's in front of the blocker.

MISSTEP

When trying to escape a blocker to the opposite side, the defender turns his shoulders and tries to run across in front of the blocker, allowing the blocker to drive him away from where he wants to go (the opposite side and gap).

CORRECTION

The defender keeps his shoulders square to the line of scrimmage and does *not* cross his feet as he shuffles across the front of the blocker. This allows the defender to keep his hands on the blocker and control the blocker's body. This also gives the defender a better position of strength because he can keep better leverage on the blocker with his hand and foot position.

Once the defender gets to the blocker's far shoulder, he can then turn to run. First, though, the defender must forcefully rip his hands away from the blocker to prevent any lingering grab. The best way to do this is by pulling himself forcefully across the front of the blocker and continuing that motion when he reaches the far side. This motion in conjunction with proper footwork will enable the defender to get across the face of the blocker and get off the block to pursue. This pulling motion is another reason why the defender must use his hands when he takes on the blocker. This technique is practiced in the hump drill.

Once the defender has disengaged from the blocker, he accelerates to get to the runner as quickly as he can. This is a critical point. The defender must consciously burst from the blocker to reach top speed as quickly as possible to pursue the ball carrier. Anything less than top speed will not be effective. Finally, the defender must finish his pursuit with proper tackling technique, or if the runner is already being tackled, by trying to strip the ball to cause a fumble. These three elements of pursuit are known as "burst, speed, finish." Use these three words to quickly remind defenders what they need to do (or what they have failed to do).

Crossing-the-Face Drill

Each player faces a partner in a two-point stance. The designated defender starts with his hands on the partner's chest, thumbs up and fingers out. He should be in a good football stance aligned slightly to the blocker's side. The defender is facing the blocker's shoulder. The blocker stands still, giving the defender a solid surface as the defender moves back and forth in front of him. On

Hump Drill

the coach's command, the defender simultaneously pulls himself across the front of the blocker while shuffling his feet, keeping feet apart and stepping first with the foot closest to the direction being traveled. The coach can use rapid multiple whistles to signal the movement (hump) back across the offensive man several times. The defender must stay in a good football stance throughout, moving his feet with short steps with feet apart, and pulling himself across each time with forceful hands.

The second step in this drill is to hump across and finish by escaping the blocker and taking several steps of pursuit. The defender can either escape and pursue straight down a line at 90 degrees to the blocker or upfield at 45 degrees from the blocker.

For the third step of the drill, the defender starts on one side. On the whistle, he humps to the other side and then immediately humps back to the starting side and rips off. This is a critical variation for defenders to learn. They must complete the hump before trying to release the blocker and turning to run. A common error is to release the blocker and turn to run before the defender is past the blocker. This variation drills this critical technique.

Success Check

- Defender remains in good football position throughout the drill.
- Defender starts moving with the foot closest to the direction he's going.
- Defender keeps his feet apart as he shuffles.
- Defender uses forceful pulls with the hands to cross the opponent's body.

LINEBACKERS AGAINST THE RUN

First let's discuss the run-pass keys for linebackers. There are two schools of thought on what a linebacker should key. Some coaches have linebackers key the backfield players. This allows defenders to see what kind of running play or pass play is developing. As with defensive linemen, it's better for linebackers to assume a play is a run until proven otherwise. However, play-action fakes will always cause linebackers to react wrong initially on a passing play. Because of this, I believe it's better for linebackers to read the offensive linemen for run-pass keys and for play direction.

The run-pass keys are the same for the linebacker as for defensive linemen. If the blocker crosses the line of scrimmage, the play is a run. If he does not, the play might be a run or a pass. In this case, the linebacker needs a secondary key: the backfield action. As the linebacker looks at his initial lineman key, he attempts to see the big picture with his peripheral vision.

Once the linebacker reads run, his key should also tell him direction. This is the same as for defensive linemen. The offensive blocker tries to get his head and body between the linebacker and the direction the ball is going. Based on his gap responsibility, the linebacker should aggressively attack any blocker toward the line of scrimmage. When he makes contact, he needs to use his hands to strike the blocker in the exact same way as the lineman does. Once he takes on the blocker, the linebacker should establish an extended arm position with shoulders parallel to the line of scrimmage (figure 8.5)—again, the same as the defensive lineman does. Moving left or right and getting off the blocker to pursue is also the same as for the defensive lineman.

Figure 8.5 LINEBACKER DEFEATING THE BLOCK

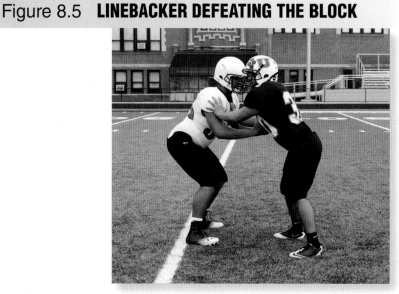

1. Linebacker makes contact with his hands
2. Linebacker extends his arms to keep the blocker away
3. Linebacker reads running play and moves to pursue the runner

DEFENSIVE BACKS AGAINST THE RUN

Defensive backs will have either primary run or pass responsibility, which determines how they initially react to their run-pass keys. In many coverages, safeties have a primary run responsibility, just like linebackers. As with linebackers, safeties with run responsibilities read offensive linemen. Because safeties usually don't line up close to the line of scrimmage, the safety will read the closest uncovered lineman. An offensive lineman who has no defender lined up on him will show his run block earlier—plus it's easier for the safety to see him.

Once the safety reads run, he attacks the closest blocking threat the same way a linebacker would. The safety attacks toward the line of scrimmage and takes on the blocker using his hands. Once the safety makes contact with the blocker, he extends his arms so he can see the play, and then gets off the block when he sees the ball carrier. From this point, the coaching points are the same as for linebackers and defensive linemen.

If the defensive back has a primary pass responsibility, he must be slow in reacting to the run key. Cornerbacks usually are in this category. Often the defender with primary pass responsibility will key a player who does not give an immediate run key. For example, a cornerback who has deep-third pass responsibility will key the quarterback or wide receiver in his area. The quarterback might fake a run and then pass, in which case the defender must not react to the run fake. The wide receiver might also come out as if to block for a run, and then take off on a pass pattern. Again, the defender must not play run first. Once the corner is positive the play is not a pass, though, he reacts immediately and takes on any blocker just as linebackers and linemen do.

MISSTEP

The defensive back assumes a play is a run and comes up to help defend, leaving his pass zone undefended.

CORRECTION

The defensive back must read his run-pass key every time a play starts. If his responsibility includes defending the run, he must see the correct key for run before he reacts to that. If his responsibility is primarily to defend the pass, he must do that first, and then react to the run play only when he's sure the play is not a pass.

Defending-the-Run Drill 1   Board Drill

This drill works the initial position necessary to take on a blocker and then getting off the block to make a tackle. Two players face each other in their appropriate stances (linemen in three-point stances, linebackers and defensive backs in two-point stances). The players straddle a 2-by-6-inch board that's about 10 feet long (either a piece of lumber or purchased from a sports equipment store).

On the coach's command, usually a snap count, both players come out of their stances and strike each other, both working to get their hands in the proper position on the opponent. The defender works to strike the offensive man's chest with his hands, keeping thumbs up and fingers out. The defender works to maintain good football position, with head below the head of the offensive man but with eyes up. Once the players strike each other, they attempt to drive the opponent backward and off the end of the board.

Emphasize proper hand and body position, especially keeping the head and eyes up. This is to avoid injury first and to aid in proper leverage second.

Also emphasize staying square (not dipping either shoulder) and keeping feet on either side of the board. This helps maintain proper leverage on the opponent.

Success Check

- The defender comes out of his stance with eyes and head up.
- The defender strikes the offensive blocker with his hands in the blocker's chest.

- The defender drives the legs and feet on contact, keeping feet apart on either side of the board.

Defending-the-Run Drill 2   Oklahoma Drill

The Oklahoma drill is a continuation of the board drill. Start with one defender, one offensive blocker, and a running back. The defender and blocker line up facing each other in their appropriate stances. The running back stands 5 yards behind the blocker. You can restrict the running back's available path by putting cones or pads on the ground 2 to 3 yards on either side of the blocker and defender. On the coach's command, the blocker and defender come out of their stances and strike each other as in the board drill. At the same time the running back attempts to run by the defender within the cones or pads. The defender strikes the blocker with proper hand placement, locks out his arms to get the blocker away from him while controlling the blocker's movement, and finds the ball carrier. Once he finds the ball carrier, the defender attempts to shed the blocker away from where the ball carrier is going and make the tackle. When shedding the blocker, the defender uses the same arm and footwork as in the hump drill.

This drill can use one, two, or three blockers and defenders.

Success Check

- The defender comes out of his stance with his eyes and head up.
- The defender strikes the offensive blocker with his hands in the blocker's chest.

- The defender drives the legs and feet on contact, keeping feet apart.
- The defender forcefully sheds the blocker away from the side the runner is on.
- The defender tackles the runner before the runner reaches a designated line.

SUCCESS SUMMARY

To defend the run, defensive players must first make the proper run-pass reads. Once they read the run, the defender protects his gap or area first and pursues out of that area only when he's sure the ball is not coming there. Next, the defender must take on blockers in such a way as to maintain control of his position and be able to get off the block to pursue to the ball. Finally, the defender must burst away from the blocker, run with top speed to the ball carrier, and finish the play using good tackling or strip-the-ball technique.

Now that we've worked on defending the run, we turn in step 9 to defending the pass. Most offensive teams use both run and pass plays. Some teams focus on the run game, some on the pass game. A defense usually must stop the run game first and foremost. If an offense can run the ball effectively, they won't need to pass the ball nearly as much. They'll avoid pass plays because more things can go wrong on a pass. Once the defense slows down or stops the opponent's run game, the offense will be forced to pass the ball. Before we shift our focus to defending the pass, answer the following questions to ensure you understand the demands of defending the run.

Before Taking the Next Step

1. How are assignments given to defensive players to defend an offense's running game?

2. What are two types of blocks a defensive lineman must defend?

3. When a defender in any position gets blocked, should he use his hands or his forearms to take on the blocker?

4. If a defender is on one side of the blocker and needs to move to the other, what technique can he use?

5. How does a defender position his eyes and head when taking on a blocker?

6. When should a defensive back come up to help stop a run play?

Defending the Pass

To effectively defend the passing game, the defender must first determine the type of passes he is defending. Does the offense employ a short three-step game, high–low routes, spacing routes, or another passing system? Your pass defense will also depend on which defensive scheme your team is best suited for. The most difficult pass defense to throw the ball against is man-to-man coverage—that is, *if* defenders are capable of executing the man technique consistently. If they are not, then zone coverage techniques should be used. In this step, we discuss pass defense coverage techniques for man and zone schemes. In man-to-man schemes, we cover both man coverage with help and blitz man coverage techniques.

ZONE COVERAGE

Let's start with zone coverage techniques used by defenders responsible for the underneath coverage zones. Generally, these are divided into the hook, curl, and flat zones (figure 9.1). Usually linebackers are responsible for the hook and curl zones and a linebacker or defensive back is responsible for the flat zones.

In zone coverage, the two basic techniques used are spot dropping and pattern match dropping.

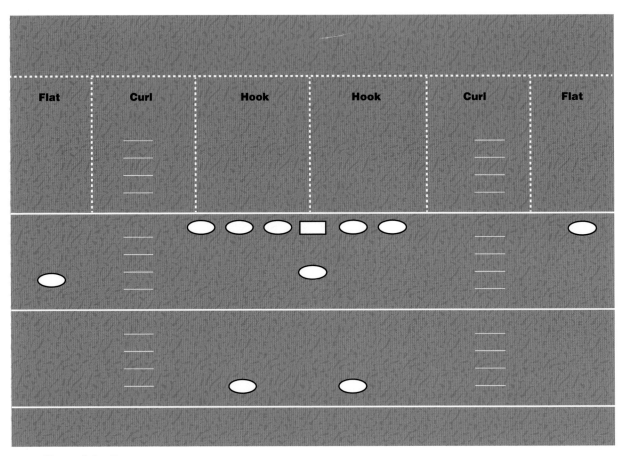

Figure 9.1 Pass coverage zones.

Spot Dropping for Underneath Zone Defenders

In spot dropping (figure 9.2), once a pass is declared, the defender drops back to a depth of 10 to 12 yards, aiming at a specific spot on the field related to the pass zone he's responsible for. For example, the player who covers the flat zone drops back to a point somewhere around the numbers painted on the field, approximately 9 yards from the sideline. This spot should be on the inside edge of the zone that the defender is responsible for.

When dropping to a zone, the defender must get back to his coverage spot as quickly as he can to be ready to react to the pass. He breaks toward the ball as quickly as possible. If he's in the process of running back to his spot when the ball is thrown, he will have to stop his momentum and redirect his movement to run to the ball. This always takes at least one step or more and, consequently, more time. That extra step and time might be all it takes for the ball to reach the receiver before the defender can get there. By getting back to his coverage spot 10 to 12 yards deep and being ready when the ball is thrown, the defender eliminates the time it takes to redirect his movement.

Why 10 to 12 yards deep? This is a general depth based on the average depth a pass is thrown. Pass routes can be 4 or 5 yards deep (three-step passing game), 10 to 15 yards deep (five-step passing game), or deeper (seven-step passing game). The

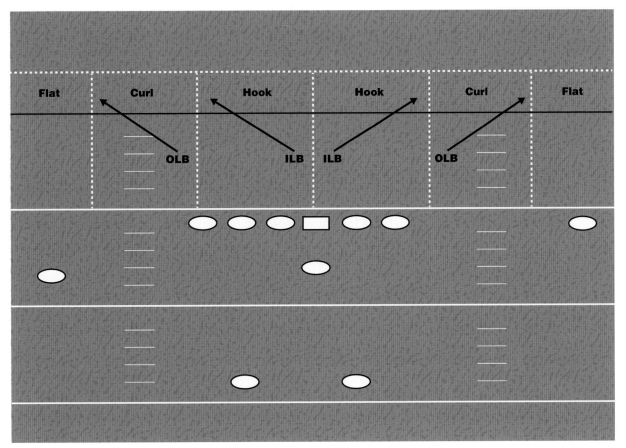

Figure 9.2 Spot drop to zones.

defender's depth should be tied to the quarterback's drop. When the quarterback is ready to throw the ball, the defender must be as deep as possible but also stopped and in a good football stance, ready to react in whatever direction the ball is thrown. On a three-step pass, the defender might get back only 5 to 7 yards. On a five- or seven-step pass, the defender should be able to get back 10 to 12 yards. On a play-action pass, the defender might be out of position initially if he reacts to the run-play fake and thus need to hustle to get as much depth as possible, because play-action patterns typically range from 10 to 15 yards or longer.

MISSTEP

The short zone defender drops back 15 yards or more, allowing the quarterback to complete a short pass and giving the receiver room to run.

CORRECTION

When dropping to his underneath zone, the defender needs to see when the quarterback stops his drop and sets to throw the ball. When the quarterback stops, the defender must also stop dropping in order to see the ball thrown and make a break to it. This will prevent the defender from dropping too deep.

Short zone defenders should not normally drop back more than 10 to 12 yards. If they drop back farther, the very short zones might be exposed to a dump pass, which can then be run for a significant gain before the defender reacts to make the tackle. This might vary, however, on a third- or fourth-down play when the offense must gain 15 yards or more for the first down. In this case, the short-zone defenders should drop deeper to defend any pass at that depth. In this situation, a completed pass and run that's shorter than the first-down distance is a win for the defense.

The fastest way for a short zone defender—such as a linebacker lined up 3 or 4 yards from the line of scrimmage—to get to his coverage spot is to turn and run back. However, if the defender turns his back on the quarterback as he runs to his spot, he can't see when the quarterback is ready to throw. Thus the defender needs to keep his head and eyes turned so he can see the quarterback during the drop. This requires the defender to have his shoulders turned slightly toward the quarterback as he crosses his legs over in a forward running motion. The defender should also keep his head on a swivel. This means he should quickly glance at the spot he's running to, then glance back at the quarterback to see where he is in his drop. The defender should continue this head swivel until he gets set at his coverage spot and can settle into a good football stance.

The negative to using the crossover technique is that if the quarterback throws the ball while the defender is running back, the defender must stop his running motion first before he can break in the direction the ball is thrown. This is why the defender must stop his drop and get in a good football stance once the quarterback has stopped *his* drop and is in position to throw the ball.

Another way to drop to a coverage zone is to backpedal (figure 9.3) until the defender reaches the designated spot. This can work if the defender does not have far to go, but it takes longer, so he can't travel as far. The positive is that the defender can see the quarterback and react as the quarterback throws the ball. In the backward crossover technique, the defender might have his head turned away when the quarterback sets to throw. This might cause the defender to be late in reacting when the ball is delivered.

Figure 9.3 Defender backpedalling to drop into zone coverage.

Once the defender has reached his designated drop spot, he stops his movement and settles into good football position. Because he should be on the inside edge of his pass zone, he turns his shoulders and hips at a 45-degree angle to the line of scrimmage. This puts him in better position to break on any pass thrown into his zone without needing to take extra steps.

Once at his spot and in good football position, the defender needs to see the quarterback while at the same time being aware of any potential receiver in his zone. Knowing that a receiver is in his zone allows the defender to anticipate the exact angle he should run to defend a pass to that receiver.

Seeing the quarterback lets the defender see exactly when the ball is thrown, allowing him to make a break to the pass as quickly as possible. Part of getting a great break toward the ball is anticipating when and where the quarterback is throwing the pass. This is done by seeing the quarterback's eyes as well as his shoulders and hands.

The quarterback's eyes tell the defender where the throw will go. The quarterback will throw the ball where he is looking every time! The quarterback's shoulders pointing in a certain direction also signals where the throw is meant to go. He must point his front shoulder in the direction he's throwing, so the defender can anticipate direction from this as well. Finally, the quarterback's hands tell the defender when he is throwing. The quarterback will hold the ball in both hands while scanning the field and looking for his receiver. The moment he decides to throw the ball and initiates the throwing motion, he'll take his nonthrowing hand off the ball to begin the motion. This is the signal for the defender to break to the point where he believes the ball is going. He picks this spot because he's aware of the potential receiver's position and because he has watched the quarterback signal the throw.

This anticipation and cue to break to the ball allows the defender to run to the correct spot at the earliest possible moment, and in the best direction. If he waits to see where the ball is actually traveling, he'll be too late in getting to the reception point and have little chance of preventing the receiver from catching the ball.

MISSTEP

The defender is consistently late breaking on passes thrown to receivers. The cause is usually the defender not seeing the pass being thrown by the quarterback.

CORRECTION

The defender must work to get to his assigned pass zone quickly and get his feet set and ready to break to wherever the ball is thrown in that zone. The defender must also keep bringing his vision back to the quarterback to watch for the signal for where the ball will be thrown.

Once the defender arrives at the receiver, he attacks the receiver to defend the pass and to ensure that the receiver doesn't get away. As he approaches the receiver attempting to catch the ball, the defender aims for the receiver's shoulder closest to the line of scrimmage. The defender should reach with his near hand (the one closest to the quarterback) to knock the pass away from the receiver. At the same time, the defender positions his far hand behind the receiver, ready to grab and tackle him should the ball be caught.

Many defenders tend to reach with their back hand (or the hand farthest from the quarterback) when they go to knock down a pass. But if the defender misses the ball, he is now positioned in front of the receiver, allowing the receiver to turn upfield and away from the defender, escaping the tackle.

If the defender feels he has a good chance to intercept the ball, then as he approaches the receiver he brings his back hand forward to catch the ball with both hands. He should do this only when he's very confident he'll get to the ball in time, because if he misses, the receiver might catch the ball and get away.

MISSTEP

The pass defender goes to the receiver to defend the pass and tries to knock the ball down with the hand away from the quarterback, allowing the receiver to catch the ball and turn upfield.

CORRECTION

When defending a pass, the defender should always approach the receiver and knock the ball down using the hand closest to the quarterback. At the same time, he must have the hand and arm away from the quarterback ready to grab the receiver and secure him in a tackle if the ball is caught.

Pattern Match Dropping

As the name implies, this technique of zone coverage involves the defender making his drop in relation to the passing pattern the receiver is running. The defender still has a pass zone to defend, just as in spot dropping. The difference is in the initial aiming point for the defender when he begins his drop. Whereas in spot dropping the defender aims for a specific spot on the field, in pattern match dropping (figure 9.4), the defender aims at a spot that's in relation to the nearest receiver threat to his zone.

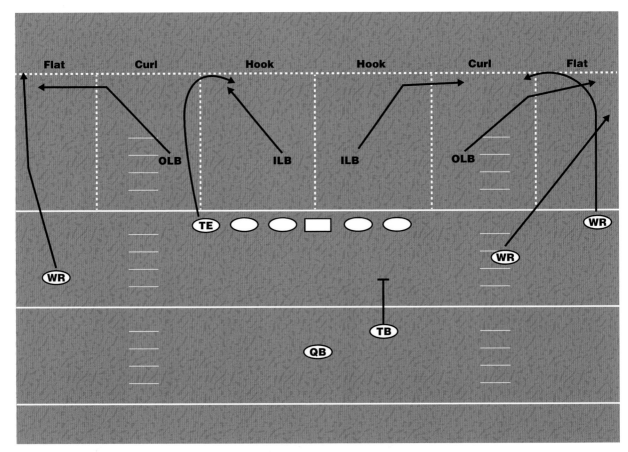

Figure 9.4   Pattern match drops.

The following are the rules for whom a defender drops toward in his initial movement:

Flat defender: Drop based on the number-one receiver (receiver farthest from the quarterback) on the defender's side of the field

Curl defender: Drop based on the number-two receiver (receiver second farthest from the quarterback)

Hook defender: Drop based on the number-three receiver (receiver third farthest from the quarterback)

As a defender identifies the receiver he's dropping toward, he identifies the aiming point for his drop. This point should be 10 to 12 yards deep and 2 or 3 yards inside the alignment of his indicated receiver. By dropping to this point, the defender ends up in close proximity to the first receiver who can threaten his zone of responsibility. This is the main advantage of pattern match dropping. In spot dropping, this is not always the case. The disadvantage of pattern match dropping is that the defender tends to keep his eyes on the receiver longer during his drop so he can end up in the right place. This can lead to the defender's failure to see the quarterback setting up to throw, delaying him in breaking on the throw.

Other than the initial aiming point, the drop and break-on-the-ball technique for pattern match dropping is identical to that of spot dropping. In either case, the defender should be as deep as he can be (up to 12 yards), be in good football position with eyes on the quarterback when the ball is thrown, and break to the receiver's upfield shoulder to defend the pass. When working on zone pass defense, focus on these three key elements.

Deep Zone Defense

So far we have focused on zone defense in the short zones. What about the deep zones? These are normally referred as the deep 1/2, deep 1/4, or deep 1/3 zones, depending on the coverage you're using. Several principles are common to each of these.

First, a deep zone cover defender needs to always stay deeper in his zone than any receiver or potential receiver. The worst sin a deep zone defender can commit is to allow a receiver to get behind him in his zone, which will nearly always result in a touchdown pass.

MISSTEP

The pass defender who has a deep zone allows a receiver to get behind him in the zone. The probable result is a touchdown pass to the receiver.

CORRECTION

The defender must be keenly aware of his zone and understand that no one can get deeper than him in that zone. He should be able to see the receiver and the quarterback beyond the receiver at the same time. He must anticipate that the receiver might try to get deeper, and must thus maintain a cushion of space behind the receiver—a distance of several yards between himself and the receiver.

The defender needs to learn how deep is deep enough without being too deep to defend receivers in the shallow part of the zone. Remember that short zone defenders will be about 10 to 12 yards deep. This means they can defend pass patterns up to about 15 to 17 yards deep. Anything deeper will fall on the deep defenders to stop. Thus any pass beyond 17 yards should be the responsibility of the deep defender. He can't just line up 25 yards deep or more to stop deep throws.

Second, the deep zone defender should be able to cover any receiver in his zone equally well. For example, if a defender is responsible for the deep outside 1/3 of the field and one receiver is running down the sideline and another is running down the hash mark, the defender must position himself so he can break to either receiver when the ball is thrown. The ball will take longer to reach the outside receiver because he's farther from the quarterback, so the defender can cheat a little toward the inside receiver.

The technique used by a zone defender in a deep zone starts with a stance that allows the defender to read his run-pass key but be able to start defending his zone from the start of the play. All deep zone defenders should defend the pass first and run second. This means the defender should never come back up to help on a run play until he's certain the play is a run and not a play-action pass. The defender can start with either a shuffle or backpedal technique.

The deep defender responsible for either a deep 1/2, middle deep 1/3, or inside deep 1/4 should start moving using a backpedal technique. This allows him to fully see the quarterback and any potential receiver threats to his zone. Once he identifies threats to his zone, he then adjusts his technique to the threat. In general, he should stay in his backpedal as long as he can so he can see the field and the quarterback. He should come out of his backpedal and turn to run only when a receiver threatens to get behind him in the zone. The point at which this occurs depends on two things: the speed of the receiver running downfield, and the ability of the defender to turn out of his backpedal and start running. This is called the transition from the backpedal, or "flipping his hips." The quicker a defender can transition or flip his hips, the closer he can allow the receiver to get before he must do so. In general, the defender should start to transition when the receiver gets 3 to 5 yards from him. Again, the speed of the receiver might dictate when this occurs. The point at which this transition should take place is called a player's cushion.

It takes practice to get a feel for knowing when this point is reached. This is a critical point to understand. A transition that's too late will allow the receiver to get behind the defender. A transition that's too soon will allow the receiver to make a break far underneath the defender for a shorter pass. Each defender will have a slightly different cushion depending on his ability to flip his hips and his overall speed. Slower players need a bigger cushion.

There are a couple of coaching points for the transition. First, the defender must be moving with his knees bent in good football position. This ensures that his body is in balance and allows efficient movement once he initiates the turn. Second, when he does make the first move, he must open up his leg and hip to the side he is turning. He should point that foot in the direction he is going. If the foot points anywhere else, his turn will be inefficient and take too much time. Third, at the same time he opens his hips, he should pull his near arm and elbow backward in the direction he's turning. This helps the body follow the movement of the hips. Finally, he needs to turn his head quickly and refocus on the receiver. A slow head turn tends to slow the whole body, creating an overall slow turn and transition.

Once the defender makes his transition, he must maintain a position on top of the receiver by about a yard. He should also be about a yard on one side—which side depends on the specific coverage requirements. Once in this position, he should attempt to look back through the receiver to the quarterback. But he must keep the receiver in his vision. It's also important to see the pass delivered, if possible. Of the two, however, seeing the receiver takes precedence.

Deep Zone Drill   Cushion Drill

The defender aligns 7 to 8 yards away from a receiver 1 to 2 yards on either side. On the coach's command, the receiver sprints straight ahead, trying to run past the defender. The defender executes the correct initial footwork technique (backpedal or shuffle). The defender attempts to stay in his initial footwork technique until the receiver gets within 3 to 5 yards of him. At this point the defender should turn and run (transition), keeping his eyes on the receiver and keeping the receiver between him and the quarterback. If the defender has trouble keeping the receiver in front after the transition, he should start his transition with the receiver farther away (4 to 6 yards). If the defender transitions and has too much room between him and the receiver (5 to 6 yards), he should start his transition with the receiver closer (2 to 3 yards). The point at which the defender can initiate his transition correlates to his ability to quickly turn his hips and get into a run.

Success Check

- The defender can stay in his initial footwork (backpedal or shuffle) for more than 5 yards.
- The defender quickly transitions from his initial footwork to a backward run without the receiver passing him.
- The defender can maintain his cushion (2 to 3 yards) as the receiver continues to sprint down field.

MAN-TO-MAN COVERAGE

Two main types of man-to-man coverage are prevalent in football: blitz man and man coverage with help. Man coverage with help can be either man free or man under. All three types of man-to-man coverage have identical elements. The main difference is whether the defender ends up on top of or underneath the receiver. Other than that, the techniques are very similar.

Blitz Man

Blitz man is used with either a six- or seven-man blitz in which each pass defender must cover a designated receiver with no help. Because they have no help, the defenders should always end up on top of the receivers. This prevents the defender from getting beat on a deep throw that could result in a touchdown pass. Let's look at alignment, initial steps, and reaction to movement for blitz man.

Because the defender has no help on blitz man, he must force the receiver to run a pass route that's either easier for the defender to defend, harder for the quarterback to throw, or both. This means forcing the receiver to the outside, away from the quarterback. This forces the quarterback to make a longer throw and puts the defender's body between the quarterback and the receiver. Sometimes this inside position makes the quarterback think the receiver is covered, and he doesn't make the throw. When the receiver can get inside the defender, the quarterback can see quickly that the receiver is open and make the easier inside throw.

The defender can start in either an off alignment or a press alignment. In either case, he needs to line up with an inside position on the receiver. When in an off position, the defender should be about 4 to 6 yards off the line of scrimmage. He also needs good eye focus on the receiver. When the receiver starts to run his route, the defender slowly backpedals out. The key word here is *slow*. If the defender backpedals too fast, the receiver can make a quick inside cut and be open for a slant pass. By being slow, the defender cuts off the quick inside route. As in zone coverage, once the receiver reaches the defender's cushion, the defender needs to transition (flip his hips) and run to a position about 1 yard on top of and 1 yard inside the receiver.

The defender's eye control is important in man coverage, as in most coverage techniques. Because the receiver usually tries to fake an initial route and run something else to get the defender out of position, it's important that the defender make as quick an adjustment as possible. It helps for the defender to focus on a part of the receiver's body that cannot be used to make his fake, such as the receiver's chest or belt buckle. Both always point in the direction the receiver is moving. The defender should *not* look at the receiver's head, arms, or feet.

MISSTEP

The pass defender in man coverage focuses on the receiver's head, allowing the receiver to make a head fake that causes the defender to take a false step. This leads to the receiver getting open past the defender.

CORRECTION

The pass defender should focus on the receiver's chest or belt. The receiver can't move these anywhere but in the direction he's running, so the defender is much less likely to follow a fake.

The defender must never lose sight of his receiver. This means the defender should never look at the quarterback or backfield unless he can also see his receiver. The only time this should happen is when the defender ends up on top of the receiver as he moves through his route. If this position allows the defender to see both the receiver and the quarterback, it's okay for him to look for the quarterback. If the defender can't see the quarterback when in position, he should never look until he knows the ball is in the air.

There are two ways to know if the ball has been thrown to the receiver. The first is when the defender's teammates make a "ball" call to alert the defender the pass has been thrown. The second is by seeing the receiver's eye focus. The receiver will look up to see a ball approaching. If the defender reads this, he can take a quick peek to see the ball. It's critical for the defender not to let himself slow down when he peeks, which is a normal reaction to turning the head. The defender forces himself to increase speed as he peeks, which will maintain his current speed.

If the receiver has managed to get past the defender, and the ball is thrown, the defender should not look for the ball. Looking only allows the receiver to get farther on top of the defender. Instead the defender reads the receiver's eyes to see if the ball is coming. When the receiver starts to reach for the coming ball, the defender reacts by quickly punching his hands up through the receiver's hands to knock the ball out.

Man Free and Man Under

When using man free or man under, the coverage man must know where the extra pass defender assigned to help on the routes is located. Usually in man free, the extra defender is located in the deep middle third of the field. In man-under coverage, the extra defenders are usually in the deep half of the field. Because the coverage man has deep help in both scenarios, he should cover the receiver accordingly. In other words, the defender should end up underneath the receiver because the helper is already on top. This means the defender must be a little slower on his initial coverage and let the receiver get slightly past him. This is called covering the low shoulder of the receiver. The defender is either inside or outside, depending on which coverage, and underneath the receiver to take away any short routes. Again, the defender must maintain about a 1-yard by 1-yard coverage (1 yard inside or outside and 1 yard underneath). Another name for this is trail technique.

This coverage can be difficult for defenders to learn, especially if you use a lot of blitz man technique. In blitz man, the defender has been programmed to never let the receiver get past him. In trail technique, he *wants* the defender to get past him. It takes many repetitions to get this ingrained to the point that the defender is comfortable letting it happen. With man free or man under, the principles of cushion and eye control are exactly the same as with blitz man.

Defending-the-Pass Drill 1   Zone Drop

This drill works the defender's technique in dropping back into his underneath zone to defend a pass. Start with one player lined up 5 yards from a coach in a good football stance. The coach designates which way the defender should drop (left or right). On the coach's command, the defender turns and drops at a 45-degree angle using backward crossover steps. The defender can aim either at a designated spot (a cone or mark on the field) or to the inside edge of his designated zone (hook, curl, or flat). As he drops, the defender quickly glances at his aim point (where he wants to end up) and back at the coach (standing in for the quarterback). When he gets to his zone, the defender throttles down and gathers himself in good football position, facing his zone but with good vision of the coach. At the same time, the defender keeps his feet moving while running in place with short, choppy steps. The coach gives a visual clue to where he's looking to throw the ball by turning his shoulders and looking at his intended target. The player anticipates which direction the coach will throw the ball to ready himself to break in that direction on the coach's throw. The coach can actually throw the ball or simulate the throwing motion and have the defender break in the intended direction.

(continued)

Defending-the-Pass Drill 1 (continued)

Success Check

- The defender gets to proper depth (10 to 12 yards) before he stops running to his zone.
- The defender runs back with knees bent, eyes looking back and forth between his aim point and the quarterback (coach).

- Once the defender gets to his zone, he settles into a good football stance, shoulders turned slightly out toward his zone.
- Once the coach throws the ball or simulates a throw, the defender reacts quickly in the correct direction.

Defending-the-Pass Drill 2
Zone Drop Versus Receiver

This is a continuation of the zone drop drill in that the defender drops to a designated spot (left or right) using correct backward crossover running technique. He keeps his head on a swivel, looking at his aim point and back at the quarterback as he drops. At the same time, a receiver runs a route into the defender's zone. The defender drops to his spot, reads the quarterback's (coach's) intentions, and breaks on the ball when it's thrown to the receiver. If the receiver runs a short route (less than 6 or 7 yards), the defender should still drop back to 10 to 12 yards deep. If the receiver is running a route toward the inside of the defender's zone, the defender should not get too much width with his drop and overrun the receiver. If the receiver is running a route toward the outside of the defender's zone, the defender must be ready to work to the outside after he gets to the correct depth (10 to 12 yards).

Success Check

- The defender drops quickly at a 45-degree angle with his head on a swivel.
- The defender gets at least 10 to 12 yards deep before he settles into a good football stance with feet chopping in place.

- The defender has good vision on the quarterback (coach) and back to his aim point as well as the receiver entering his zone.
- The defender breaks quickly once the ball is thrown to the receiver.

Defending-the-Pass Drill 3   Break on the Ball

This drill works the phase of pass defense when the ball is actually thrown. This assumes the defender has already dropped to his designated zone and is reading the quarterback for pass clues, ready to break to the ball when it's thrown. The defender aligns 15 yards from the coach, 12 yards for the defender's drop plus a few yards to simulate the quarterback's drop depth. The defender can either face the coach or turn 45-degrees left or right to simulate facing his pass zone. The coach brings the ball up in a ready-to-throw position.

Success Check

- The defender has his eyes on the quarterback (coach) for clues to the direction the ball will be thrown.
- The defender is in a good football stance, ready to react to the throw.

At the same time, the defender starts running in place with short, choppy steps. The defender reads the coach for the intended pass direction. The coach (quarterback) throws the ball about 10 yards to either side of the defender. Once the coach throws the ball, the defender breaks as quickly as possible and attempts to catch the ball. As the defender gets better at making a good break, the coach can throw the ball slightly farther away, forcing the defender to get a quicker break and run faster to catch the ball.

- The defender is able to start his break to the ball immediately after the quarterback starts his throw, not after the ball leaves the quarterback's hands.
- The defender is able to get to the ball and catch it.

Defending-the-Pass Drill 4   Swat Drill

This drill practices the act of knocking down a pass while securing a possible tackle of the receiver. Start with the defender about 10 yards from the coach; the receiver is about 11 yards from the coach and slightly to the right of the defender. On command, both players run to their right, perpendicular to the coach. The coach throws a pass

Success Check

- The defender is able to knock the ball down with his near hand while keeping his far arm and hand behind the receiver.

to the receiver. As the ball approaches the receiver, the defender tries to knock the pass down with his right hand (the hand closest to the coach). At the same time, the defender should have his left hand and arm ready to grab the receiver if the ball is caught. Repeat the drill with the defender and receiver running both directions to work on both hands.

- The defender does not touch the receiver while knocking down the pass.
- If the defender misses the pass, he's able to grab the receiver with his back arm and hand.

SUCCESS SUMMARY

In step 9, we have discussed the two main types of pass defense: zone coverage and man coverage. We have covered two types of underneath zone coverage: spot dropping and pattern match dropping. We've also reviewed techniques used in covering the deep zones by the defensive backs. In the last part of the step we looked at the two types of man coverage versus the pass: blitz man and man coverage with help.

Before moving on to step 10 on kicking and punting, review step 9 by answering the following questions.

Before Taking the Next Step

1. What are the five underneath pass zones?

2. What are two types of underneath zone coverage drop techniques?

3. When dropping to an underneath zone, should the defender turn and run back to the zone with his back to the quarterback?

4. What does pattern match zone defense mean?

5. After dropping to your pass zone responsibility, what do you key on to be able to make a quick break to where the ball is thrown?

Kicking and Punting

The skills of kicking and punting the ball have a great impact on special teams play. The ability to kick a field goal or PAT (point after touchdown) is often the difference between winning and losing. Likewise, effective kickoffs and punts that result in good field position for your defense makes their job a lot easier and frequently result in good field position for your offense.

FIELD GOALS AND PATS

The three kicks in football are the kickoff, the field goal, and the PAT. As we noted in step 1, the kicks for field goals and PATs share many similarities in technique. On a kickoff, the kicker is not limited in any way to how long he takes or how far away from the ball he starts. On a field goal or PAT attempt, the kicker is limited by time and space—to put points on the board, he must kick the ball between the uprights before a defender can block the kick. Thus it's mainly the kicker's approach in each situation that distinguishes one kick from another. The actual skill of kicking the ball is the same. We'll discuss this first.

In modern football, the vast majority of kickers are soccer-style kickers. That is, they approach the football from a slight angle and kick the ball with the inside top of the foot as a soccer player would. Before soccer style became the rage, all kickers used their toes to kick the ball, with the ankle locked in a 90-degree angle and the toes pointed up. Soccer style has become the dominant technique because the force generated is much greater, which makes the ball go farther. The accuracy of soccer-style kicking tends to be slightly lower than straight-on kicking, but this has not slowed its proliferation.

Because the moment the foot strikes the ball is key to a good kickoff, field goal, or PAT, we'll briefly discuss soccer-style kicking from the point the foot makes contact. The foot contacts the ball on the inside top of the arch near the ankle. On contact, the big toe is pointed at the ground and at a slight inside-to-out angle. The ankle is locked out, with the foot pointing down and away from the kicker's body. The inside of the arch contacts the ball. The exact point of contact is slightly below the middle of the ball (figure 10.1).

Figure 10.1   FOOT CONTACT ON A SOCCER-STYLE KICK

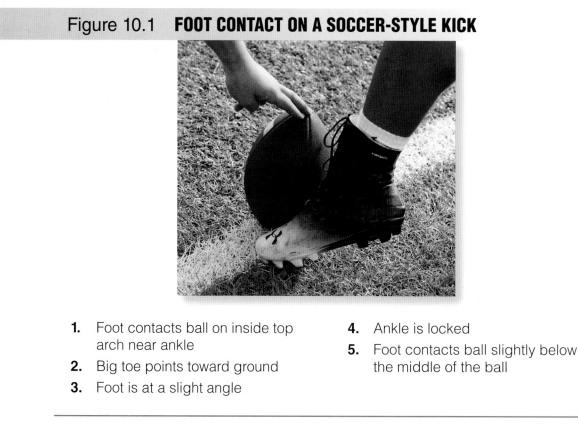

1. Foot contacts ball on inside top arch near ankle
2. Big toe points toward ground
3. Foot is at a slight angle

4. Ankle is locked
5. Foot contacts ball slightly below the middle of the ball

Getting to the point of good contact begins with the right approach, which we discuss next.

Approach for the Kick

The approach to the ball is different for field goals or PATs and for kickoffs. As mentioned, time is critical on field goals and PATs. The defense is allowed to come across the line of scrimmage to block these kicks, so the ball must be kicked as quickly as possible without sacrificing technique. In normal circumstances, the kick should take 1.3 to 1.4 seconds from the snap to the kick in order to avoid being blocked. We'll discuss this more later, after we cover the technique of the approach steps.

To kick the ball on time, the kicker should use two steps on his approach. So, a right-footed kicker steps with his right foot first, and a left-footed kicker steps first with his left foot. The toe of the stepping foot should point directly at the ball (figure 10.2a). The second step brings the plant foot down, with the ball of the foot even with the football and toes pointed slightly toward the ball (figure 10.2b). The kicker's body leans away from the ball. While taking the second step, the kicker bends his kicking leg, bringing the heel of his kicking foot back by his butt. As the kicker plants his front foot, he starts moving the kicking leg forward. He contacts the ball just as the kicking leg reaches knee-lock position. This maximizes the full extension of the leg as well as it's swing speed to create as much leg speed as possible at contact. At the point of contact, the kicker must keep his eyes focused on the ball. He wants to see his kicking foot contact the ball.

As the kicker starts his steps, he leans forward slightly, with weight on his front (kicking) foot. As he takes his second step (the plant-foot step), he brings the arm opposite the ball up and out at shoulder level away from the ball. This helps start the body rotation that must take place as he kicks the ball.

To start in the correct place, kickers must experiment with their alignment steps. Most kickers start at the ball, pointing the toe of the kicking foot at the target line or goal post opening. They take two steps back and either two or two and a half steps to the side, depending on body type and size. All kickers should experiment with what gets them in correct position to be able to take their normal approach to the ball.

Figure 10.2 FIELD GOAL OR PAT ATTEMPT

First Step

1. Left-footed kicker steps with left foot first
2. Toe of stepping foot points at ball

Plant Step

1. Ball of plant foot is even with the ball
2. Toes of nonkicking foot point at the goal post target
3. Body leans away from the ball
4. Kicking foot is brought back toward butt

(continued)

Figure 10.2 (continued)

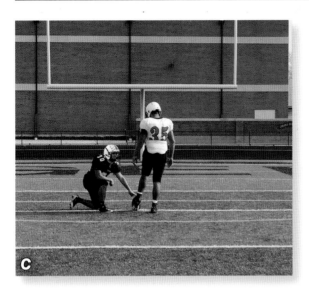

Contact

1. Big toe of kicking foot points toward the ground
2. Ankle is locked
3. Kicking leg is extended
4. Foot makes contact slightly below the middle of the ball
5. Body leans away from the ball
6. Hips turn slightly to the left (for a left-footed kicker)

Follow-Through

1. Kicking leg naturally moves up and across the body
2. Short skip on plant foot

Contact on the Kick

On contact, the kicker's kicking leg should be fully extended with no knee-bend on contact with the ball (figure 10.2c). This is called leg lock. The kicker's body should be on the side, leaning away from the ball. This lean allows the kicker to fully extend his leg with the ankle locked and to contact the ball in the proper position. The opposite foot should be aligned with the ball of the foot about even with the point of the ball; toes point directly at the target. The hips need to be turned slightly on contact—to the right for a right-footed kicker, to the left for a left-footed kicker. This is to ensure that the kicking foot is perpendicular to the aiming point. Any deviation of the plant foot in its aim will result in the kick being off line in the direction the toe is pointing. The plant-foot heel should be about 6 to 10 inches from the ball to the side. The exact spot depends on the individual kicker.

A side note on the position of the ball: When kicking soccer style on kickoffs, field goals, or PATs, the ball should lean slightly away from the target and slightly away from the kicker. The exact amount of lean depends on individual preference. For field goals and PATs, whether the kicker uses a kicking tee or kicks from the ground is also a factor.

Follow-Through on the Kick

The kicker must allow his foot to follow through. Any physical deviation from a normal follow-through will reveal any mistakes the kicker has made. As the foot contacts the ball and begins to follow through, the natural circular motion of the leg and hips should bring the leg up and across the body toward the nonkicking leg (figure 10.2d). With his arm up and away from his kicking leg and his body lean away from the ball, he follows through with a short skip with his plant foot forward and away from the ball.

Kicking Drills

Kickers must know their strengths and weaknesses. They should keep track of their makes and misses during practice so they know what they need to work on and which spot to try to kick from in games. For instance, if during practices they make a higher percentage of kicks from the left hash mark than from the right hash mark, during a game the coaching staff can run plays to the left when they suspect a field goal will soon be attempted. A note about practice: Kickers must take care not to overkick. Too much full kicking in practice will wear out the kicker's leg and lead to muscle fatigue. Kickers should take time off now and then to let their legs recover and stay fresh.

Field Goal and PAT Drill 1
No-Step, Leg-Lock Drill

The kicker places his plant foot in proper position next to the ball. With the plant foot stationary, he kicks the ball without a step. The focus is on foot position, ball contact with the foot, and the leg lock at the point of contact. This is a great warm-up drill and reinforces getting the proper leg lock.

Success Check

- Plant foot is in proper position next to the ball.

- Achieve leg lock on contact with the ball.

Field Goal and PAT Drill 2 **Plant-Step Drill**

The plant-step drill is a continuation of the no-step, leg-lock drill. The kicker starts with the plant foot in proper position next to the ball, as in the no-step, leg-lock drill. He takes one step back with his plant foot. He takes the plant step, putting his foot in its proper spot,

Success Check

- Plant foot is in proper position.

and kicks the ball. Again, emphasis is on foot position, contact position on the foot, and leg lock. Also evaluate the position of the arm on the nonkicking side and the upper body as contact is made.

- Achieve leg lock on contact with the ball.

Field Goal and PAT Drill 3
Making Close Field Goals

This is a good drill for developing height on the kick. Move the ball up to a spot very close to the goal post. The kicker tries to kick the ball through the uprights. Start on the goal line and

Success Check

- The kicked ball gets immediate height and clears the goal post bar.

move the ball up as the kicker continues to make the kick. The goal is to get inside of 5 yards from the goal post. This is a good competitive drill for kickers to do together.

- Maintain proper alignment and steps throughout the drill.

Field Goal and PAT Drill 4
Field Goal Accuracy

This drill develops accuracy and can be done as a competition between kickers. Start with the ball on the sideline at

To Increase Difficulty

- Move the ball closer to the end line, cutting down on the angle even more. Or move the ball out into the field in a semicircle.

the junction of the sideline and the goal line. Kickers try to make a field goal from this angle.

Success Check

- Maintain good kicking technique.
- Ball is kicked between the up--rights.

KICKOFFS

Kicking off is slightly different from kicking field goals or PATs. On kickoffs, you want to get a lot more power into the kick, and pinpoint accuracy is not as important. The approach on the kickoff is longer, resulting in more body speed at the ball. Kickers should experiment with the number of steps they need to take to get to maximum body speed while maintaining the control needed to execute the kickoff with repeatable precision. Start 7 to 10 yards away from the ball to see what works best.

The point of contact is the same on kickoffs as on field goals and PATs; the same part of the foot makes contact just below the center line of the ball.

The approach and follow-through for the kickoff are slightly different than for field goals and PATs. To get more power and speed at contact, the kicker puts more of his upper body into the kickoff. As he approaches the ball and starts to plant his nonkicking foot, he brings the arm opposite his kicking foot up and away, as in a field goal or PAT attempt. As he starts the kick, however, he attempts to crunch his upper body forward as he would in a sit-up, pulling his upper body down and forward to create more forward power than in a field goal or PAT attempt. This technique, done properly, creates tremendous forward movement (figure 10.3), causing the kicker to land on his kicking foot in the direction of the kick. Compare this to the field goal, in which the kicker skips forward and to the side with his plant foot.

Figure 10.3 **FOLLOW-THROUGH AFTER KICKOFF**

1. Body is moving forward after the kick
2. Kicking leg continues forward
3. Kicking foot lands first, in direction of the kick

Kickoff Drills

As is true of any technique, breaking the kickoff down to its component parts and drilling these components leads to improved technique. Following are several drills that develop technique for the kickoff.

Kickoff Drill 1   Step Drill

This drill works on the approach steps of the kickoff to make them repeatable. The kicker starts 8 to 10 yards away from the kicking tee (no ball on the tee). He aligns slightly to the side (left side for right-footed kickers; right side for left-footed kickers) and mark this spot so he can reproduce it. He approaches the ball and simulates the kick, taking note where he is when he steps with his plant foot and swings his kicking leg. He should make sure to approach the tee with the same speed and force he would if actually kicking the ball. If it appears the plant foot or kicking leg is not in correct position at the tee, he adjusts his initial alignment accordingly. It helps to have someone stand to the side and look for this as well. Once he has the correct starting spot, the kicker works on the steps it takes to reach that spot from the tee. He should be exact in how many steps he takes, how long they are, and in what direction they are to reach his starting spot. Making sure these steps are exact and repeatable will help ensure his approach and kickoff are consistent each time.

Success Check

- The same steps are taken each time. Kicker starts at the tee and ends up at the same start spot for his kickoff approach.

- The plant foot is in the same spot at the tee, with the ball of the foot even with the tee.
- Follow through after the simulated kick by landing on the kicking foot.

Kickoff Drill 2   Full Kicks

After establishing his start point, the kicker kicks six or seven full kicks, working on consistently making contact with his plant foot in the same spot each time. Again, it helps to have someone else stand to the side and look for the placement of the plant foot. The kicker should not kick too many full kickoffs in a row. Full kickoffs are strenuous on the leg if too many are done in succession.

Success Check

- Steps and contact point are consistent each time. Verify by the distance and height of the kick; also have a partner visually check each kick.

- Kicking foot is at full extension at contact with the ball.
- The kicker's body is leaning away from the ball.
- The kicker makes contact with the top inside of the arch of his kicking foot.

Kickoff Drill 3   Accuracy Drill

Kickers sometimes want to place their kickoffs at specific spots on the field. Place a cone downfield from the kicking spot at the desired target for the ball to land. Place several cones at different locations based on where you want the kick to be aimed. Kickers kick practice kicks, attempting to have the ball land within 5 yards of a designated cone.

Success Check

- The kicked ball lands within 5 yards of the target cone.

Kickoff Drill 4   Competitive Accuracy Drill

Each kicker competes against himself or against another kicker. To compete against himself, the kicker keeps track of how many balls fall within 5 yards of his target cone. For example, he might try to hit the 5-yard target three times before moving to another cone. He can also keep track of how many kicks are within 5 yards of the cone when kicking two or three balls at each target. If four targets are used, the kicker's goal is to get 80 percent of his total kicks within 5 yards of a cone.

To compete against another kicker, each kicker kicks two or three balls at each target; keep track of who is the most accurate.

Success Check

- The ball lands within 5 yards of the designated cone.

PUNTS

Like the field goal, the punt is a scrimmage kick, meaning the defense can rush in an attempt to block it. Thus the ball must be punted quickly but with proper technique.

Kicking and punting share many similarities. First, the ball must be consistently positioned for the foot to make contact in the same correct spot every time. Second, to maximize leg power, the foot must contact the ball at the moment the leg achieves leg lock. Third, a proper follow-through allows the body to move in a way that maximizes its power potential throughout the punting motion.

The major difference in kicking and punting is that the punter holds the ball and kicks it shortly after he drops it. This point is one of the biggest issues in developing a punter. The ball drop from the hands to foot contact is probably the most important sequence in punting. We'll discuss catching the snap of the ball, moving into the drop of the ball, the ball drop, and completing the punt.

Catching the Snap

When catching the snap, the punter must have his body directly in front of the ball. If the ball is slightly off center, he can simply reach to the ball and bring it back to proper position as he begins to step. But if the ball is outside the framework of his body, he must move sideways to catch the ball within the framework of his body. This is done with a quick shuffle step, keeping shoulders and hips square to the line of scrimmage. If he doesn't catch the ball within the framework of his body, he must reset his body before the punt, which usually leads to a blocked punt.

Moving Into the Drop

Once he catches the ball, the punter must do two things at once. He starts his steps while holding the ball in proper position to make the drop to kick it. Punters may be two-step punters or three-step punters. Either way, the ball must be kicked quickly to avoid a block. The normal get-off time from snap to punt is about 2.0 to 2.2 seconds.

A two-step punter catches the ball and then takes his first step with his kicking foot (right foot for right-footed kicker; left foot for left-footed kicker). The first step should be 10 to 12 inches long, with the upper body leaning forward over the toes. The foot should either land flat or with weight slightly on the ball of the foot. The second step is a natural step, again with weight forward. The punter lands either flat-footed or with his weight slightly on the ball of his foot. By keeping weight forward, steps will be shorter and quicker, which helps prevent a slow punt. Keeping weight forward is also critical to the leg swing and follow-through.

A three-step punter will take a step as he catches the ball. This is fine as long as he still takes two steps after the catch.

As the punter starts his steps, he must get the ball in position to make the drop. There are many theories on how to hold the ball for the drop. Most important, when the punter begins to drop the ball, the ball must be steady and in the same position every time. I recommend holding the ball with the hand on the kicking side underneath and slightly to the outside and the ball slightly extended out into the fingertips. The hand on the nonkicking side should be on the inside of the ball, applying just enough pressure to keep the ball steady but not enough to affect its position. The ball should be held with the hand on the kicking side extended with a slight bend in the elbow. The hand and ball must be held directly in line with the kicking leg. The elbow on the kicking side must point at the ground, which keeps the arm aligned over the kicking leg. The arm should be held at about belly height.

Dropping the Ball

As the punter takes his steps, he must prepare to release the ball. A consistent drop is critical for a consistent punt. The punter takes two steps after catching the ball. The first step is with the kicking leg. Both hands remain on the ball during this step.

The second step is with the nonkicking leg, or the plant leg. As the second step takes place, the punter removes the hand on the nonkicking side from the ball by pulling it straight away to the side. This hand must not affect the ball's alignment or direction in any way.

As the plant leg hits the ground, the kicking leg extends back, with the foot bending toward the punter's butt, as in a field goal. At the same time, the hand and arm on the kicking side extend to full extension away from the body in a level line with where the ball was being held. As the arm reaches full extension, the release takes place. Think of holding the ball on the top of a table. As the punter extends his arm, pushing the ball toward the edge of the table, the ball should not change position. As the ball gets to the edge, the punter pulls his hand away and lets gravity start to pull it down. Again, the kicking hand must not affect the position of the ball as it's released. The punter opens his fingers, releases the ball from his fingertips first, and pulls his hand away and to the side.

Completing the Punt

The release occurs at about the same time the kicking foot begins to come forward (figure 10.4a). The kicking foot contacts the ball with leg fully extended in a leg lock (figure 10.4b). Leg lock is critical to transmit the maximum amount of force from the leg to the ball. The point of leg lock should come somewhere between the punter's knee and hip. Anything lower, and the leg cannot get to a locked position, causing loss of power and height.

The ball should contact the extended foot (toe down) on top, striking the arch. The point of the ball can be slightly turned in so it points at the big toe, with the back point of the ball pointing at the outside ankle bone. The point should also be just slightly down. This helps the ball strike the foot flush with the arch.

The punter must not try to swing his kicking leg across the ball to impart spin on the ball. It might do that, but doing so will cut way down on the power being imparted on the ball. By placing the ball with the correct orientation on the foot and directly on the arch, the ball will naturally have spin as it comes off the foot. The leg must swing straight up through the natural arc of the hip joint to allow the maximum transfer of power to the ball.

Very important in an effective punt is the follow-through, which depends directly on the two approach steps and the body lean leading up to ball contact. If the two steps prior to contact are with the correct foot position (flat footed or weight slightly on the ball of the foot), with the upper body relatively upright, then as the ball is kicked the punter's hips can pass over his plant foot. This motion allows the punter to follow through by having his weight forcefully move straight forward with a resulting skip of the plant foot.

Figure 10.4 **PUNTING THE BALL**

a

Release

1. Plant foot hits the ground
2. Kicking leg begins forward
3. Ball is released from the fingertips

b

Contact

1. Ball contacts top of arch
2. Point of ball points to big toe and slightly down

MISSTEP

The punter's steps are too long, causing him to lean back as he swings his contact leg to the ball, creating a lack of power on the punt. The long strides also delay the punter in getting the punt off.

CORRECTION

The punter must make sure he steps with his weight on the balls of his feet. This will automatically cause him to keep his weight forward and shorten his steps. Keeping his weight forward will help get his hips through the punt. Taking shorter steps will ensure the punt gets off more quickly.

A common mistake of many punters is to take steps that are too long leading up to contact, which tends to force the body to lean back. With the weight behind the plant foot, the plant leg pushes back into the body, stopping its forward movement. This stopping motion prevents the body's full momentum from being transmitted to the ball, which makes for a weaker punt.

Pooch Punt

Part of the skill of punting involves a specialty punt called the pooch punt, which is used when the line of scrimmage is close to the opponent's goal line but too far away for a field goal try. Normally, this is from the 40- to the 30-yard line.

When punting in this situation, the objective is for the punter to put the ball as close to the goal line as possible without going into the end zone for a touchback. Three methods can be used in this situation. The first is the corner kick. In a corner kick, the punter attempts to kick the ball out of bounds on one side of the field as close to the goal line as possible. This is strictly an accuracy punt and requires great control and practice.

The second type is the punch punt. In a punch punt, the punter punts the ball just hard enough to get it over the heads of all players at the line of scrimmage. The ball hits the ground and rolls toward the goal line. This punt is a matter of feel and takes practice to develop. The punch punt poses a couple of potential problems. First, the punt might not go far enough, allowing the return team to catch the ball farther upfield than desired. Second, this punt doesn't give the punting team's coverage players time to block and release downfield so they can quickly cover the returner.

The third type of punt, the standard pooch punt, is the most widely used. This punt is a high kick anywhere downfield but preferably inside the opponent's 10- to 20-yard line. Punting the ball high gives the coverage team time to run downfield and cover a potential returner. A pooch punt often leads to a fair catch called by the returner inside the 20-yard line, fulfilling the goal of the punt. Sometimes this punt results in the returner letting the ball go, hoping it will hit the ground and roll into the end zone.

To prevent this, the punter can alter his drop technique to make the ball land and roll back away from the goal line. The punter holds the point of the ball up slightly and a little higher in relation to his body. This change in the hold and drop causes the ball to come off his foot with the point up in the air, which results in a shorter punt that will likely roll back when it hits the ground. Holding the ball higher promotes a higher trajectory as the ball comes off the foot, giving the coverage players more time to get downfield to down the ball before it enters the end zone.

Punting Drills

Like kickers, punters should not punt all-out too many times a day during practice. Punters can overkick and risk injury, not to mention the loss in power when legs are tired. These drills can be done on a daily basis without full-out punting.

Punt Drill 1   **Line Drill**

A young punter should work on his drop more than anything. This is a good drill to work the drop and initial steps.

The punter starts with the ball in both hands as if he has just caught the snap. He takes two steps leading up to the punt, focusing on proper foot placement and body lean. As he takes the final plant step, he extends the hand on the side of his kicking foot and releases the ball, noting its correct position and focusing on the ball maintaining the correct position as it drops. He lets the ball fall to the ground. The ball should bounce off the ground in the exact same way every time. This indicates that the drop was proper and consistent. The punter starts on the sideline and steps down a yard line, repeating the steps and drop all the way across the field and back.

Success Check

- The ball is in correct position on release.

- The ball bounces off the ground the same way each time, back and to the right (for a right-footed punter).

Punt Drill 2   **Leg-Lock Drill**

This drill works the leg lock required for full power on the kick. Have a partner hold the ball with both hands on top of the ball and fingers out of the way at the spot where contact with the ball should occur. The punter sets his plant foot, with his kicking foot back behind. He rocks his weight forward as he swings his kicking leg up to the ball. Note his foot position as well as the leg lock (at the knee) on contact with the ball. Repeat 8 to 10 times in a row, then rest and repeat.

Success Check

- Punter has his kicking leg locked as his foot contacts the ball.

- Punter keeps weight slightly forward during the punt.

Punt Drill 3   **Punting Catch**

Another good warm-up drill that focuses on the drop and contact with leg lock is to play catch with another punter. Punters start about 15 yards apart and pass the ball to each other by punting it. The focus is on controlling the path of the ball to the partner. Punters don't go for

height; the focus is on accuracy and proper technique. Punters gradually back up until 30 to 40 yards apart. The farther apart, the more height they'll get on their kicks, but accuracy should not be compromised. Look for proper leg lock on contact with the ball.

Success Check

- The ball has a spiral.
- The punt is accurate to the partner, without a lot of height.

- Each partner focuses on a good drop of the ball and getting leg lock at contact.

Punt Drill 4   **Bad-Snap Drill**

This is a basic drill that punters should do every day. A partner stands 10 to 15 yards from the punter and throws the ball underhanded to the punter, simulating a snap. The partner should vary his throws, forcing the punter to catch the ball at various spots. The punter works on seeing the ball as he catches it and quickly moving the ball back into position for a good drop as he starts his steps. (He doesn't actually punt the

ball.) If the ball is so far outside that he must move his feet to catch it, he should take quick shuffle steps to the side, keeping his shoulders and hips as square to the line of scrimmage as possible. The punter should note where the punt scheme needs his contact point to be in relation to the protection. He works to get back to that point as he takes his steps. Punters should run this drill 20 to 30 times a day.

Success Check

- The punter catches the ball with his body in front of it each time (that is, he should receive the ball within the framework of his body, as described earlier).

- The punter uses good knee-bend on low snaps, getting his hands down to the ball.
- After catching the ball, the punter quickly brings it back to ready position.

SUCCESS SUMMARY

In step 10 we have looked at the skills involved in successfully kicking the football on kickoffs, field goals, and PATs. We have covered the techniques for punting the ball correctly. For kicking, we have discussed the proper footwork required be in the right position at the ball. We have stressed the importance of the leg lock at the point the foot contacts the ball. For punting, we have emphasized proper footwork, a consistent drop of the ball, and locking the leg on contact.

In step 11 we progress to discussing complete offensive systems and schemes. Before turning to that step, answer the following questions to review the key points on kicking and punting the football.

Before Taking the Next Step

1. When kicking a field goal or PAT, with what part of the foot should a soccer-style kicker contact the ball?

2. For field goals and PATs, what body part points at the center of the goal posts at point of contact with the ball?

3. How is the follow-through on a kickoff different from the follow-through on a field goal or PAT?

4. When dropping the ball on a punt, should the point of the ball be level, pointed slightly down, or pointed slightly up?

5. If a punter is not getting his hips through the punt when he swings his leg through, what can he do with his footwork to solve this problem?

Offensive Strategies

Many offensive systems are used in football today. The variety of offenses is limited only by the number of players you can use at one time, the coach's imagination, and a few rules. Possibilities range from systems that emphasize the run game to ones that emphasize the pass game—and everything in between. What is the best system? That's the million dollar question, but no one has the definitive answer. Several variables come into play for a coach when considering which offensive system to use with his team.

When selecting a system, an offensive coach looks at three main elements of the game. First, he considers his own personal philosophy of what the game of football is about. If a coach believes in controlling the football and playing great defense to win games, he probably will lean toward a run-oriented offensive scheme. If a coach loves to score as many points as possible and believes that his teams should be explosive, he'll lean toward a pass-oriented scheme.

The second element to consider is team personnel. If a coach has an abundance of offensive players who are bigger and stronger than most opponents, he might choose an offensive scheme that gears on physical dominance. Usually, this is a run-oriented offense. If a coach has smaller, faster, more athletic players, he might choose a scheme based on speed and deception. He might consider passing schemes or even an option offense.

The third element for a coach to consider is the kinds of offense he completely understands. This is a critical point. The coach must understand the key facets of an offensive scheme before he can succeed with the scheme. He must understand the offense well enough so that when a part of it doesn't work, either in practice or in a game, he knows how to fix it. Too often, coaches try to install an offense that's in vogue at the time without understanding its intricacies. These teams seem never to adjust during a game, and they fail to improve as the season progresses.

RUNNING GAME

The three basic types of running-game offenses are gap scheme, zone scheme, and option scheme. We'll look at each in some detail.

Gap Schemes

The gap scheme offense focuses on running plays that feature a lead blocker for the running back. This scheme uses blocking rules that spell out exactly who each lineman will block. All of this is identified prior to the play. In our discussion of gap scheme offensive plays, I'll describe a play and then explain how the play fits into this category. The plays included will cover a representative sample, but we can't cover every possible play.

ISOLATION PLAY

In the isolation play, the offensive line blocks the defensive linemen at the point of attack, leaving the nearest linebacker for the lead blocker to attack (figure 11.1).

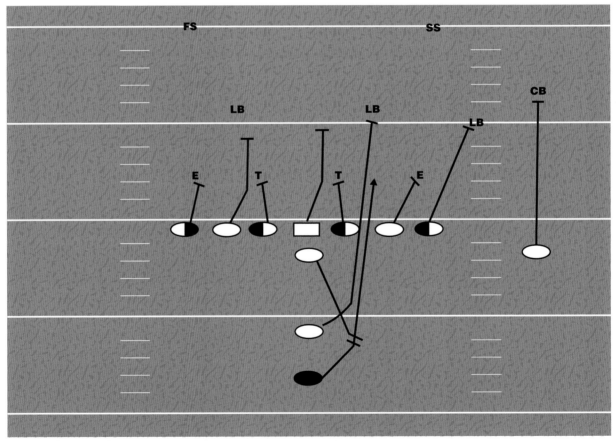

Figure 11.1 Isolation play gap scheme to a 5 technique.

Here are the blocking rules for the isolation play:

      Right tight end: Block first man on, outside.

      Right tackle: Block first man inside, on, outside.

Right guard: Block first man inside, on, outside.

Center: Block first man front-side gap, on, back, near linebacker.

Left guard: Block first man inside, on, outside.

Left tackle: Block first man inside, on, outside, near linebacker.

Left tight end: Block first man inside, on, outside.

Fullback: Versus 5 technique, lateral step to B gap, lead block on near linebacker; versus 3 technique, lead through A gap to near linebacker.

Figure 11.2 shows the same play to a 3 technique. The same blocking rules apply.

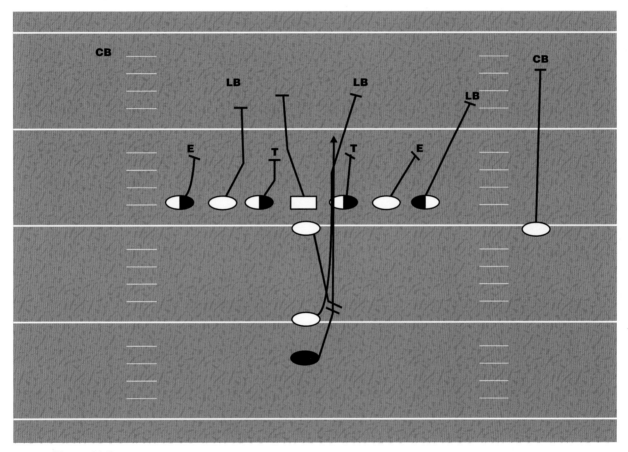

Figure 11.2   Isolation play gap scheme to a 3 technique.

POWER PLAY

The power play (figure 11.3) is similar to an isolation play in that the fullback lead-blocks on a defender. The difference is that his block is on the end man on the line of scrimmage, and the backside guard will pull to the front side and add his block to the point of attack. The other basic difference is that the offensive guard away from the play pulls to the front side and blocks the first inside-linebacker threat. The other difference is in the tight end–offensive tackle block. They double team a 5-technique defensive lineman just inside the designated play hole.

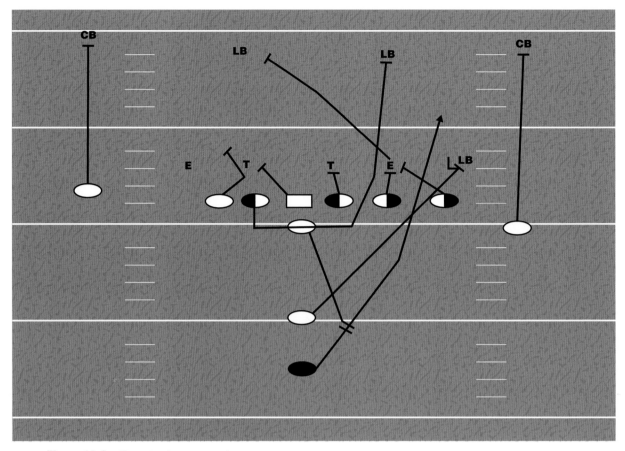

Figure 11.3 Power play gap scheme.

Here are the blocking rules for the power play:

Right tight end: Block first inside, possibly double team with offensive tackle.

Right offensive tackle: Block outside, on, inside; possibly double team on outside with tight end.

Right offensive guard: Block outside, on, inside, near linebacker.

Center: Block back (cover offensive guard), on, near linebacker.

Left offensive guard: Pull play side, block first linebacker off line of scrimmage inside tight end.

Right offensive tackle: Block inside, on, outside, near linebacker.

Right tight end: Block inside, on, outside, near linebacker.

TOSS

The toss play is a third type of gap scheme play that attempts to get the ball carrier outside the perimeter of the defense with one or two lead blockers on the linebackers and defensive backs. This play involves a toss of the ball from the quarterback to the tailback as the tailback sprints for the perimeter. This gets the ball carrier to the outside faster than a regular handoff would.

There are several ways to block the front side of this play. The simplest is to have the entire offensive line block the first threat to their outside, with the fullback lead blocking around the outside for the tailback (figure 11.4).

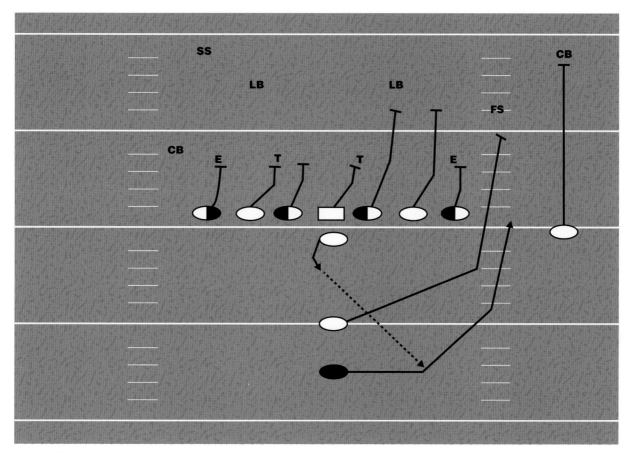

Figure 11.4   Toss play gap scheme. Offensive linemen block first threat to the outside.

A variation of the toss play has one or more offensive linemen pulling to the outside to block any additional defensive players who may be outside (figure 11.5). In this variation, one or more linemen pull to the play side of the formation and block, based on the team's offensive philosophy and the ability of the linemen to execute the pull. Linemen need a degree of athleticism to execute this.

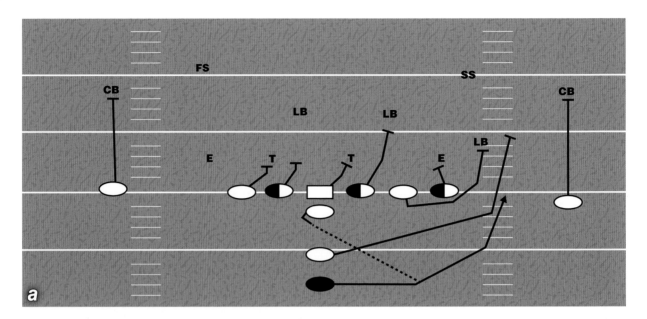

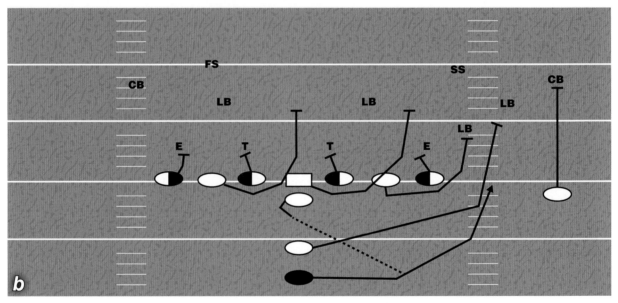

Figure 11.5 Toss play gap scheme. *(a)* The offensive tackle pulls to the outside; *(b)* the offensive guard, center, and tackle pull to the outside.

COUNTER

Another example of a gap scheme play is the counter (figure 11.6). This play works well in conjunction with the isolation play and the power play because as the counter play starts it resembles both of these plays in an attempt to get the defense to react in that direction. The counter play then reverses the direction of the play to catch the defense off guard.

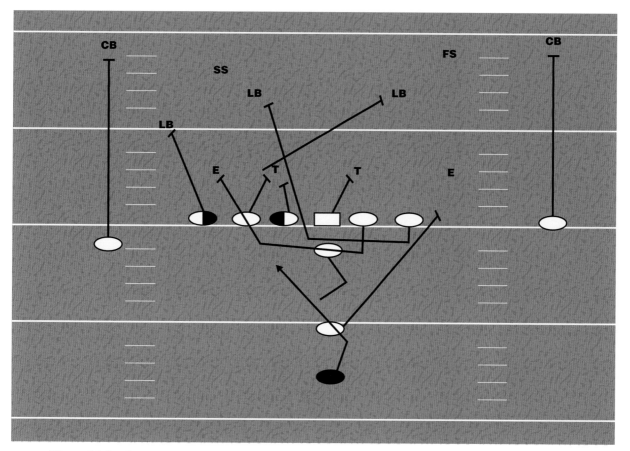

Figure 11.6 Counter play gap scheme.

There are several ways to run the counter as to who the pulling blockers are. In figure 11.6, the offensive guard and tackle are the pulling blockers. You can substitute for the tackle with the tight end if the tight end is better at pulling (figure 11.7a). You can also use the fullback to pull instead of the tackle (figure 11.7b).

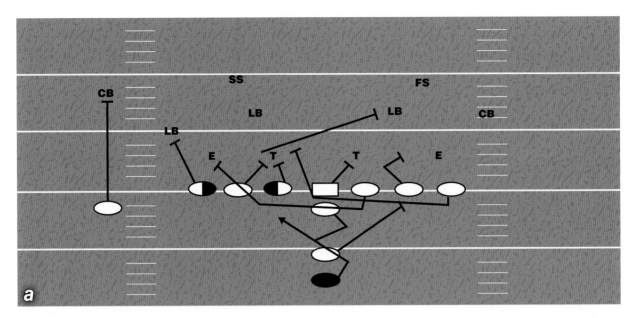

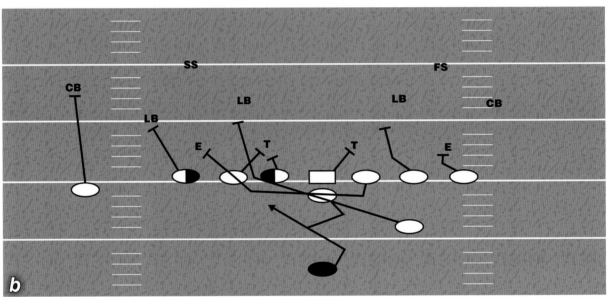

Figure 11.7 Counter play variations: *(a)* counter OY (tight end pulling); *(b)* counter OF (fullback pulling).

FULLBACK TRAP

Usually, the fullback won't get as many running plays in a gap scheme offense as the tailback will. The fullback's primary job is to block. One of the few plays designed for him is the fullback trap (figure 11.8). Again, this is a misdirection play. The tailback fakes a toss play and then executes a quick handoff to the fullback. At the same time, one of the offensive guards pulls to trap the down linemen just outside the designated hole. If the linebackers take the bait of the tailback's fake, this can be a very effective play, especially in short-yardage situations.

We've looked at some of the more traditional gap scheme plays. Many other such plays are possible, limited only by the coach's imagination.

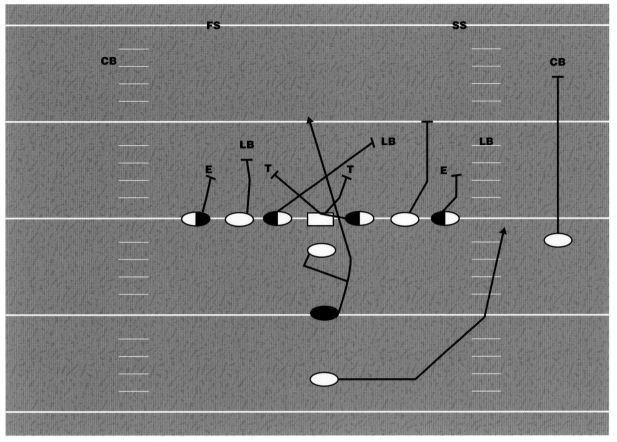

Figure 11.8 Fullback trap.

Zone Schemes

The second basic type of running attack is the zone scheme. In this scheme, the offensive blockers at the line of scrimmage are assigned an area rather than a specific man to block. Whoever shows up in that area is the man the offensive blocker is responsible for. This requires the offensive man to be patient as he moves to his area to identify the defender he must block. Blockers must make this identification and execute blocks on the fly.

INSIDE ZONE

The most basic running play in the zone scheme is the inside zone (figure 11.9). Basically, the inside zone is a running back dive play that can hit any of several possible gaps. The deciding factor on which gap the running back takes is based solely on which gap is open. Defenders often make mistakes and protect the wrong gap, leaving a gap open. In a zone scheme play, after receiving the handoff from the quarterback, the running back looks for an open gap as he prepares to attack the line of scrimmage. When the gap opens, the running back makes a quick decision and cuts to that open area. The blockers at the line of scrimmage don't care who they block, as long as the defender is in the area the blocker is assigned.

By having the running back cut to the open gap based on what the defense does, the running back should always be able to run to the best hole.

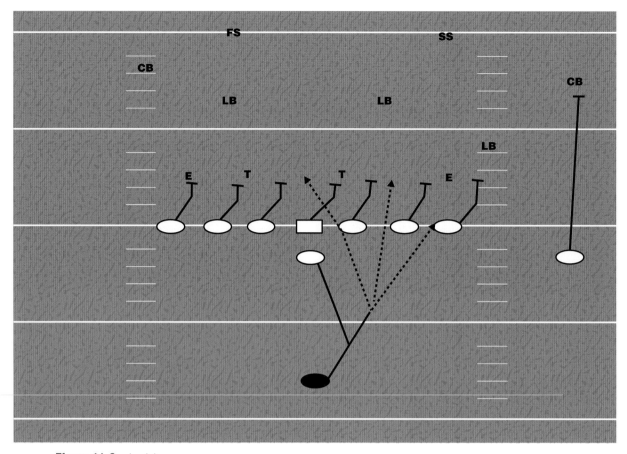

Figure 11.9 Inside zone.

The inside zone can be run from many formations and personnel groups. It can be run with the quarterback under center, as shown in figure 11.9, or in the shotgun position.

Here are the blocking rules for the inside zone:

Right tight end: Block first man on or off the line of scrimmage from head up to outside.

Right offensive tackle: Block first man on or off the line of scrimmage from head up to outside.

Right offensive guard: Block first man on or off the line of scrimmage from head up to outside.

Center: Block first man on or off the line of scrimmage from head up to play side.

Left offensive guard: Block first man on or off the line of scrimmage from inside to head up.

Right offensive guard: Block first man on or off the line of scrimmage from inside to head up.

Left tight end: Block first man on or off the line of scrimmage from inside to head up.

ZONE READ

In today's game, one of the most popular plays is the zone read, which gives the quarterback the option of handing the ball off to the running back on a zone play or keeping the ball himself. The zone read can be designed to go anywhere along the line of scrimmage. The original zone read was designed to run either the zone inside or the quarterback outside the offensive tackle position. On this play, the quarterback reads the defensive end. The defensive end is left unblocked on the play, so the defensive end can either take the running back on the zone play or stay put to take the quarterback. Whichever way the defensive end goes, the quarterback decides the opposite. If the defensive end turns to take the running back on the zone, the quarterback keeps the ball (figure 11.10a). If the defensive end stays square facing the quarterback, the quarterback hands the ball off to the running back (figure 11.10b). By leaving the defensive end unblocked, the offense can add one blocker to the other run defenders, essentially gaining a one-man advantage.

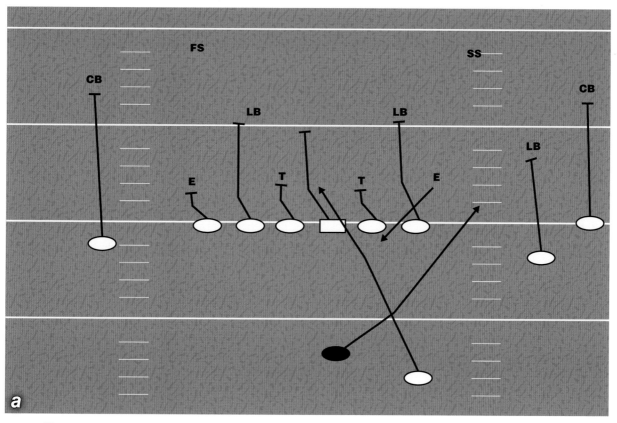

Figure 11.10   Zone read: *(a)* quarterback keep.

(continued)

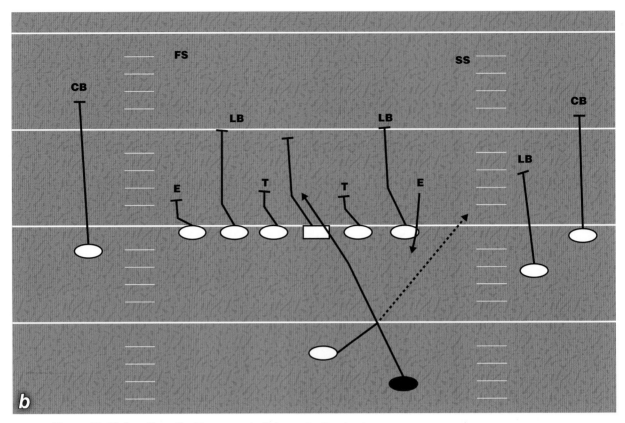

Figure 11.10 *(continued)* Zone read: *(b)* quarterback give.

If the defense has a defender aligned outside the defensive end, the zone read can be defended fairly easily. The defensive end goes directly to the dive, tackling that running back, which forces the quarterback to keep the ball (figure 11.11). The defense then has the defender aligned outside the defensive end take the quarterback.

If this occurs, the offense can add an element to the play to put the defense in a difficult situation. The offense can do one of three things: block the outside linebacker with a wide receiver, run an option play versus the outside linebacker, or throw a bubble pass to the offensive linebacker's side.

The zone read with a wide receiver block (figure 11.12) is a good solution if the offense has a wide receiver who's a good blocker. If this is not the case, the offense might best use either the option or the bubble pass as a third part of this play.

Running an option play off the zone read forces the outside linebacker to either take the quarterback or the pitch to the running back, leaving the other part of the option open. If the quarterback is asked to make the read on the zone-keep play, then the play becomes a triple option—zone, quarterback keep, or option pitch. The option part of this play can be run from any of several different looks. Figure 11.13 shows the two-back look. Figure 11.14 shows how a wide receiver can motion into the backfield and become the pitch man on the option phase.

In both variations of the option, the quarterback reads the outside linebacker. If the outside linebacker comes to tackle the quarterback, the quarterback pitches the ball to the wide receiver who has motioned in to a running back position. If the outside linebacker goes to the pitch man, the quarterback keeps the ball.

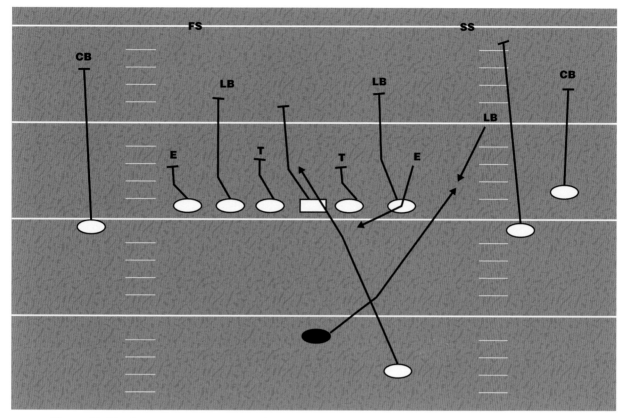

Figure 11.11 Linebacker outside defensive end forces quarterback keep.

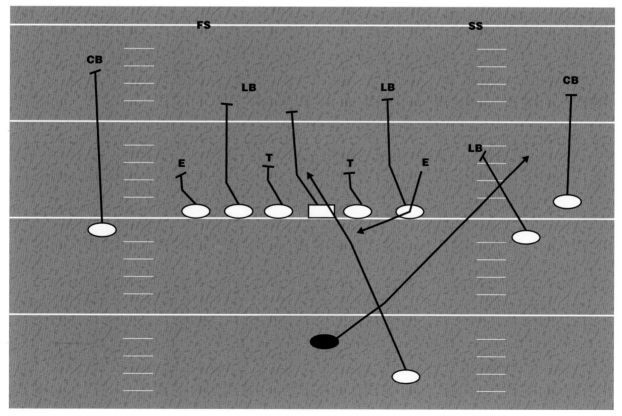

Figure 11.12 Zone read with wide receiver blocking outside linebacker.

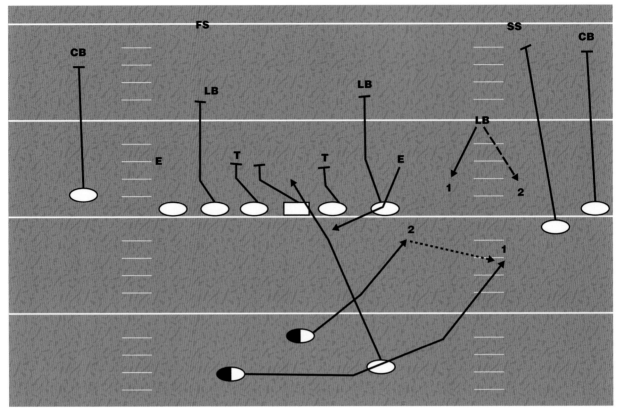

Figure 11.13 Option versus the outside linebacker, two-back look.

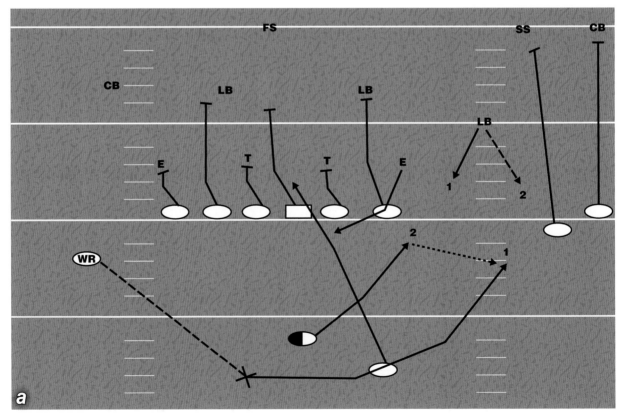

Figure 11.14 *(a)* Wide receiver motions from left.

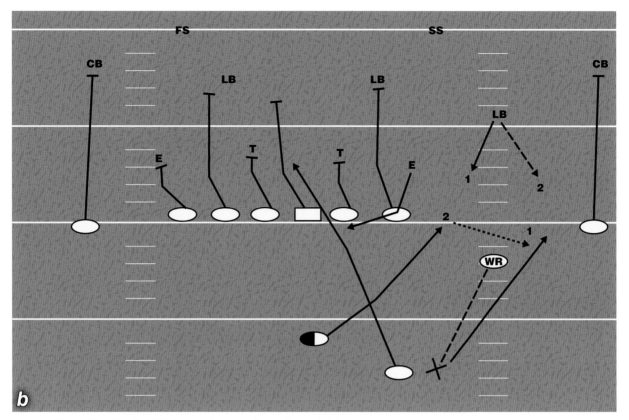

Figure 11.14 *(b)* Wide receiver motions from right.

A variation of this play is to have the wide receiver run a bubble pass route (figure 11.15). The quarterback makes the same read as he does with the option. If the outside linebacker comes to him, the quarterback throws the bubble pass to the wide receiver. If the outside linebacker goes to cover the bubble pass, the quarterback keeps the ball.

A final variation of this play creates more difficulty for the defense. A second wide receiver lines up wide to the right of the formation (figure 11.16). This wide receiver runs a 5- to 10-yard slant, or inside route. Instead of throwing the bubble pass, the quarterback reads the outside linebacker and throws the slant pass if the outside linebacker comes to take him. If the outside linebacker goes out, the quarterback can still keep the ball as he does on the bubble read.

The inside wide receiver still runs the bubble pass route, which acts as a diversion and makes the outside linebacker go to defend that pass, especially if the offense has thrown the bubble pass with success on a prior play.

This brings up an important point of offensive philosophy. The offensive system needs to be developed so that plays build off each other. If a play looks like a different play in the system to the defense, the defense will have a hard time reacting correctly. Likewise, in the passing game, the play itself and the patterns run by the wide receivers should take advantage of the defense's reaction to the initial look of the play. Along the same lines, if the offensive system has flexibility in its design, it can open up many possibilities for different plays to attack what the defense is doing. An offense's ability to adjust to defensive reactions as the play progresses makes the play more difficult to defend.

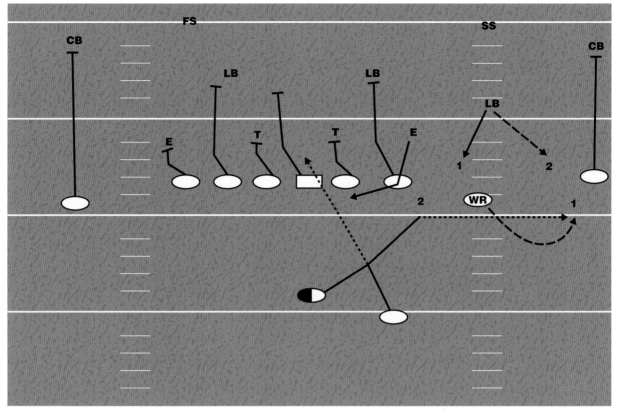

Figure 11.15 Bubble pass option on zone read.

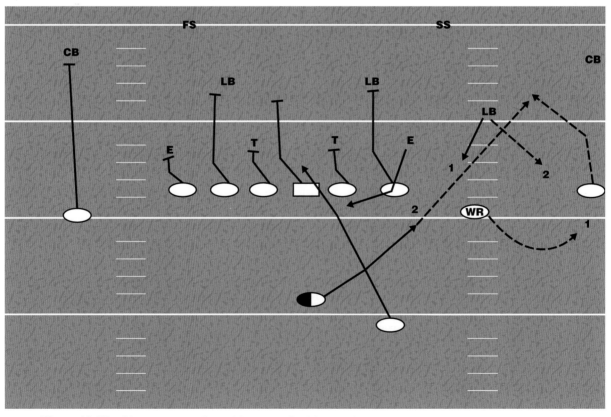

Figure 11.16 Slant pass option with second wide receiver.

Option Scheme

We discussed earlier the option play as part of the zone scheme. Prior to the option being incorporated into the zone scheme system, it was a prominent stand-alone system that took several forms. The most popular form of the option in recent years is the triple-option schemes used by some of the military service academies, predominantly Air Force and Navy. A triple-option play has three elements: the dive, the quarterback keep, and the pitch. As the play begins, any one of the three may occur based on what the defense does. It's the quarterback's job to make two reads and decide either to hand the ball to the fullback on the dive, keep the ball himself, or pitch the ball to the halfback on the option. The quarterback's reads are based on the reaction of the defense to each phase of the play. The offensive blocking scheme on the triple option is designed to leave two defenders unblocked to defend the three phases of the play.

Blocking for the dive play is shown in figure 11.17.

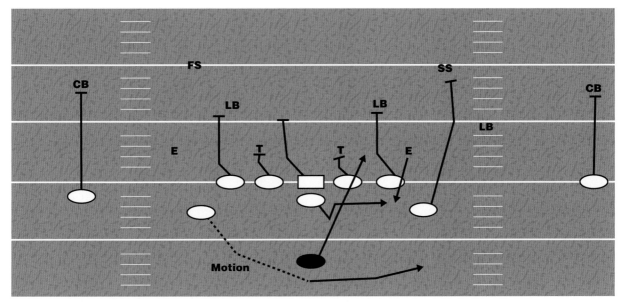

Figure 11.17 Blocking for the dive option play.

By leaving the defensive end unblocked, the offense can add one more blocker to the other defenders with good angles. If the defensive end closes down and tackles the fullback on the dive, the quarterback keeps the ball and moves out to the pitch-or-keep phase of the play. If the defensive end does not close down, the quarterback hands the ball to the fullback on the dive play.

If the quarterback keeps the ball, he shifts his next read to the next defender to the outside who is also unblocked. If this defender closes down to take the quarterback, he pitches the ball to the running back (figure 11.18).

If the outside defender does not close down, or if he moves out to take the running back getting the pitch, the quarterback keeps the ball himself (figure 11.19).

These are a few examples of running schemes an offensive can employ. There are many more, such as the traditional triple-option offense, the wing T, and their many variations.

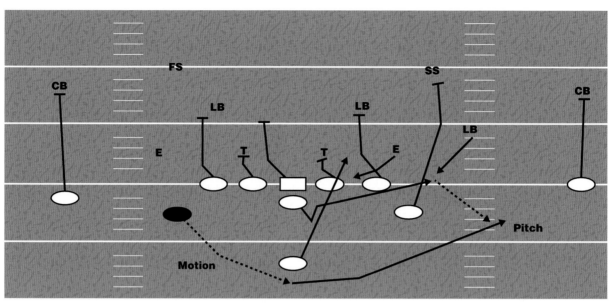

Figure 11.18 Pitch to the running back.

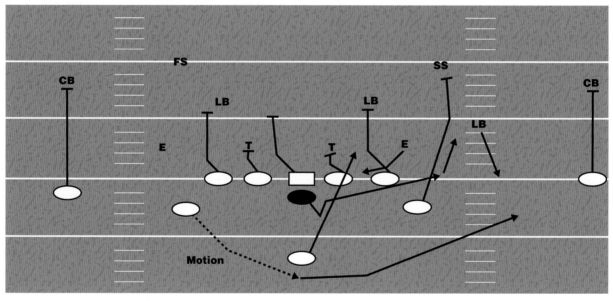

Figure 11.19 Quarterback keep on the option.

PASSING GAME

The passing game also presents multiple systems for offensive coaches to choose from, including the three-step pass, the five- to seven-step pass, the play-action pass, and the boot or misdirection pass. Within these systems are several common passing concepts that can be classified in a couple of ways.

Horizontal Concepts

The first way to look at patterns and pattern combinations is by how they are distributed on the field itself—horizontal or vertical concepts. In horizontal concepts, the pattern combinations develop in such a way as to attack pass zones horizontally across the field. This spreads defenders out in a way that allows the offense to take advantage. The basic concept is to run more receivers into a specific zone, or across the under zones, than the defense has defenders to stop.

CURL–FLAT CONCEPT

The curl–flat concept is used to stretch the outside defenders in the curl and flat zones. The idea is to create a play so the defender of the curl zone, usually the inside linebacker, will not be able to get out to his zone before the ball is thrown, and the flat defender cannot cover both the curl and flat zones at the same time. In figure 11.20, the curl route is run in the wide part of the curl zone, as far away from the inside linebacker as possible. The quarterback reads the player defending the flat zone (the outside linebacker) and throws to the receiver not covered by the outside linebacker. If the outside linebacker goes directly to the flat route, the curl will be open until the inside linebacker can get there. If the outside linebacker goes to the curl route, the flat route will be open.

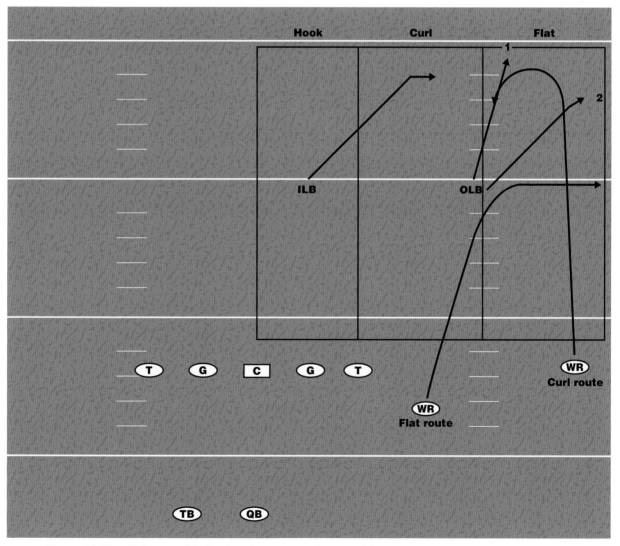

Figure 11.20 If the outside linebacker covers the curl (1), the quarterback throws to the flat route. If the outside linebacker covers the flat (2), the quarterback throws to the curl route before the inside linebacker can get there.

ALL CURLS

A similar concept has all receivers running curl routes (figure 11.21). As they complete the curl, the receiver slides to the open area between the two adjacent defenders. Again, the quarterback reads a particular defender and throws away from him in the zone.

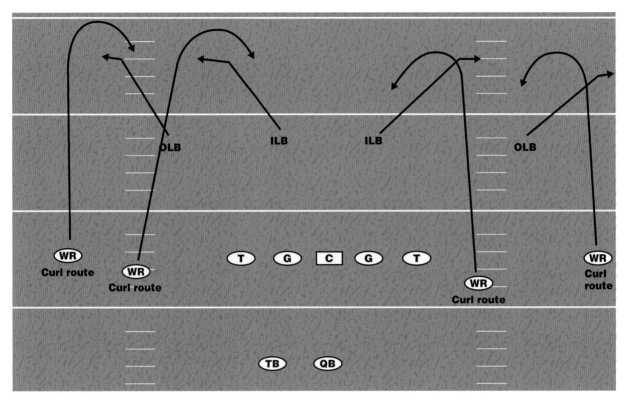

Figure 11.21 All curl routes.

An additional element can be included: The tailback releases inside the two inside linebackers and adds to the pattern. This can be done if the pass protection by the five offensive linemen is adequate without using the tailback as an additional blocker.

Vertical Concepts

A second class of pattern combinations is the vertical route combinations, which try to stretch the pass defense either within a specific zone or throughout the entire coverage.

HIGH–LOW CONCEPT

The high–low pattern concept tries to take a specific pass zone, usually an underneath zone, and attack the depth of the cover defender. The high route is run about 15 yards deep. The low route is run about 5 yards deep. If the defender covers the short low route, the deep high route is open. If the defender covers the deep route, the short route is open. Figure 11.22 shows the high–low against an inside linebacker.

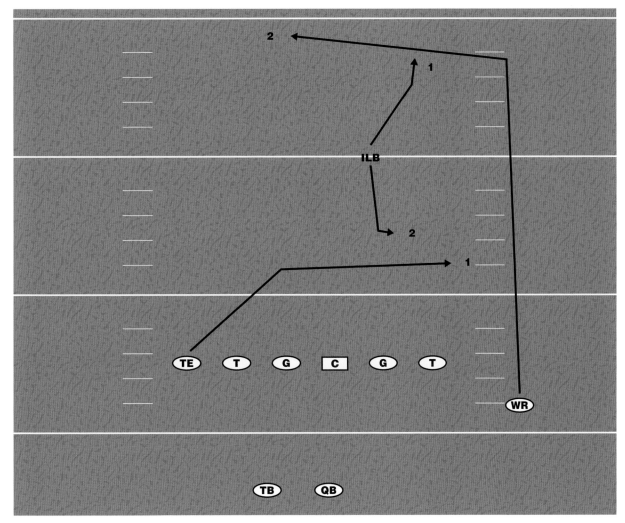

Figure 11.22   High–low versus inside linebacker.

The same pattern concept can be run versus the flat defender, in this case the outside linebacker. If the defender covers the short route, the quarterback should throw to the deep route. If the defender covers the deep route, the quarterback throws to the short route (figure 11.23).

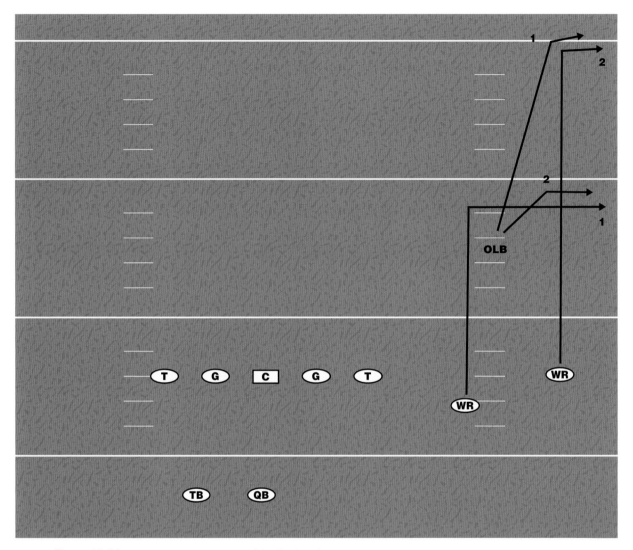

Figure 11.23 High–low versus outside linebacker.

THREE-LEVEL HIGH–LOW CONCEPT

The three-level high–low pattern concept attacks both the under cover defender as well as the deep cover defender. The attack can be run either versus the flat defender and deep outside defender (figure 11.24) or between the hook or curl defenders and the deep middle defenders (figure 11.25).

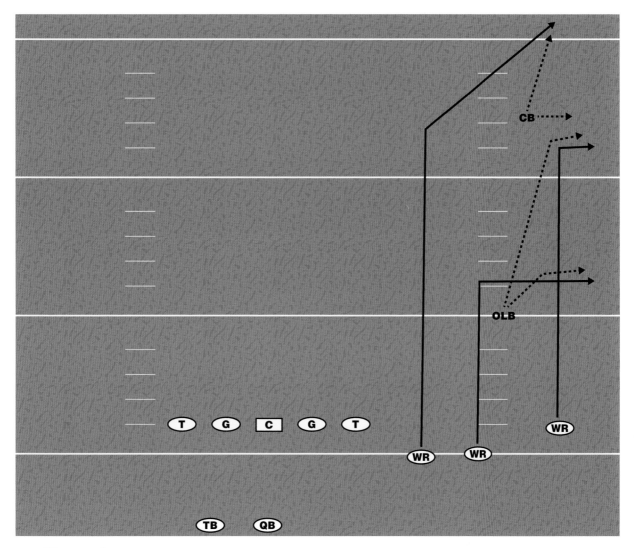

Figure 11.24 Three-level high–low versus flat defender and deep outside defender, sometimes called a flood pattern.

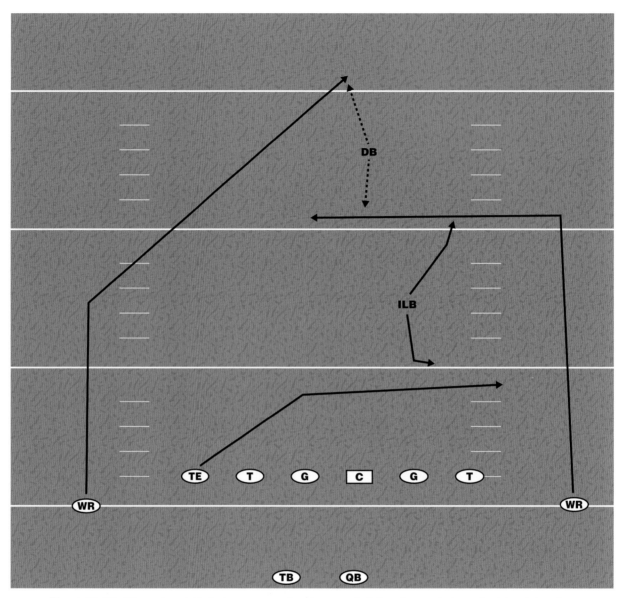

Figure 11.25 Three-level high–low versus hook or curl defender and deep inside defender, sometimes called the NCAA route.

Backfield Action

All of the pattern concepts can be run with several types of backfield action, from drop back, to play action, to sprint out. What type of backfield action to use depends on the down-and-distance situation, the offensive and defensive personnel, and the type of play.

For example, on first or second down or on third down with short yardage, downs when you may usually run the ball, you might want to use a play-action pass. This causes the under cover defenders, usually the linebackers, to defend the run first, keeping them from getting back into their pass zones quickly.

On obvious passing downs, such as third and long, you'll most likely want to use drop-back action rather than play action. The drop-back action allows the quarterback to get his eyes downfield to see his reads more quickly. It also allows running backs to get their eyes on any potential men they might have to pass block.

The sprint out and boot actions are good options for a shorter quarterback who has trouble seeing downfield from the pocket, or if the offensive line is not as adept at pass protection. The sprint out and boot actions move the quarterback outside the pocket where he can see better and puts him in position to run away from pass rushers. The patterns used for these backfield actions need to be concentrated in an area associated with the action. For example, if you are using a sprint-out action, the flood pattern can be a good one to use. The flood pattern likewise can be paired with a boot action.

A big quarterback who is not a strong runner probably needs to pair the pattern concepts with both play action and drop-back actions.

As with the running game, there are hundreds of different patterns, pattern combinations, and backfield actions that can be used in the offensive passing game. The only limits are the imagination of the coach and the abilities of the players. One of the easiest pitfalls a coach can fall into when developing a scheme is to try to do too much. Whatever running or passing scheme he chooses, it won't work if the players cannot remember it or are not able to execute it. The scheme must be manageable in size and learning ease and must suit the kinds of players on the team. The coach must spend a great deal of time considering the best scheme for his team before he begins to draw up plays.

The other pitfall a coach can easily fall into is changing the scheme from week to week. It might appear that based on what the next opponent does on defense, the team would be better off running plays outside the normal package. On the surface, this seems logical, but in reality, a play's effectiveness is tied much closer to the offense's ability to execute it than to the play's superiority over the defensive scheme. A poorly executed play will seldom work, even if it's the perfect call. A well-executed play will succeed more often than not because the players will be playing with superior confidence, speed, and effort, based on their familiarity with the play and practice running it. It's usually better to do less, but to do it well. That said, a team must also have enough offensive plays to be able to adjust if an opponent succeeds in stopping the offense's main plays. This is where coaching and making game adjustments comes in.

SUCCESS SUMMARY

In step 11 we have covered basic offensive schemes and plays for both a running game and a passing game. Many possible variations, and other systems, exist. For a running attack, we have reviewed gap schemes, zone schemes, and option schemes. For a passing attack, we have introduced common pass route concepts. These have all been presented for coaches to build on.

Before moving on to step 12, which covers defensive schemes, review and answer the following questions to make sure you have a solid grasp of the offensive schemes covered in step 11.

Before Taking the Next Step

1. What are the three basic offensive running game schemes?

2. What is one play that fits into the gap scheme system?

3. How can the counter play be modified to take advantage of the abilities of the offensive players available?

4. What concept does the zone read play depend on in regard to the defensive reaction to the play?

5. What pass concept can be added to the zone read play to take advantage of an aggressive outside linebacker?

6. Can you list and draw up examples of one horizontal pass concept that you like?

7. Can you list and draw up examples of a vertical pass concept that you like?

Defensive Strategies

Whether a team is offense oriented or defense oriented is often a reflection of the head coach. A defense-minded coach does not like giving up points. He believes football games are won primarily on defense. A look at many of the last decade's most successful teams—at all levels of the sport—supports the idea that a team usually requires a strong defense to win a championship. The challenge for a coach is finding the defensive scheme that works best for his team. Before deciding on a defensive scheme, a coach must consider the abilities of his players to execute the scheme, the type of offensive schemes his team will be facing, and his own knowledge and understanding of the defense. Once a basic scheme has been determined, there are hundreds of variations that can be built into it.

Defensive schemes are usually classified by the number of defensive linemen and linebackers used. For example, there are 4-3 defenses, 4-2 defenses, 3-4 defenses, 5-2 defenses, 3-3 defenses, and so on. Within a specific scheme, there are multiple ways to line up the run defenders (defensive linemen and linebackers) and many coverage concepts that can be used. In this step, we'll look at some of the more common overall schemes and coverages as well as ways to switch them up to give your team the best chance of success.

CHARACTERISTICS OF A GOOD DEFENSE

Several basic concepts are critical to an effective defense. First, the defense must be able to stop (or slow down) the opponent's running game. If the defense can't stop the running game, the offense will control the ball and the clock and keep your offense off the field. An offense that can run the ball effectively can quickly dishearten a defense. The running game is associated with the physical nature and toughness of a team. When a defense can't slow down an opponent's running game, they can be defeated mentally well before the game is over.

Second, the defensive scheme must be able to adjust to the many possible offensive formations the opponent can use. To some extent, the coach can control this by knowing what personnel the offense has on the field at any given time. For example, if an offense has three tight ends and two running backs in the game, it's almost certain the offense will attempt to run the ball and likely use the extra tight ends to do so. With this knowledge, the defensive coach can make appropriate calls. Likewise, if an offense has five wide receivers in the game and no tight ends or running backs, the defense can count on seeing almost all pass plays. Knowing the offensive personnel helps the defense adjust to match up, assuming they have the players they need to do so. This is one factor the coach must take into account as he develops his system.

Third, and maybe most important, the coach must make sure his players are capable of executing the chosen defensive scheme. Do they have the physical ability, the confidence, and the effort? A complex defensive scheme usually results in hesitant defensive play because players are focused on remembering what to do rather than playing hard. This leads to mistakes caused by mental errors, as well as playing slow and hesitant. The defensive scheme must fit the personnel. For example, a blitzing defense is a bad idea for a team whose defensive backs are not quick, fast, or athletic enough to play man coverage. Smaller linemen and linebackers will struggle if asked to play straight-up on bigger, stronger offensive blockers. In this case, the linemen and linebackers should be moving when the ball is snapped to take advantage of their relative speed and quickness and to minimize the size difference.

Another important concept involves the running gaps created by the alignment of the offensive linemen. On every play, there are up to eight possible gaps to run the ball to (figure 12.1).

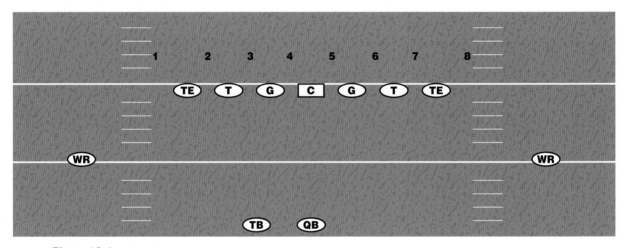

Figure 12.1 Possible running gaps.

To soundly defend an offense's running game, the defense must defend all eight running gaps with at least one defender assigned to each gap. Any defensive scheme needs to have this built in.

Whatever scheme a defensive coach chooses to use, he must intimately understand the ins and outs. During games and practices, the offense will have success at times. When players fail to execute the defensive scheme, the coach must recognize the problem immediately and know how to fix it. Sometimes the coach won't actually see the problem player and must deduce the problem based on the play that was run or where the ball went. A coach who cannot recognize what an offense is doing and why they are successful has no chance to make corrections or changes on defense to stop the offense.

A final factor in selecting a defensive scheme is deciding how the front seven players, the defensive linemen and linebackers, will play their technique versus running plays. When referring to run-gap responsibilities, we usually assign a letter designation to each gap for identification purposes (figure 12.2).

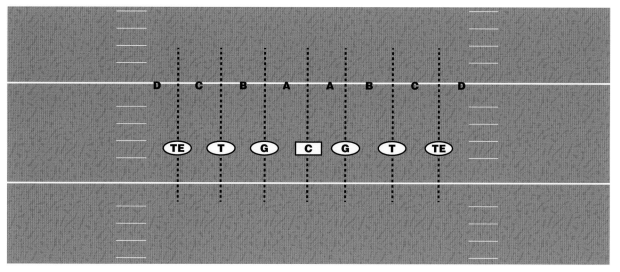

Figure 12.2 Run-gap identification.

There are two basic possibilities. In the first, the defensive linemen try to penetrate through their designated gaps into the offensive backfield. At the same time, the linebackers read the direction of the play and attack their designated gaps, carrying the responsibility only for that one gap. This is called a 1-gap defense; everyone up front is responsible for only one gap once the play develops (figure 12.3).

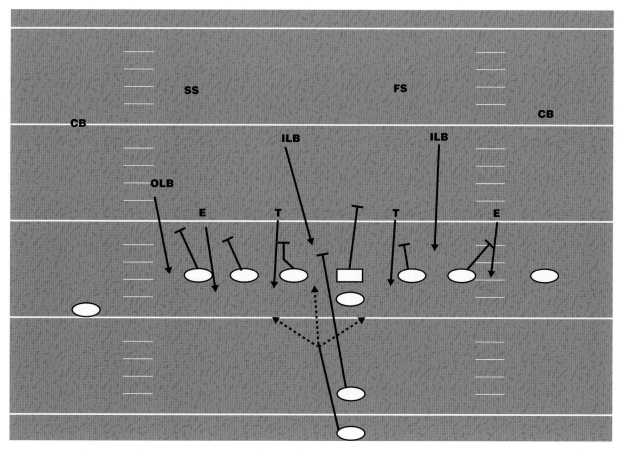

Figure 12.3 1-gap defense versus isolation play.

Here are the gap responsibility rules for the 1-gap defense:

Outside linebacker: On run play, press and defend the D gap.

Defensive end: On run play, press and defend the C gap.

Defensive tackle (to tight end): Press and defend the A gap.

Defensive tackle (to split end): Press and defend the B gap.

Inside linebacker (to tight end): Press and defend the B gap.

Inside linebacker (to split end): Press and defend the A gap.

In the second possibility, each defensive lineman attacks a designated offensive lineman, favoring the side to the defensive lineman's assigned gap. The idea is for the defensive lineman to keep the offensive lineman from releasing off the line of scrimmage. The defensive lineman is still responsible for a particular gap, but he tries to force the blocker in such a way as to minimize the opposite gap that the linebacker is responsible for. If possible, the defensive lineman, after he makes sure the ball is not being run in his gap, crosses the face of the offensive blocker and helps the linebacker in the adjacent gap. By using this 2-gap technique (figure 12.4), the defensive lineman makes it possible for the linebacker to help in more than one gap. Because the linebacker doesn't need to quickly attack his assigned gap, he can shuffle along behind the line of scrimmage and attack wherever the ball is going.

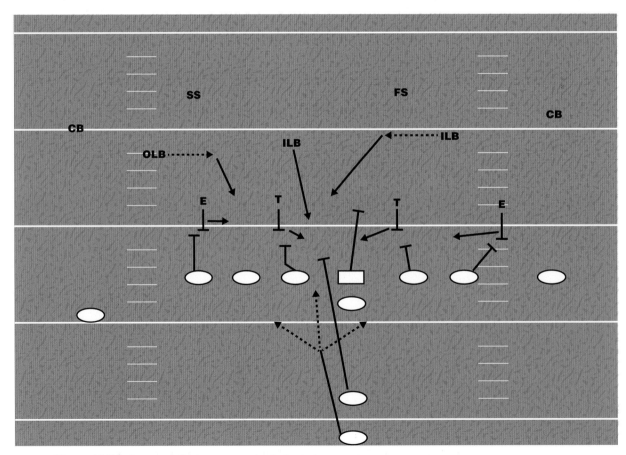

Figure 12.4   2-gap defense versus isolation play.

Here are the gap responsibility rules for the 2-gap defense:

Outside linebacker: On run, squeeze tight end back into C gap. Check D gap first. Cross face blocker to inside play.

Defensive end (to tight end): Attack tight end. Check C gap first. Cross face blocker to inside play.

Defensive end (to split end): Attack offensive tackle. Squeeze tackle back into B gap. Check C gap first. Cross face offensive tackle to inside play.

Defensive tackle (to split end): Attack offensive center. Squeeze center back into far A gap. Check A gap first. Cross face offensive center for play away.

Defensive tackle (to tight end): Attack offensive guard. Squeeze guard back into A gap. Check B gap first. Cross face guard for play away.

Inside linebacker (to tight end): Run flow to. Check A gap. Run flow away. Shuffle to ball. Attack runner where he attacks line of scrimmage.

Inside linebacker (to split end): Run flow to. Check B gap. Run flow away. Shuffle to ball. Attack runner where he attacks line of scrimmage.

When playing a 1-gap technique, each player makes sure he is in his assigned gap only. The defensive linemen try to penetrate into the offensive line as they are covering their gaps. The linebackers must be able to handle their one gap alone with little or no help from the linemen. More so than the 2-gap technique, this technique requires athletic defensive linemen who can make plays at the line of scrimmage. The advantage is that each player can be assertive in attacking his gap.

When playing the 2-gap technique, the defensive lineman's main job is to protect his gap while keeping the offensive lineman from releasing up to the linebackers. The linebackers are then free to go wherever the ball goes. This requires defensive linemen who are bigger and stronger and are able to play their gaps and hold up the offensive linemen.

Whichever base technique is used, the defensive linemen and linebackers must be on the same page. If the linemen are playing a 1-gap technique and the linebackers a 2-gap technique, the linebackers will be soft attacking their assigned gaps.

Now let's look at some of the most common defensive schemes in football.

MISSTEP

The defensive linemen play a 1-gap technique and penetrate upfield past the offensive blocker while the linebackers play a shuffle technique and flow to the gap they feel the running back is attacking. This leads to the offensive blockers assigned to the linebackers being able to get upfield on the linebackers and create a large bubble of space between the defensive linemen and linebackers. This bubble allows the running back a lot of room to make his cuts.

CORRECTION

The defensive linemen and linebackers must execute compatible techniques. If the linemen are penetrating, the linebackers must attack downhill toward the line of scrimmage. If the linemen are playing a 2-gap technique, trying to hold up the offensive blockers, the linebackers can then play a shuffle technique and flow to where the ball is attacking.

4-3 SCHEME

The 4-3 scheme is probably the most common defensive scheme used in football today. It involves four down linemen, three linebackers, and four defensive backs. There are many ways to arrange the players in a 4-3; two of the most common are the 4-3 Stack (figure 12.5a) and 4-3 Eagle (figure 12.5b).

Here are the alignment and run responsibilities for the 4-3 stack:

Outside linebacker (to tight end): Align over offensive tackle, 4 yards deep. On a run, defend the C gap.

Inside linebacker: Align over A gap to tight end 4 yards deep. On a run, defend the A gap.

Outside linebacker (to split end): Align over offensive tackle, 4 yards deep. On a run, defend the B gap.

Defensive end (to tight end): Align in 9 technique (outside shoulder of tight end). On a run, defend the D gap. (Refer to step 2 for alignment techniques.)

Defensive end (to split end): Align in 5 technique (outside of offensive tackle). On a run, defend the C gap.

Defensive tackle (to tight end): Align in 3 technique (outside shoulder of offensive guard). On a run, defend the B gap.

Defensive tackle (to split end): Align in 2I technique (inside shoulder of offensive guard). On a run, defend the A gap.

Here are the alignment and run responsibilities for the 4-3 Eagle:

Outside linebacker (to tight end): Align in 9 technique (on line of scrimmage). On a run, defend the D gap.

Inside linebacker (to tight end): Align over offensive guard. On a run, defend the B gap.

Inside linebacker (to split end): Align over offensive guard. On a run, defend the A gap.

Defensive end (to tight end): Align in 5 technique. On a run, defend the C gap.

Defensive end (to split end): Align in 5 technique. On a run, defend the C gap.

Defensive tackle (to tight end): Align in 1 technique. On a run, defend the A gap.

Defensive tackle (to split end): Align in 3 technique. On a run, defend the B gap.

In the 4-3 Stack, fewer players line up directly on the offensive linemen, so it appears to have more holes in the front part of the defense. This means the linebackers must play aggressively downhill anytime a run threatens their gaps. In the 4-3 Eagle, this is not as much the case because more defenders line up directly on the offensive linemen. The 4-3 Stack is the most common alignment used in a 1-gap scheme defense. The 4-3 Eagle is the most common 2-gap defensive alignment.

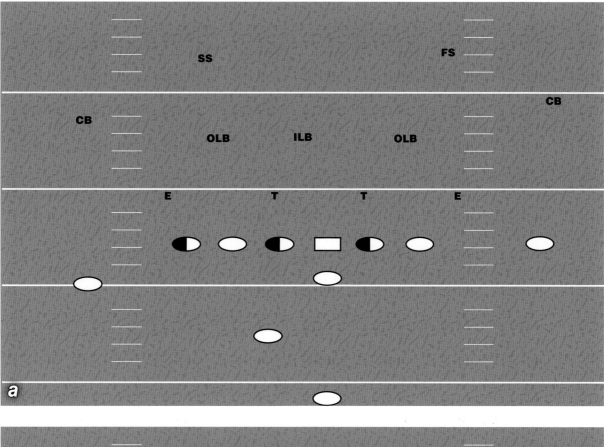

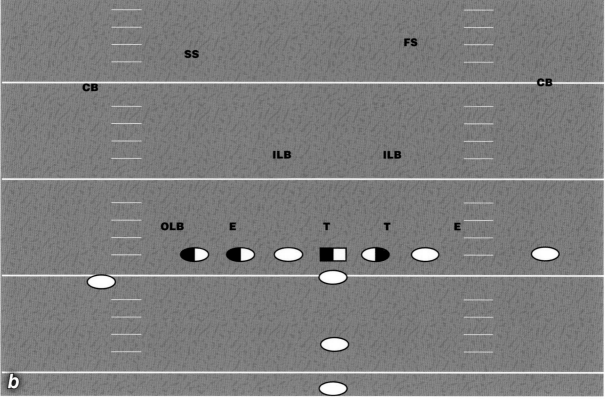

Figure 12.5 4-3 defenses: *(a)* 4-3 Stack; *(b)* 4-3 Eagle.

The 4-3 schemes give the defense the ability to line up seven, eight, or nine defenders in proximity to the offensive line. Sometimes this is called the run box, or simply the box. These schemes give the defense the chance to maximize their ability to defend running plays. The 4-3 Stack is also very flexible in allowing linebackers to adjust their alignments against three, four, and five wide receiver offensive sets. The three linebackers simply slide whichever way they need to in order to cover the wide Here are the alignment and run responsibilities for 4-3 Stack to trips formation (figure 12.6a):

Outside linebacker (to trips): Align on inside shoulder of number-two receiver 4 yards deep. On a run to, defend the D Gap. On a run away, defend the cutback to the C gap.

Inside linebacker: Align in strong side C gap 4 yards deep. On a run to, defend the strong side C gap. On a run away, defend the near A gap.

Outside linebacker (away from trips): Align over offensive guard and offensive tackle gap (B gap), 4 yards deep. On a run to, defend the B Gap. On a run away, defend the far A gap.

Defensive end (to tight end): Align in 9 technique. On a run, defend the D gap.

Defensive end (to split end): Align in 5 technique. On a run, defend the C gap.

Defensive tackle (to tight end): Align in 3 technique. On a run, defend the B gap.

Defensive tackle (to split end): Align in 2I technique. On a run, play the A gap.

Here are the alignment and run responsibilities for 4-3 Stack to twins pro formation (figure 12.6b):

Outside linebacker (to twins): Align on inside shoulder of number-two receiver 4 yards deep. On a run to, defend the D gap. On a run away, defend the cutback to the B gap.

Inside linebacker: Align in strong side B gap 4 yards deep. On a run to, defend the near B gap. On a run away, defend the far A gap.

Outside linebacker (away from twins): Align over tackle and tight end gap (C gap), 4 yards deep. On a run to, defend the C gap. On a run away, defend the A gap.

Defensive end (to tight end): Align in 9 technique. On a run, defend the D gap.

Defensive end (to split end): Align in 5 technique. On a run, defend the C gap.

Defensive tackle (to tight end): Align in 3 technique. On a run, defend the B gap.

Defensive tackle (to split end): Align in 2I technique. On a run, play the A gap.

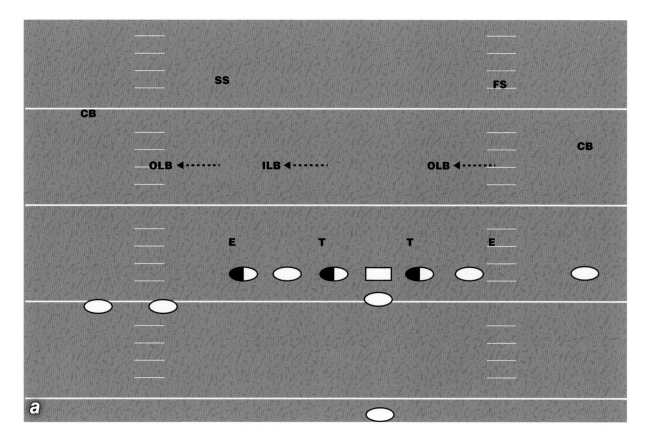

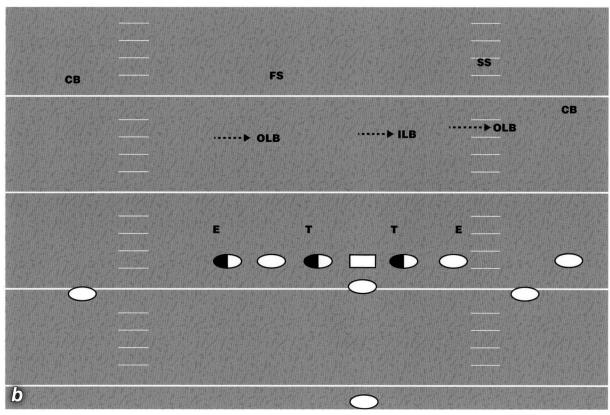

Figure 12.6 4-3 Stack adjustments to split wide receivers: *(a)* 4-3 Stack to trips formation; *(b)* 4-3 Stack to twins pro formation.

It's a little more difficult to adjust the 4-3 Eagle to these formations. Because the outside linebacker is lined up on the tight end, when he adjusts out to cover any wide receivers on his side, the defensive tackle and defensive end on his side need to adjust out as well (figure 12.7) so the defensive front can maintain its integrity against the run. This is a little more difficult to do, but possible with practice.

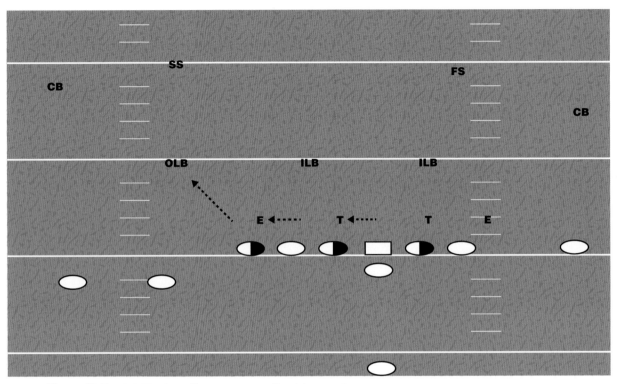

Figure 12.7 4-3 Eagle adjustment to split wide receivers.

Here are the alignment and run responsibilities for the 4-3 Eagle adjustment to split wide receivers:

Outside linebacker (to strength): Align in inside shoulder of number-two receiver, 4 yards off line of scrimmage. On a run to, defend the D gap. On a run away, defend the cutback or reverse play.

Outside linebacker (away from strength): Align over offensive guard, 4 yards deep. On a run to, defend near A gap to outside. On a run away, defend A gap cutback to front side.

Inside linebacker: Align over offensive guard, 4 yards deep. On a run to, defend the B gap. On a run away, defend the far A gap.

Defensive end (to strength): Align in 7 technique. On a run to, defend the C gap.

Defensive end (away from strength): Align in 5 technique. On a run to, defend the C gap.

Defensive tackle (to strength): Align in 2I technique. On a run to, defend the A gap.

Defensive tackle (away from strength): Align in 3 technique. On a run to, defend the B gap.

3-4 SCHEME

The 3-4 scheme has many of the same strengths of the 4-3 Stack and 4-3 Eagle. The 3-4 features three defensive linemen, four linebackers, and four defensive backs. Depending on how the 3-4 is designed, it could be similar to the 4-3 Eagle, or it could be similar to what many call the 5-2 scheme, a defense not used much anymore.

The 3-4 can be a good alternative to the 4-3 if it is difficult to find enough good defensive linemen, especially defensive ends. The outside linebackers in the 3-4 perform both the duties of the defensive ends and the outside linebackers in the 4-3. Figure 12.8 shows the base alignment for the 3-4 defense. The main issue in using the straight 3-4 is that you either need to slant the defensive line in one direction or you need the nose tackle or defensive ends to play a 2-gap technique in order to have enough defenders to cover the available run gaps from offensive tackle to offensive tackle.

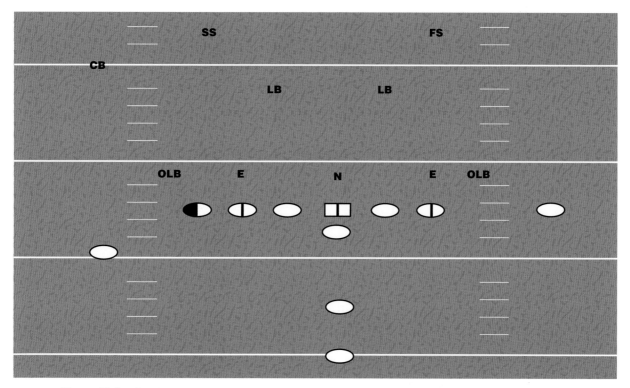

Figure 12.8   Straight 3-4.

Here are the alignment and run responsibilities for the straight 3-4:

> **Outside linebacker (to tight end):** Align in 9 technique (on line of scrimmage). On a run, defend the D gap.
>
> **Outside linebacker (to split end):** Align off the line of scrimmage 3 to 4 yards deep and 2 yards outside the defensive end. On a run, defend the D gap.
>
> **Inside linebacker:** Align over the offensive guard, 4 yards off the line of scrimmage. On a run to, defend the near B gap. On a run away, defend the near A gap to play side.

Defensive end: Align head up on offensive tackles. On a run, play the gap to the side of the play.

Nose tackle: Align head up on offensive center. On a run, play the A gap to the side of the play.

By slanting the defensive line and one outside linebacker in one direction, you declare the gaps each man is responsible for defending. By slanting one outside linebacker, you include him in defending one of the six inside gaps. This leaves two inside gaps for the two inside linebackers to defender. You can slant the line in either direction to achieve this 1-gap strategy. Figure 12.9a shows the 3-4 slant to the offensive formation's strength. Here are the alignment and run responsibilities for 3-4 slant strong:

Outside linebacker (to tight end): Align in 9 technique (on line of scrimmage). On a run, defend D Gap.

Outside linebacker (to split end): Align on line of scrimmage outside offensive tackle. On snap, slant inside; aim at tackle's outside hip. Defend C Gap.

Inside linebacker (to tight end): Align over offensive guard. On a run to, defend B Gap. On a run away, defend far A gap.

Inside linebacker (to split end): Align over offensive guard. On a run to, defend A gap. On a run away, shuffle to that side and play ball inside out.

Defensive end (to tight end): Align in 5 technique. On snap, slant to outside gap. On a run, defend C gap.

Defensive end (to split end): Align in 5 technique. On snap, slant to inside gap. On a run, defend B gap.

Nose tackle: Align in 0 technique. On snap, slant to strong-side gap. On a run, defend A Gap.

Figure 12.9b shows the 3-4 slant away from the offensive formation's strength. Here are the alignment and run responsibilities for 3-4 slant weak:

Outside linebacker (to tight end): Align in 9 technique (on line of scrimmage). On snap, slant inside, aim at offensive tackle's near hip. On a run, defend C Gap.

Outside linebacker (to split end): Align on line of scrimmage outside offensive tackle. Defend C Gap.

Inside linebacker (to tight end): Align over offensive guard. On a run to, defend A Gap. On a run away, shuffle to that side and defend cutback.

Inside linebacker (to split end): Align over offensive guard. On a run to, defend B Gap. On a run away, defend far A Gap.

Defensive end (to tight end): Align in 5 technique. On snap, slant to inside gap. On a run, defend B gap.

Defensive end (to split end): Align in 5 technique. On snap, slant to outside gap. On a run, defend C Gap.

Nose tackle: Align in 0 technique. On snap, slant to weak-side gap. On a run, defend A Gap.

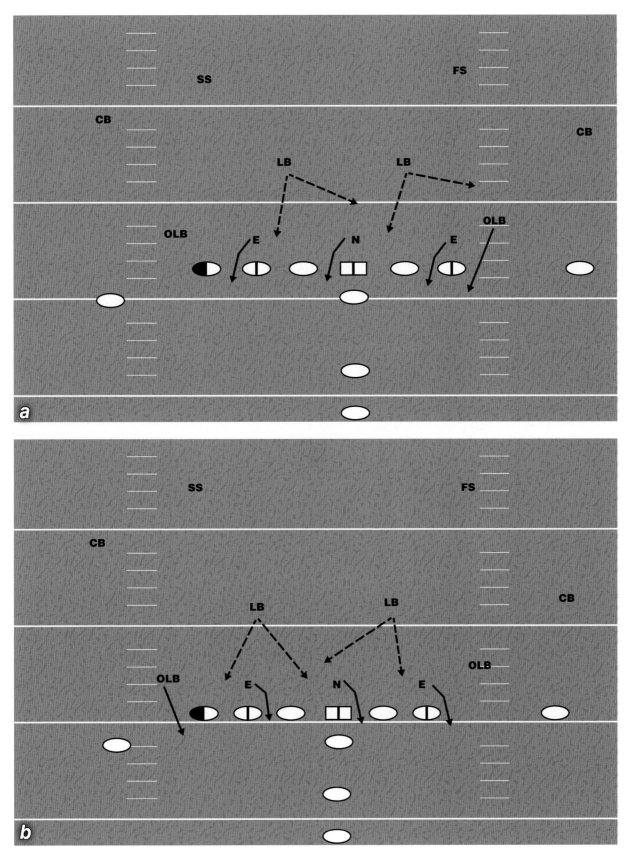

Figure 12.9 *(a)* 3-4 slant strong; *(b)* 3-4 slant weak.

MISSTEP

The defensive linemen slant in different directions, creating an extra open running gap and allowing the offensive runner to hit that gap.

CORRECTION

Communication is critical when slanting the entire defensive line. Assign one defensive player (usually one of the inside linebackers) to make the call, and make sure he echoes that call two or three times. Have defensive linemen tap their hips to indicate they heard the call. This helps the linebacker making the call know the call was heard.

An alternative way to play the 3-4 slant scheme is to predetermine which gaps the defensive linemen and outside linebackers will defend and have them line up in those gaps. One example is the 3-4 Eagle front (figure 12.10). By aligning each man in the designated gap, the defense declares before the snap which gaps each defender needs to defend.

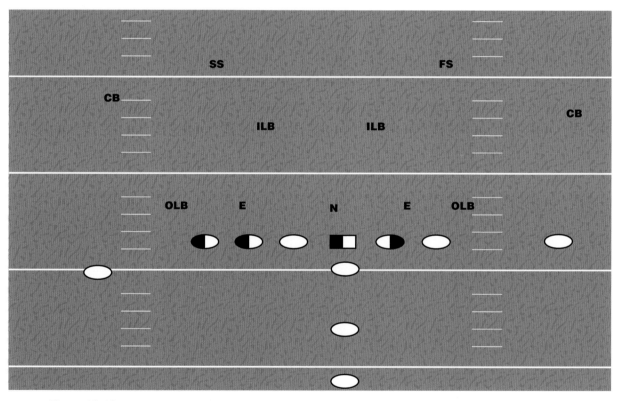

Figure 12.10 3-4 Eagle.

Here are the alignment and run responsibilities for the 3-4 Eagle:

Outside Linebacker (to tight end): Align in 9 technique (on line of scrimmage). On a run, defend the D gap.

Inside linebacker (to tight end): Align over offensive guard. On a run, defend the B gap.

Inside linebacker (to split end): Align over offensive guard. On a run, defend the A gap.

Defensive end (to tight end): Align in 5 technique. On a run, defend the C gap.

Outside linebacker (to split end): Align in 5 technique. On a run, defend the C gap.

Defensive tackle (to tight end): Align in 1 technique. On a run, defend the A gap.

Defensive tackle (to split end): Align in 3 technique. On a run, defend the B gap.

A second way to solve the gap number issue in a 3-4 defense is to play everyone straight and have the nose and defensive ends play two gaps each (figure 12.11). They align head-up on their designated players and, on the snap, work to the play-side gap of their men. The play-side gap is the side the offensive blocker is attempting to block. The best way for the defender to know which side the blocker is blocking is to observe the direction to which the blocker works his head. This is the play-side gap. The outside linebackers defend the outside gaps to their sides while the inside linebackers defend the remaining gaps inside that the nose and defensive ends do not take.

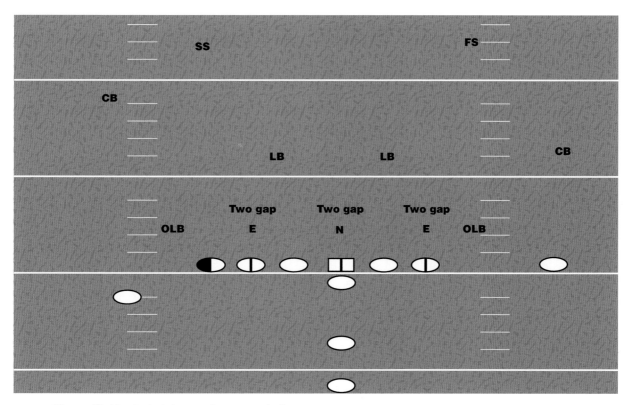

Figure 12.11 3-4 defense, 2-gap technique.

Here are the alignment and run responsibilities for the straight 3-4 using the 2-gap technique:

Outside linebacker (to tight end): Align in 9 technique (on line of scrimmage). On a run, defend D gap.

Outside linebacker (to split end): Align off line of scrimmage 3 to 4 yards deep and 2 yards outside defensive end. On a run, defend D gap.

Inside linebacker: Align over offensive guard, 4 yards off line of scrimmage. On a run to, defend near B Gap. On a run away, defend near A Gap to play side.

Defensive end: Align head up on offensive tackle. On a run, play 2 gap on tackle and work to play-side gap.

Nose tackle: Align head up on offensive center. On a run, play A gap to side of play.

In order to play the 3-4 2-gap scheme, the nose and defensive ends must be strong enough to take on their blockers and move to either side of them during the block. This takes good strength and technique. If the defensive linemen do not have good strength and technique, it's better to use the 3-4 Slant or 3-4 Eagle schemes since they require each player to step to and defend only one run gap.

3-3 STACK DEFENSE

The 3-3 Stack, sometimes called a 3-5 defense, is a relatively new development in football, although it's based on some older concepts that have been out of vogue in recent years. When offenses in the past focused on running the ball the majority of the time, a popular defensive front many teams used was the 5-3 defense: five defensive linemen, three linebackers, and three defensive backs (figure 12.12).

The 5-3 defense was designed to stop the running game. With only three defensive backs, it lacked the flexibility to adjust to today's passing offenses and thus fell out of favor. In its place has come the 3-3 or 3-5 defense. Essentially, these are the same defense as the 5-3, but with only three defensive linemen and four or five defensive backs. The extra defensive backs or linebackers take the place of two of the defensive linemen. These added pass defenders make the scheme flexible enough to cover any passing formation. Figure 12.13 shows the 3-3 Stack defense.

Here are the alignment and responsibilities for the 3-3 Stack:

Defensive end: Align in 5 technique. Defend C Gap.

Nose tackle: Align in 0 technique. Defend A Gap away from play direction.

Inside linebacker: Align over offensive center, 4 yards deep. Defend play-side A Gap.

Outside linebacker: Align over offensive tackle, 4 yards deep. Defend B Gap.

Strong safety: Align 3 yards outside the tight end position on your side, 5 yards off the line of scrimmage. Based on coverage called, defend D gap, or play force (contain run play).

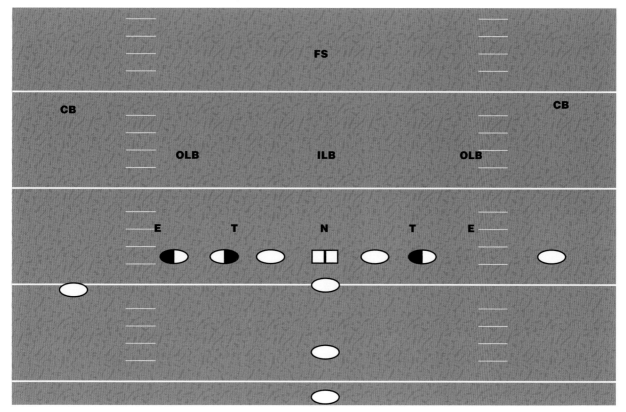

Figure 12.12 5-3 defense.

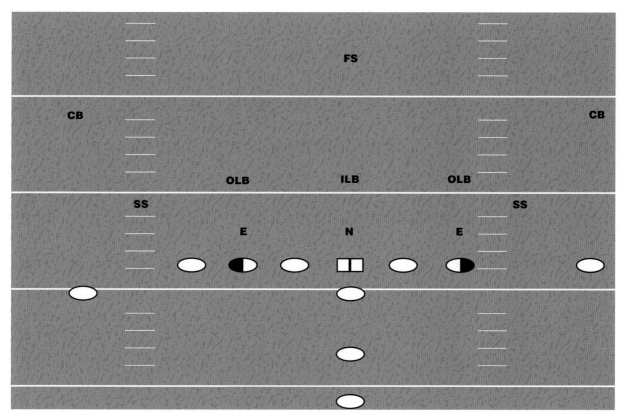

Figure 12.13 3-3 Stack.

There are two main advantages to using the 3-3. First is the alignment flexibility. When playing the 3-3, defenders can adjust easily to any number of passing schemes and formations. It allows for dropping at least eight defenders into pass coverage, making it very difficult for the quarterback to find an open receiver downfield. Against the running game, there are five players—three linebackers and two strong safeties—aligned in such a way to defend multiple running gaps. The negative of the 3-3 is that the five players are aligned off the line of scrimmage, giving the offense an initial couple of yards to come off and execute their blocks. The bubbles in the defense are areas that must be attacked by defenders to stop or slow the running game.

The other advantage of the 3-3 front is that it allows a lot of line movement and blitzing from five possible players. This front creates a complex problem for the offense.

PASSING DEFENSE

As with defensive fronts, pass coverages encompass a large range of possibilities. Zone, man, and combination zone–man coverages are possible. Within the zone-coverage category, there are three-deep zones, two-deep zones, three-deep zones with man under, two-deep zones with man under, and four-deep zones. There are also zone blitz schemes with three-deep, three-under zones or two-deep, four-under zones.

Within the man schemes, there are man free schemes and blitz man schemes. Within each of these subclasses are many variations. As with offensive schemes, the number of variations is limited only by the coach's imagination and the team's ability to execute. Whatever is done, the team's ability to execute the techniques required in the scheme is critical. If a team doesn't have players adept at the quick change of direction and reaction required by man coverages, they should probably not use a lot of these coverages.

Zone Coverage

First we'll look at the basic zone coverage schemes, focusing on the major assignments and the fundamental techniques used. These techniques were covered in detail in step 9 on defending the pass. Before getting specific with coverages, let's review the defensive coverage zones that are used as reference points: three-deep coverage, two-deep coverage, and four-deep coverage.

THREE-DEEP ZONE

The strength of a three-deep zone coverage (figure 12.14) is that the defense has three deep defenders who can defend the width of the field fairly easily. Each player covers an area 17 yards wide. If the deep 1/3 defenders stay deeper than the receivers in their zones, and if they do a good job of seeing the ball when it's thrown, they should be able to defend their 17 yards effectively.

A secondary advantage of the three-deep defense is that there's always a player (the free safety) aligned over the ball who can help stop any long running plays that the defensive linemen and linebackers fail to stop.

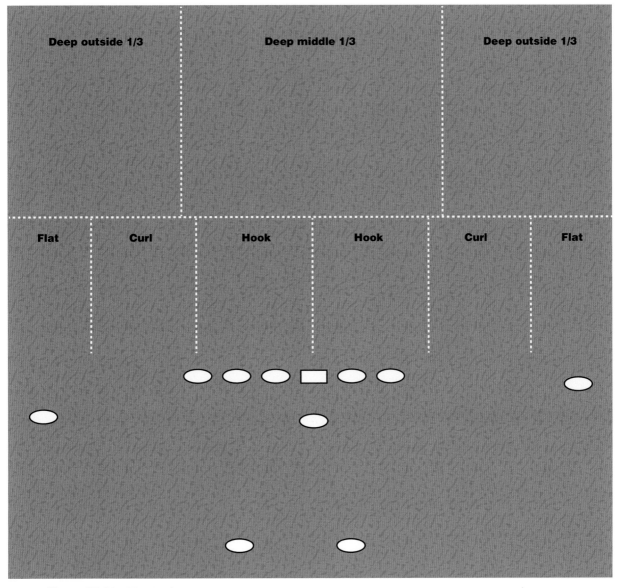

Figure 12.14 Three-deep zone.

The main pass weakness is that there are only four defenders to cover the six underneath zones (in 4-3 and 3-4 schemes). Combine this with the fact that the offense has five possible receivers to run routes in those underneath zones, and the defense can be at a disadvantage versus shorter routes if the offense sends out more than three or four receivers (figure 12.15).

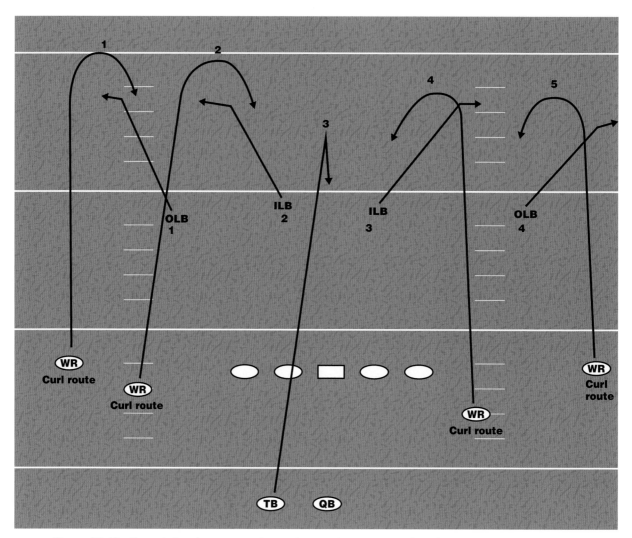

Figure 12.15 Four defenders cover the underneath zones—a disadvantage against five potential receivers.

Here are the alignments and responsibilities for a three-deep zone:

Cornerback: Align over number-one receiver 7 to 8 yards deep. On pass, stay deeper than deepest threat in your outside 1/3 zone.

Free safety: Align 12 yards deep, splitting the offensive formation. On pass, stay deeper than deepest threat to your middle 1/3 zone.

Inside linebacker: Align based on front called. On pass, drop to inside edge of hook zone, expand out to curl zone if no immediate threat in hook.

Outside linebacker: Align based on front called. On pass, drop to inside edge of curl zone, expand out to flat zone if no immediate threat in curl. Reroute toward the outside anyone running vertical route through curl zone.

No matter what the defense does, one of the five receivers will be open. The key to using a three-deep zone is to understand this weakness and drop to the under zones in such a way as to minimize this weakness. This is done by dropping back and covering the possible routes inside out. The easier passes to throw are to the closer receivers, those inside. The more difficult and more time-consuming passes to throw are to the outside receivers. By covering the receivers from the inside out, the defense forces the quarterback to consider the hardest pass first (the outside throw) and is defending the easier pass. By dropping inside out, the defenders take away the easier throws, forcing the quarterback to look to the outside throws. After dropping to stop the inside throw, the defenders slide outside to defend the harder and longer outside passes. This gives them a chance to defend those passes as well.

Even though a three-deep coverage has enough defenders for most deep patterns, if the offense sends four receivers downfield, there are more receivers than can be defended. The most common four-man route versus a three-deep zone is the four-vertical route (figure 12.16). This places a receiver running vertically downfield on each sideline, stretching the cornerbacks as far as possible, and two more receivers running vertically downfield at each hash mark, putting the free safety in a bind if the cornerbacks move out too far.

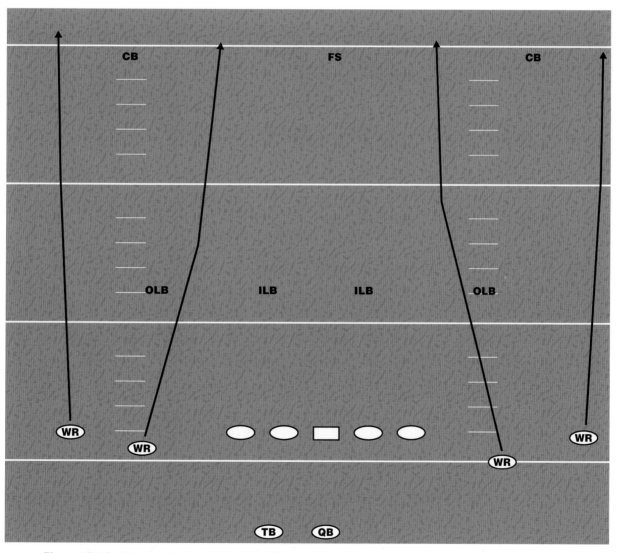

Figure 12.16 Four-vertical route versus three-deep zone.

The idea is for the outside receivers to draw either or both cornerbacks out with them and put the free safety on an island. The quarterback can then throw to either inside receiver. Likewise, if one of the cornerbacks cheats toward the inside receiver too far, the outside receiver will be open.

To defend against this Cover 3 beater, the defense must force the two receivers running down the hash marks either out toward the cornerbacks or in toward the free safety. This forces two of the receivers into one zone, allowing the man defending that zone to cover both receivers equally well. This is called rerouting the receiver. The technique involves an underneath defender hitting and forcing the receiver either in or out. The player who is rerouting must make contact with the receiver about 10 yards from the line of scrimmage (figure 12.17). This makes it difficult for the receiver to bend back into his original path before he gets upfield close to the deep-zone defender. If the rerouting takes place too soon, the receiver can bend his path back to the hash marks in time for the ball to be thrown before the receiver gets too deep.

The nearest under cover man should perform the reroute, as long as he can still get to his assigned coverage zone.

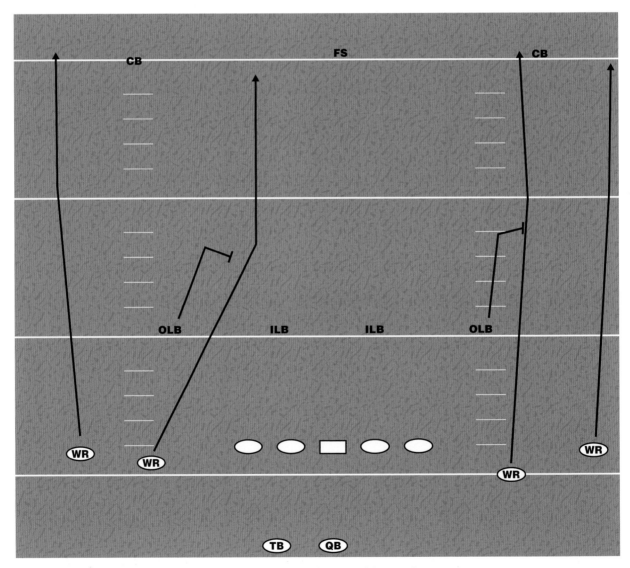

Figure 12.17 Outside linebacker reroutes the inside wide receiver.

TWO-DEEP ZONE

If the offense shows a lot of underneath zone routes or has four or five receivers going out on patterns, the defense may want to try a two-deep zone coverage (figure 12.18), which uses five under-zone cover men and two deep-zone cover men. The five under-zone defenders help stop the shorter routes. However, this opens up the deep zones because now only two defenders must cover the width of the field, about 25 yards apiece. A key for this coverage is to have the under-zone cover men reroute any receiver attempting to run a route into a vacant deep zone (middle or outside). It's also important to have one or two of the under-zone cover men help on deeper routes when they don't have a threat to their under zone.

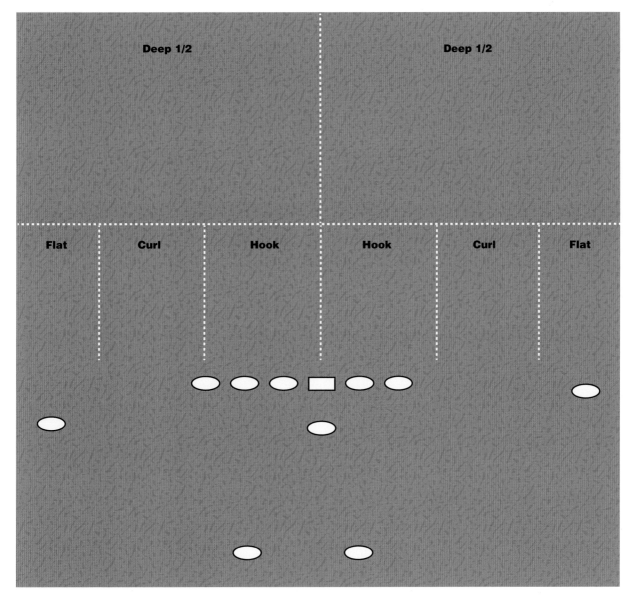

Figure 12.18 Two-deep zone.

This is done in one of two ways. The first involves the cornerbacks. Their basic technique is to first reroute the outside receiver to the inside toward the deep half safety. The cornerback then looks for any receiver running a short route into his zone (flat). If no receiver threatens his flat, the cornerback sinks deep and to the outside at a 45-degree angle to help the half safety on any corner routes (figure 12.19).

MISSTEP

The cornerback fails to reroute the wide receiver running through his flat zone, allowing the wide receiver to get outside and upfield into the deep outside zone unhindered. This makes it very difficult for the free safety on that side to cover a 15- to 20-yard pass to the receiver by the sideline.

CORRECTION

The cornerback must always reroute the receiver who's trying to release outside him and up the field. The cornerback must stay square to the receiver. The cornerback must also move his feet quickly (shuffle technique) to stay in front of the receiver while jamming the receiver (rerouting) trying to release.

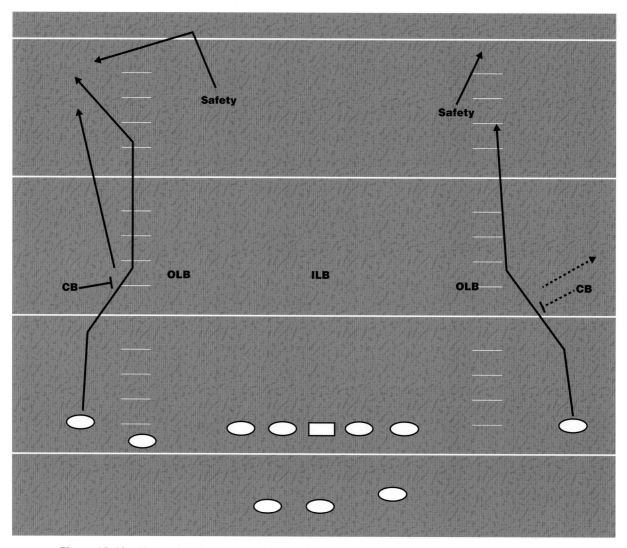

Figure 12.19   Cornerback reroutes the outside receivers toward the deep half safeties.

Here are the alignments and responsibilities for the two-deep zone:

Cornerback: Align 5 yards from line of scrimmage on outside shoulder of number-one receiver. On snap, reroute receiver to the inside toward the safety. After receiver clears, expand back to defend flat.

Safety: Align 12 to 14 yards deep and 2 yards outside the near hash. On snap, backpedal while keying your run-pass key. Stay deeper than deepest receiver in your half field zone.

Inside linebacker: Align based on front called. On pass, drop back to inside of hook zone to three-man side (the side where three receivers are running routes). Play hook, but be ready to run with number-three receiver vertical route.

Outside linebacker: Align based on front called. On pass, drop to curl, reroute number-two receiver to your side out toward safeties.

Unlike the reroutes in three-deep zones, Cover 2 reroutes by the cornerbacks should take place at about 5 yards and continue for several yards before the cornerback comes off.

The second way to help the deep safeties in two-deep zones is for the inside linebacker to cover any deep middle pass route (figure 12.20). This allows the two safeties to widen their alignments by about 2 yards each; they can then more easily cover an outside threat to their half of the field.

This allows the safeties to focus on the outside threats. However, this solution might pit the inside linebacker against a better athlete in coverage. It also reduces the number of defenders for the under routes to four, although this happens only if the inside linebacker has to cover someone deep. If no receiver is attacking the deep middle, the inside linebacker stays in his short zone.

FOUR-DEEP ZONE

A four-deep zone (figure 12.21) is very similar to a two-deep zone. The main difference is in the play of the cornerbacks. In a four-deep zone, the cornerbacks do not try to reroute the outside receivers as they come off, and the cornerbacks are not responsible for the flat zones. Instead, the cornerbacks sink into their deep outside 1/4 zones to cover any routes attacking the outside. Because there are now four deep defenders, each needs to cover only about 12 or 13 yards of the width of the field. This makes completing a deep-route pass very difficult for the quarterback. Thus a four-deep zone coverage is good in long-yardage situations or when the defense doesn't care if the offense completes a short pass, such as at the end of the game.

On the other hand, because there are four deep defenders, this leaves only three defenders to cover the six underneath zones in a conventional 4-3 defense. A variation of the four-deep zone has the cornerbacks playing a combination of the two-deep concept and the four-deep concept. This basically means the cornerbacks cover anyone who comes into the flat, but if no one does so, they sink to the deep outside zones.

Man Coverage

The two basic types of man coverage are blitz man and man free. Blitz man is used when the defense blitzes at least six men, leaving five defenders to cover the five eligible receivers. The objective of the blitz is to get to the quarterback quickly and tackle

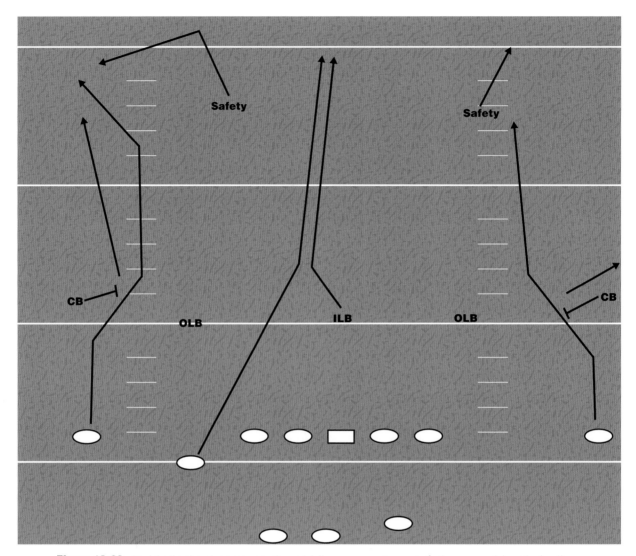

Figure 12.20 Inside linebacker covers the middle pass route so safeties can widen their alignments.

him before he gets the pass off. Because they don't want the quarterback to get off a quick throw, defenders must cover all receivers closely to deter a rapid pass after the snap. This is called press coverage. The defenders use the aggressive man technique described in step 9. The strength of this coverage is that defenders are very close to their receivers, making it difficult for the quarterback to complete a pass. The weakness is that the defenders have no help in coverage. If a receiver manages to escape his defender, an easy reception and a big play for the offense might result—unless the blitz reaches the quarterback early enough. Blitzing requires players who can get in on the rush quickly, either to tackle the quarterback or force him to get rid of the ball before he wants to. If the blitzing players take too long to get to the quarterback, pass defenders have a more difficult time sustaining coverage on their receivers.

A variation of blitz man is called man free coverage. There are two variations of man free coverage. The first involves blitzing five men (or five-man pressure) instead of the six with regular blitz man. By blitzing five men, the defense is trying to overload the offensive blockers while retaining a free pass defender to help any defender who loses his man. The free defender lines up in the deep middle of the field, the

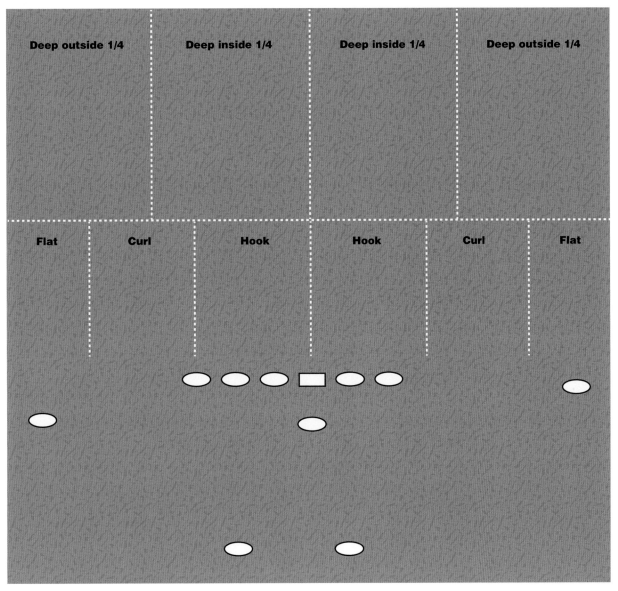

Figure 12.21 Four-deep zone.

same as a Cover 3 free safety. The coverage men try to force their receivers inside toward the free defender (figure 12.22). If the pass defender loses his man, it will be toward the free defender, allowing him to help on the receiver. This coverage is effective only if the blitzers can get to the quarterback fairly quickly.

MISSTEP

A pass defender in man free coverage allows his receiver to get outside him to run his route, preventing the free safety from being able to help defend a deep route.

CORRECTION

The pass defender must stay on the outside of his receiver throughout the pass route. The defender must work hard to force the receiver to run to the defender's inside at all times.

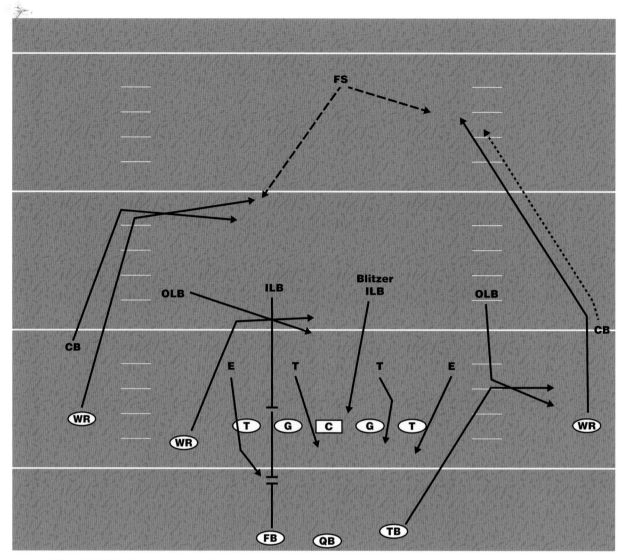

Figure 12.22 Pressure man free.

The second type of man free involves no blitz. The defense has only four defensive linemen rushing the passer, as in any normal zone coverage. This leaves two free pass defenders, usually one deep and one shallow, to help the man-coverage defenders (figure 12.23). As in the five-man blitz, in regular man free the defenders take away any outside routes from the receivers, forcing the receivers to run inside routes. If the receivers do get free, there are two free defenders to help out.

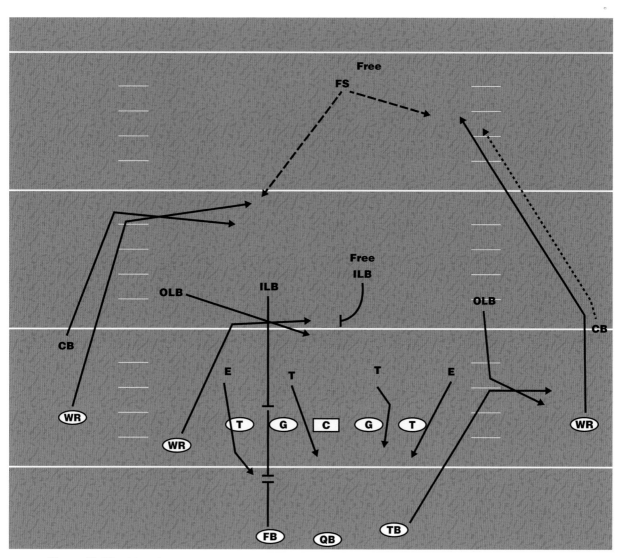

Figure 12.23 Man free.

SUCCESS SUMMARY

In step 12 we have looked at some basic defensive schemes used in football. By no means have we covered every scheme out there. We have covered the basic fronts: 4-3, 3-4, and 3-3. We have also discussed the five traditional coverage schemes: three-deep zone, two-deep zone, four-deep zone, man blitz, and man free.

Before moving on to step 13, answer the following questions to check your understanding of the concepts discussed in step 12.

Before Taking the Next Step

1. In a 4-3 scheme, how many defensive linemen, linebackers, and backs are used?

2. In a 3-4 scheme, how many defensive linemen, linebackers, and backs are used?

3. What is one advantage of using a 4-3 Stack defensive scheme?

4. What is one disadvantage of using a 4-3 Stack defensive scheme?

5. In a three-deep zone coverage, how many pass defenders are there to cover the five underneath pass zones?

6. What is one technique of the underneath pass defenders that can be used to help the deep-zone pass defenders?

7. What is one difference between blitz man pass coverage and man free pass coverage?

Special Teams

Between 20 and 25 percent of most games is spent on special-team plays. Special team-plays can accumulate more yardage than all offensive plays combined. Some of the biggest plays in a game take place on special teams, such as 100-yard kickoff returns or blocked punts taken in for touchdowns. This means teams must spend an appropriate amount of practice on special teams, both in basic fundamentals (see step 10) and in scheme practice. In this step we focus on the basic fundamentals needed in each of the six phases of special teams: punt and punt return; kickoff and kickoff return; field goal and PAT (point after touchdown) attempts; and field goal and PAT block attempts.

PUNT

The punt play might be the most important of the special-team plays because more punts (and punt returns) occur in a game than any other special-team play. Most punts also result in a major change in field position—usually a 30- to 40-yard change. A blocked punt can be a game-changing play. Because of its impact, the punting game is usually allocated more practice time than any other play on special teams.

The punting team has two critical responsibilities: to protect the punter as he punts the ball and to cover downfield after the punt to prevent the punt returner from gaining yardage on his return. A breakdown on either play can spell catastrophe. As with offensive and defensive schemes, many different systems can be used in the punting game. We'll look at two main alignments and two main blocking schemes. The two alignments are the spread punt and the shield punt. The two main blocking systems used with any punt alignments are zone protection and man protection.

Spread Punt Alignment

The spread punt has been the most popular alignment in the last 10 to 15 years. In the spread punt alignment (figure 13.1), two players split out their alignment with the intent of covering downfield immediately on the snap, trying to get to the returner before or as he catches the punt. By getting there quickly, these cover men, called gunners, can minimize the return. The remaining punting team members must block for the punter before they can release downfield to cover.

The gunners split 5 to 15 yards from the main formation. The punter is aligned 13 to 15 yards behind the snapper. The personal protector (PP) is aligned 5 yards behind the line of scrimmage to the punter's kicking-foot side. The wings can line

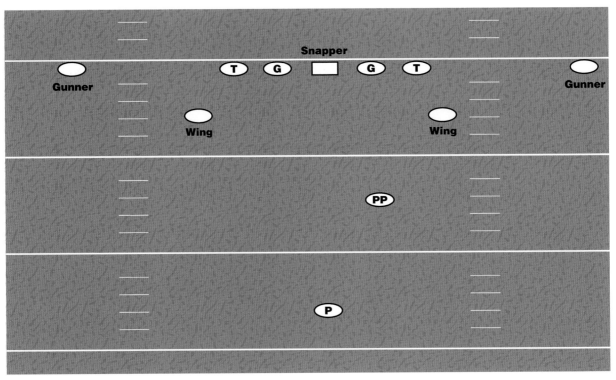

Figure 13.1 Spread punt alignment.

up as shown in figure 13.1, just off the line of scrimmage and outside the offensive tackles, or they can be 4 to 5 yards deep, just outside the offensive tackles, as shown in figure 13.2.

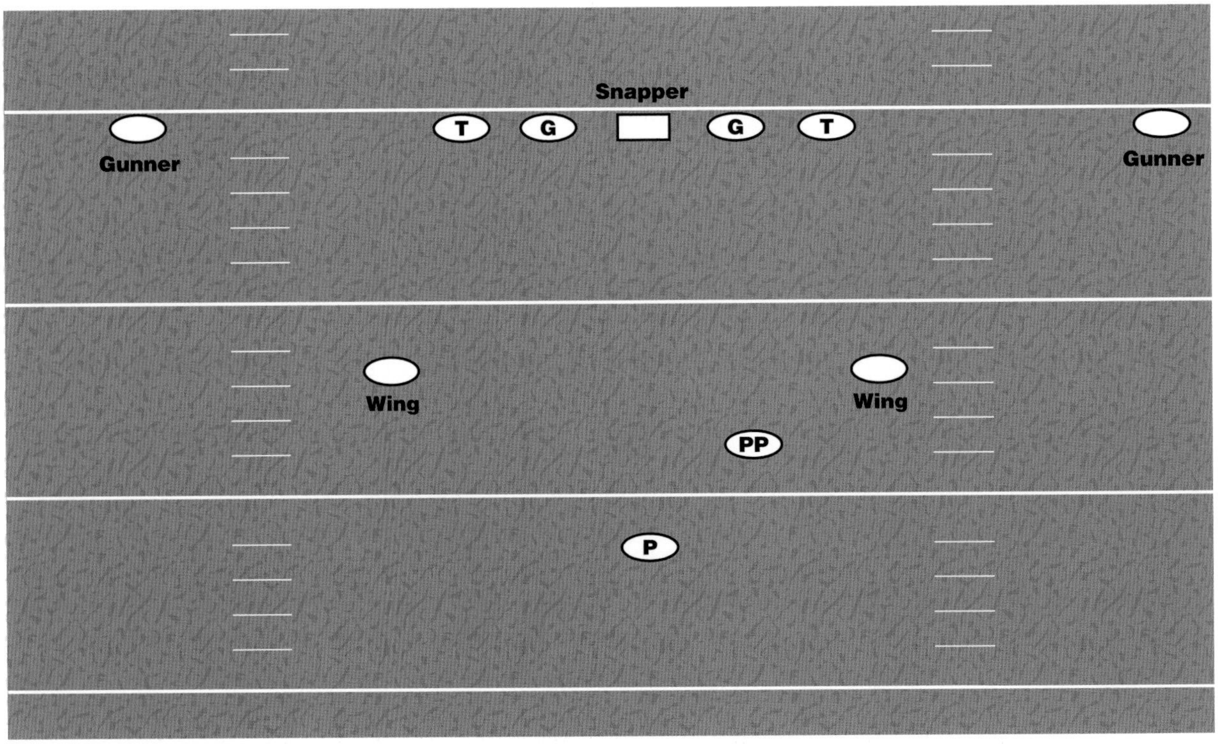

Figure 13.2 Spread punt alignment, wings 5 yards deep.

When the ball is snapped, the core blockers—the offensive linemen and the wings—shuffle straight back, getting ready to block an area or a man, depending on the type of scheme used. If the wings align 4 to 5 yards deep, they avoid having to shuffle back. On the snap, the gunners release immediately to cover downfield. They have no blocking responsibility.

Shield Punt Alignment

The shield punt alignment (figure 13.3) is an older punting alignment that has now regained popularity. In this alignment, three players line up 5 yards behind the line of scrimmage directly in front of the punter. These three players are usually larger, stronger players, often linemen or linebackers, who present a solid wall of protection directly in front of the punter. The rest of the punt-coverage team aligns anywhere from 1 yard to 7 or 8 yards apart. Aligning linemen 7 to 8 yards wide helps to spread the punt-return defenders to the point they can't rush the punter and get there before the ball is kicked. Once defenders are more than 10 yards or more wide, the distance to the punter is too great for them to get to him. The wider splits by the punting team give them more room to release off the hold-up blocks of the defenders as they release to cover the punt. The wider splits also automatically put the coverage men in their prescribed coverage lanes. All they must do is cover directly to the returner, keeping him on their inside shoulders as they squeeze to him.

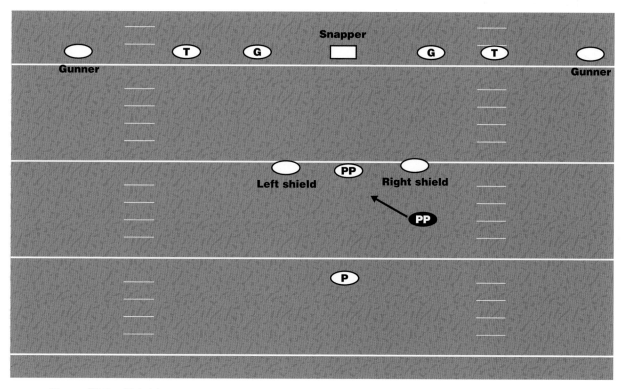

Figure 13.3 Shield punt alignment.

The PP aligns off center, behind the right shield blocker, before and as the ball is snapped. Once the snap passes him, the PP moves quickly into the position shown in figure 13.3.

The splits between the linemen can be as wide as 7 or 8 yards (or more), depending on the coach's philosophy. Some coaches worry a defender can slide inside at the last minute and get within that 10-yard distance and have a chance to get to the punt. If a blocker recognizes that his defender is going to move in, he can tighten his alignment to compensate so he can block the rusher. The width of the shield also makes it difficult for any free rusher to get around the blocker to the punter's contact point.

The shield punt alignment can use either zone-protection rules or man-protection rules, whichever the coach prefers. The protection rules for either scheme are similar to the rules for the spread punt formation.

Zone Scheme

In a zone scheme, the punt blockers use a blocking rule similar to an offense running a zone play. Usually the blockers (offensive linemen and wings) are responsible for blocking the area from head-up on them to the next man outside. The snapper (offensive center) is usually assigned the gap to the side to which he can move the best, whereas the PP takes the opposite center–guard gap.

When the ball is snapped, everyone but the PP takes at least two shuffle steps back and blocks the rusher who shows up in his gap. One of the key techniques blockers must master is recognizing when the rusher is actually rushing to block the punt and when he's simply trying to hold up the blocker he's rushing. If a blocker is simply being held up, the blocker must react quickly to try to release downfield and get away from the rusher. If the rusher is actually rushing to block the punt, the blocker must stay with his block until he knows the ball has been punted.

Once the ball is punted, all blockers release off their defenders and cover downfield. Each cover man must know which area of the field he must cover as he runs to the returner. Each man is responsible for a lane. Figure 13.4 depicts proper lane responsibilities for each man. In most systems, the coverage lanes are as follows:

Gunners: Cover directly to the punt returner. Aim for his near number.

Wings: Cover to the numbers. Contain all returns.

Tackles: Cover to midpoint from the numbers to the hash mark.

Guards: Cover to just inside the hash mark to your side.

Snapper: Cover to the ball. Force the returner to go left or right.

Personal protector: Cover to the ball.

Punter: Cover to the ball. Act as safety 15 yards from ball.

When covering to his lane, each man should expand from his alignment to the aiming point, reaching that point by 10 yards downfield. From that aiming point, each man should start to squeeze down toward the returner as he runs downfield. As he approaches the returner, he should keep the returner on his inside shoulder.

Gunners do not have lane responsibilities. It's their job to get to the punt-return man and tackle him as soon as possible.

Man Scheme

A second basic scheme used with punt formations is the man blocking scheme. As the name implies, each blocker is responsible for blocking a specific rusher based on a set of rules. There are several possibilities:

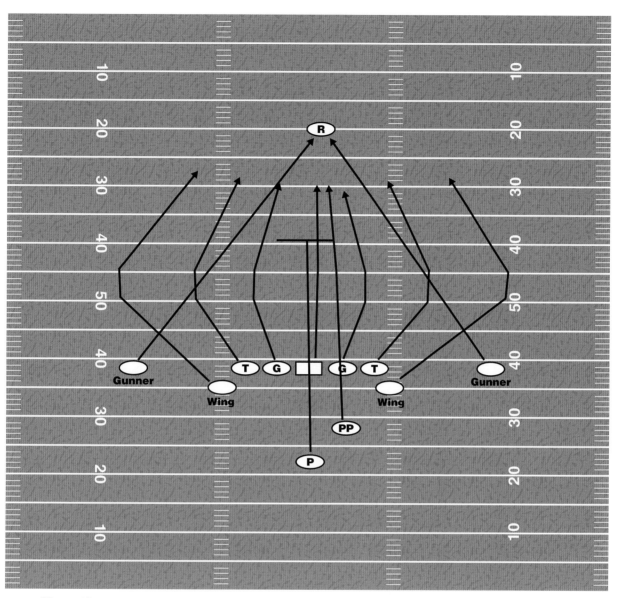

Figure 13.4 Punt-coverage lanes in a zone scheme.

Gunners: Cover directly to the ball. If your man creeps to a rush position inside of you, call "tight" and move to an alignment 1 yard outside the wing. Block number 1 (most outside man to your side).

Wings: Block number 2. If number 2 is in press on gunner, release into coverage.

Tackles: Block number 3.

Guards: Block number 4.

Snapper: Block number 5 to the left.

Personal protector: Block number 5 to the right. Help.

Count the rushers from the outside in, starting with the defender lining up on the gunners (figure 13.5).

If the rushers stack and change positions as they rush (figure 13.6), each blocker picks up the rusher who becomes his man. This is the main reason for the shuffle steps back: to give the blocker time and space to identify the correct rusher.

The advantage of blocking man is that the blocker might be able to recognize earlier if his man is rushing or dropping into coverage. If the rusher is dropping into coverage, the blocker can quickly abort his shuffle and get into coverage. In the zone scheme, the blocker must stay in his shuffle until the ball is kicked to ensure someone does not rush through his area. This delays his release to cover downfield. The weakness of man blocking is that the rushing team can line up in many different alignments to confuse the blockers in their recognition.

PUNT RETURN

The punt return is another common play on special teams. As the punting team can have 6 to 12 plays a game, so will the punt return team. The object of the punt-return unit is to give the offensive unit the best field position possible. This can be done through an effective return or by blocking the opponent's punt. This is the first thing the punt return coach must decide: What kind of punt-return unit does he want, a return unit or a blocking unit? This decision has changed somewhat in recent years with the advent of the shield punt alignment. The shield makes it more difficult to block a punt, so most teams choose to be primarily return teams versus shield punt teams. This is not to say it's impossible to block a shield punt—it is possible, just more difficult.

Many types of returns can be effective, but key to any successful punt return is how well defenders can prevent the coverage men from getting to the returner. Obviously, the returner's skill has much to do with the success of the return as well, particularly his ability to catch the punt and hold onto the ball. Many a good punt return has been foiled by a dropped ball, made even worse, of course, if the opponent recovers the fumble.

When learning to hold up a punt-coverage man, defenders must remember four main points:

1. The hold-up at the line of scrimmage
2. The blocker's transition to his release
3. The shadow-and-stab technique as the man covers downfield
4. The final block at the returner

First, when the ball is snapped, the defender must attack the man he is to hold up and attempt to drive him back as far as possible. The defender attacks with knees bent, in good football position, with his hands inside the blocker's hands on his chest. As he drives the blocker back toward the punter, the defender must maintain his balance and keep his head up. He must be able to see and feel the point at which the blocker stops blocking and attempts to release off the defender to go downfield.

This leads to the second key technique for effective returns: If the defender has too much weight forward while trying to drive the blocker back, he won't be able to react properly when the blocker transitions into his release. The defender might even

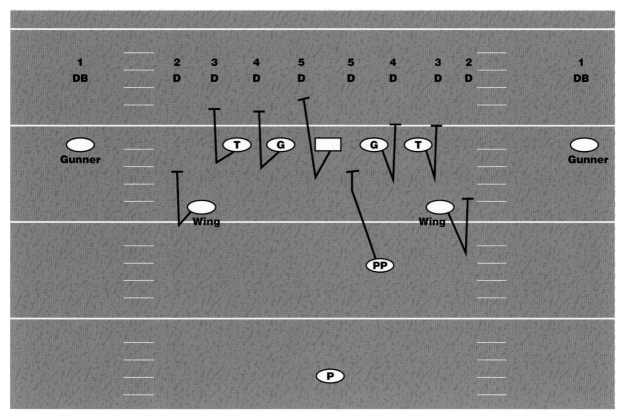

Figure 13.5 Man punt blocking scheme with rushers numbered.

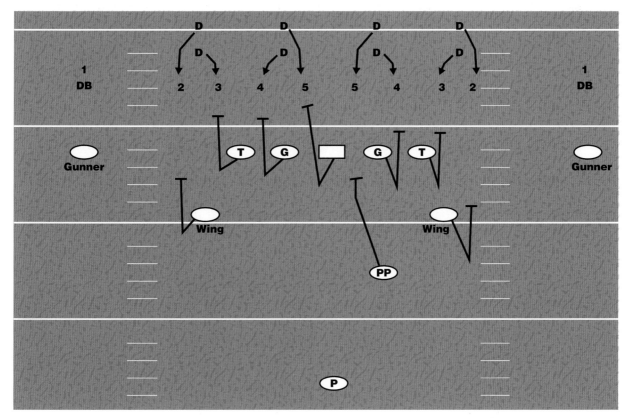

Figure 13.6 Punt rushers change positions; blockers adjust.

lose balance and completely lose contact with the blocker as the blocker releases. With proper balance and awareness of the release taking place, the defender can gather himself and prepare for his next responsibility. A good coaching point for the defender is that for every yard he can drive his blocker back before the release, he's forcing the blocker to cover 2 more yards downfield. Even 1 extra yard is sometimes all it takes to spring the returner free for a long return.

The third technique for the defender is the shadow-and-stab technique, which takes place while the coverage man is running downfield to cover the punt. As the name implies, this technique involves running downfield next to the coverage man and trying to "stab" him to move his coverage lane in a desired direction. The technique is simply running next to the coverage man and punching him on the shoulder pad to widen his path. The more the defender can punch and widen the coverage man's path, the better. If the punch is successful, running lanes are created for the returner. An important coaching point for the defender is to contact on the side and not the back of the coverage man. Hitting him in the back draws a clipping penalty. Also, if the coverage man gets ahead of the defender to the point the stab is not possible, the defender should sprint to catch up, staying 2 or 3 yards to the inside of the coverage man. As the coverage man nears the returner, he'll slow down slightly and gather himself to make the tackle. At this point, the defender can catch up, get his head in front of his man, and make the final block as the returner passes. This is the fourth technique the defender must execute in an effective punt return.

There are many ways to design a punt return. Basically, the return team must account for all the players who can release downfield and assign a blocker to each. The return team must be able to hold them up at the line of scrimmage, divert their paths downfield , and make good, solid blocks to spring the returner. The design of the return depends on several factors: the ability and general direction tendency of the punter; the coverage ability of the punting team; the weather conditions; and the overall scheme used by the punting team. For example, in a shield punt scheme, the shield blockers are seldom effective coverage men because they are aligned deeper, cannot release until the ball is punted, and are usually bigger and slower players. Thus the punt-return scheme might not try to block all of them, freeing up a blocker to help on the better coverage men.

An important coaching point that must be covered with every punt-return team is what to do if the punt is short and coming down near the blockers. If a punt touches any player on the return team, it becomes a free ball that anyone can recover. If a defender is busy holding up a coverage man and does not see a short punt come down, he might get hit by the ball, freeing it to be recovered by the punting team. It is the returner's responsibility to make a call to everyone if he sees this happening. Any code word that everyone understands will work. The most common two words used are "Peter" and "Poison." The word *poison* is an obvious one. Why *Peter* is used is unknown, but it's a clear word, easy to call out, and easily understood. Whatever word is used, the returner must yell it loudly and repeatedly to let his return team know to stop blocking, look up to find the ball, and get away from it. If the ball hits the ground and rolls to a stop without touching anyone, it will be whistled dead by the official.

Another important coaching point is to make sure the returner knows how deep he should go toward his own goal line to attempt to catch a punt. Most punts that land inside the 10-yard line will roll into the end zone for a touchback if allowed to. This brings the ball back out to the 20-yard line for the offense. For this reason, the returner should never back up inside his own 10-yard line to catch a punt. If he does, the odds are against him being able to return the ball back to the 20-yard line. The returner should be taught to stand with his heels on the 10-yard line and never back up to catch the punt. If the ball is obviously going to be over his head, he should move left or right away from it and try to look like he is attempting to catch the ball in a different spot. This fake might get the coverage men to follow him, which might prevent them from downing the ball before it enters the end zone. The returner should not fake a fair catch in this situation because this allows the coverage men to ignore him and look for the ball. By acting as if he will catch the ball and run, the returner forces the coverage men to honor his position.

Many schemes can be drawn up to block a punt. Whatever scheme is used, the technique of the rushers is critical to success. These include the following three points:

1. The get-off

2. Angle of attack to the ball and block point of the punt

3. Hand and body position on the block

The get-off is critical in blocking a punt. The blocker should be in an elongated stance with his feet at least heel to toe in relation to each other. His weight needs to be heavily on his down hand, with his free arm to the side and slightly back. The blocker's focus must be on the ball. At the slightest movement backward of the punt-block man, the punt blocker explodes out of his stance, staying low, driving his back foot and free hand forward to initiate movement. He rushes forward like a sprinter, turning his chest away from blockers to reduce the blocking surface as he tries to run under the blockers' hands.

The punt blocker must know where the punter's contact point is. This is the spot in relation to the snapper where the punter's foot contacts the ball. For most punters who line up at 15 yards (a standard for many teams), the contact point is usually 8-1/2 to 10 yards behind the snapper. This must be studied from opponent film and practiced during the week. Knowing the contact point allows the blocker to take the most direct line possible to that point. His path needs to be as straight as possible. Any bending of the path makes him take longer to get there.

Once the blocker gets to the contact point, he must keep his eyes open. It is a normal reaction to close the eyes when close to the punter's foot at contact. But the blocker needs to see the ball and foot in order to put his hands in the exact spot. The blocker reaches out and down with his hands together, thumbs touching. He tries to hit the ball as it contacts the punter's foot. A common error is to reach up with the hands to block the ball as it comes off the punter's foot, which increases the margin for error.

MISSTEP

The punt rusher trying to block a punt raises his hands up to about shoulder height as he passes the contact point of the punter. This allows the punted ball to pass underneath the blocker's hands, unblocked.

CORRECTION

The punt blocker must focus on looking at the punter's foot and ball at contact, and try to tap the top of the punter's kicking foot. This will ensure the blocker's hands are down low enough not to allow any room for the ball to slip through.

The blocker's body must not pass through the contact point spot. If it does, and if he misses touching the ball, he'll probably hit the punter's foot, which leads to a penalty for roughing the punter. This penalty typically results in a first down for the punting team and a lost offensive series for the punt-return team. A good rule for the punt blocker is to run in front of the punter if he's coming from the tackle position or wider (figures 13.7a and 13.7b). If he's rushing from the tackle–guard gap or center–guard gap, the rusher should pass to the side of the punter as he reaches for the ball (figure 13.7c).

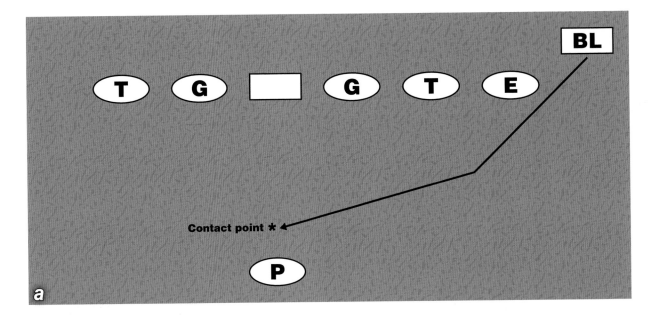

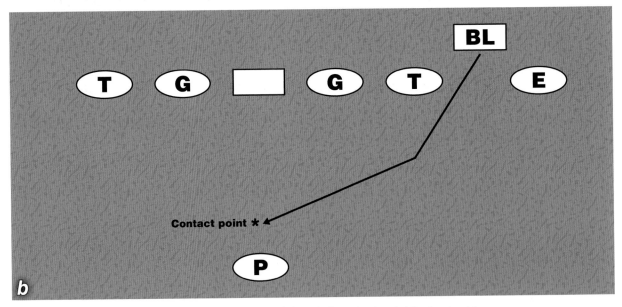

Figure 13.7 Punt blocks: *(a)* wide rush; *(b)* rush from just outside the tackle.

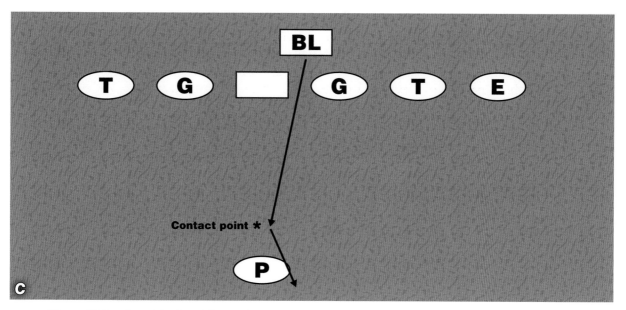

Figure 13.7 Punt blocks: *(c)* rush from the center–guard gap.

KICKOFF

The kickoff is similar to the punt in that the main purpose of the team kicking off is to minimize the return to give the return team poor field position. To cover downfield in a secure manner, the kickoff team must spread the field to allow only minimal gaps in coverage. There are several ways to accomplish this task.

Kickoff Alignment

Most kickoff schemes have 8 to 10 of the 11 men covering downfield to make the tackle while the remaining 1 to 3 serve as safeties in case the front line of coverage misses the returner. To start with, the 11 men align in such a way as to cover the width of the field completely. We'll name the coverage men with their side and number from the outside: L1, L2, L3, L4, L5, R5, R4, R3, R3, R1, and the kicker. Figure 13.8 shows a typical line-up prior to the kicker approaching the ball to kick it.

The outside cover men align 5 yards from the sideline. Each succeeding man lines up 5 yards from the man to the outside. This provides an even coverage of the field with the kicking team as a starting point.

In college football, the ball is kicked off from the 35-yard line. In high school football, it's the 40-yard line. Various alignments are possible. In some, the entire kickoff team lines up 5 yards from the kicking line, facing in toward the kicker. When the kicker passes the kicking line, all the cover men turn and start to run to the designated kicking line. Another variation has the outside men lined up 5 yards from the kicking line, with each succeeding player 1 to 2 yards farther back. Again, each player turns and starts running toward the kicking line when the kicker passes him. New rules at the college level do not allow this variation. In college, all players must be at the 30-yard line or closer to the ball prior to the kick.

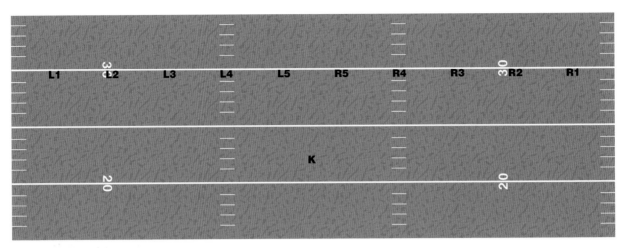

Figure 13.8 Kickoff alignment of kicking team.

Successful Kickoff Coverage

The kickoff team must focus on these four points to maximize its chance of a successful kickoff:

1. The get-off
2. Speed covering downfield
3. Avoidance of blockers
4. Tackle of the returner, keeping him inside and in front of the coverage

The first element, the get-off, refers to the point at which the ball is kicked and where each cover man is at that instant. Ideally, each man should be as close to the kicking line as possible, running at top speed. That gives each cover man the maximum chance to be as far downfield as possible and going as fast as possible when the kick is caught.

The second major element in a successful kickoff is the speed of the cover men running downfield. Ideally, each man is running at top speed. The farther downfield the coverage can get before the returner catches the kick, the better. A good way for a coach to measure an individual's effort and speed is to watch the entire cover team from the side at a point 20 yards downfield. For college, this is at the far 45-yard line. For high school, it's the far 40-yard line. If everyone has a good get-off and is running at full speed, all cover men should be within 1 or 2 yards of each other downfield. Anyone back farther than 2 yards either didn't get a good get-off or is not running at full speed. Use video to show your players. A good drill to work during the week combines the get-off with speed. The kicking team simulates a kickoff, working on each player getting a good get-off, then sprints 30 yards downfield. The coaches watch to see if everyone is within 1 or 2 yards of each other.

The third element of effective kickoff coverage is avoiding blockers. When covering downfield, each cover man must stay in his position relative to the rest of the cover team. This is called his cover lane. When each cover man stays in his cover lane, no large spaces remain for the returner to slip through.

When a cover man comes to a return-team man who is blocking, he can either run around to avoid the blocker or take on the blocker and wait to see where the returner is going before attempting to get away from the blocker. If the cover man is more than 15 yards away from the returner, he should avoid the blocker and get back into his cover lane. If the cover man is 15 yards or closer to the returner, he should take on the blocker using a 2-gap technique and wait to see which way the returner runs. If the cover man attempts to avoid a blocker when he's close to the returner, he might not be able to get around the blocker and back into his cover lane in time to get to the returner. This opens up a hole in the cover team's coverage lanes, which should be avoided. When the cover man avoids a blocker farther than 15 yards from the returner, he usually has time to get around the blocker and back into his cover lane before getting to the returner—thus the 15-yard rule. Remember these rules:

- If more than 15 yards from the returner, avoid the blocker.

- If 15 yards or closer to the returner, use a 2-gap technique on the blocker and wait for the returner to commit to a direction. When he does, get off the blocker in that direction.

The 2-gap technique means that the cover man takes on the blocker in a head-up position, punching the blocker with both hands in the blocker's chest. The cover man stays in good football position, driving his feet with short, choppy steps, attempting to drive the blocker back toward the returner. While doing this, he keeps his shoulders square and tries to see the returner. When the returner commits to a direction, the cover man uses his hands to shed the blocker and come off him in the direction of the returner.

MISSTEP

A kickoff coverage player avoids a blocker who's 20 yards in front of the returner. After avoiding the block, the coverage player fails to move back into the same coverage lane he started in prior to avoiding the block. This results in the returner running through the area the coverage man was assigned to.

CORRECTION

Anytime the coverage man avoids a block, he must move back into the same coverage lane from which he started. He avoids the blocker close to the body (to avoid running too far out of the lane) and moves to get back immediately in his original lane.

The final element in kickoff coverage is making the tackle. As the cover men approach the returner, they must maintain their coverage lanes as they each squeeze the returner's possible avenues of escape. This is called keeping the returner inside and in front. This means that each cover man keeps the returner on his inside shoulder—don't let the returner cross your face to the outside—as well as in front of him as he approaches the returner. Ideally, the cover team will form a semicircle around the returner and gradually squeeze the circle down until someone can make the tackle. The inside–in front drill works on this point.

Focusing on these four elements of successful kickoff coverage—the get-off, speed, avoidance, and inside–in front—will maximize a kicking team's chances of good coverage.

Kickoff Strategy

Several strategies involve the kicker and the way he kicks off. Statistics show that if the kicker can place his kickoff outside the hash marks around the numbers, the kickoff coverage team will be more successful than if the ball ends up in the middle of the field. By squeezing the kick returner into the corner, you essentially cut off half the field from his return.

The kicker also can use a specialty kick to help in a successful cover. One of these is the pooch kick, which is a short, high kickoff that lands near the opponent's 20- to 25-yard line, again by the numbers. A short, high kick means the cover team won't have as far to cover, and usually can tackle the returner quickly. This kick also forces the return team to communicate about who should catch the ball, sometimes leading to confusion and a fumble.

Another specialty kick is the squib, in which the kicker attempts to execute a line-drive kick so the ball hits the ground and skids downfield. The hope is that the ball will take some wild bounces, making it difficult for the return team to field it for the return. Ideally, the kicker should attempt to kick a squib kick into a gap in the return team's alignment so that no one can pick it up too quickly.

The final specialty kick every kickoff team needs in its arsenal is the onside kick. This kick is designed to go the minimum 10 yards downfield and bounce in such a way that the return team is unable to catch it before the kicking team can recover it themselves. The onside kick is typically used late in a game after a team scores but is still behind. The team using the onside kick is betting they can recover the kick and get another chance to score. The onside kick is usually kicked across the field from one hash to the other, giving the cover team time to cover the 10 yards before the ball is caught. Once the ball goes past 10 yards, it's a free ball for either team. By kicking the top half of the ball, the kicker can impart overspin, which might cause the ball to take a large hop at about 10 yards. This gives the kicking team a better chance to get it. Note that the rules of football stipulate that at least four cover men must be lined up on each side of the kicker as he kicks the ball. Figure 13.9 shows a typical onside kick formation.

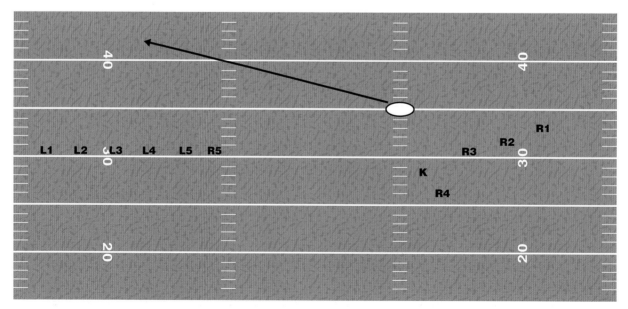

Figure 13.9 Onside kick formation.

Kickoff Drill 1   Get-Off Speed

This drill works reaching maximum speed at the kick line (35-yard line) as the ball is kicked. The entire team lines up. On the coach's command, the kicker takes his normal approach to kick the ball. The coverage players learn when to start running based on where the kicker is in his approach. Each player's start might be slightly different. Have a coach watch from the sideline, looking down the kick line to see if anyone is off side or too far back when the ball is kicked. Make sure each cover player sprints at least 5 yards past the kick line to ensure he's at top speed at the kick line.

Success Check

- Each coverage player is within 1 yard of the kick line when the ball is kicked, running at top speed.

Kickoff Drill 2   Get-Off and Initial Speed

This is a continuation of the get-off speed drill. The setup is the same, and the drill starts the same way. Here, though, instead of sprinting only 5 yards past the kick line, the cover team sprints 25 yards past the kick line. Have a coach at the line 20 yards from the kick line on the side to check to see that each player crosses the 20-yard line within 1 to 2 yards of each other. If everyone is sprinting at top speed, they should all be within 1 to 2 yards of each other. Anyone farther back than 2 yards needs to be encouraged to run harder or make sure he gets a good get-off at the kick line.

Success Check

- Each cover player is at top speed within 1 yard of the kick line when the ball is kicked.

- Each cover player is within 1 to 2 yards of everyone else 20 yards downfield from the kick line.

Kickoff Drill 3   Inside–In Front Drill

Four lines of cover men line up at the 30-yard line. A line stands on each number, and a line on each hash mark. A ball carrier stands at the goal line. On the coach's command, the cover men start running toward the returner, gradually squeezing together as they approach the runner. When the cover men get to the 20-yard line, the returner starts running. The runner should attempt to change direction several times and either run around to the outside of the cover men or run straight ahead and split them. As the cover men get to within 5 yards of the returner, they get into good football position with their inside foot and hip up. They shuffle their feet as they squeeze down the returner's running lanes, keeping him on their inside shoulders. If the returner tries to run around to their outside, they press forward and cut off his path. Finish with the nearest cover man tackling the runner.

(continued)

Kickoff Drill 3 (continued)

Success Check

- The returner executes several changes of direction, and the cover men react correctly.
- When within 5 yards of the returner, the cover men get into good football position.

- The cover men work together to close the returner's running lane.
- The drill ends with the closest cover man tackling the returner.

Kickoff Drill 4   Avoid Drill

This drill works avoiding blocks on a kickoff and getting back to the correct coverage lane. Start the drill by lining up players as shown in figure 13.10. Prior to giving his command, the coach tells the blocker which way he should block the cover man. On command, the blocker drops back 10 yards and turns to block the cover man in the indicated direction. The cover man runs downfield toward the blocker. When he reaches the blocker, the cover man should avoid the block, going around behind the blocker's back. After going

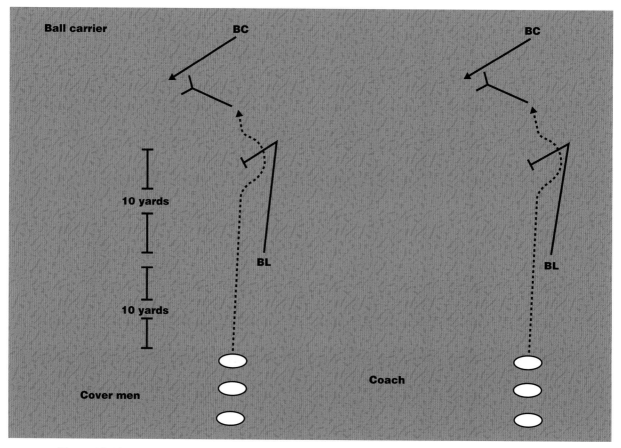

Figure 13.10   Avoid drill.

around the blocker, the cover man should get back into his original cover lane. Having the cover man run down a yard line helps to identify his cover lane. After the cover man returns to his cover lane, the running back simulating the returner makes a break in either direction at a 45-degree angle. The cover man settles his hips and executes an open-field tackle.

Success Check

- The cover man successfully avoids the block then returns to his cover lane.

- The cover man stays in his cover lane, using the yard line as a guide.
- The drills ends with the cover man executing a good open-field tackle on the returner.

KICKOFF RETURN

The objective of the kickoff-return team is to catch the kickoff and return it as far downfield as possible, either to score or to give the offense the best field position possible. As in offensive scheme development, a multitude of possible return schemes can be drawn up.

An effective return includes some basic elements. First, the return team must field the ball so the kicking team cannot recover an uncaught ball. Remember that once the ball goes 10 yards on a kickoff, it can be recovered by either team. With this in mind, the receiving team must have enough men close to the kicker so he can't execute an onside kick. The receiving team must also cover the field with their initial alignment in a way that makes them able to field a kick that occurs anywhere on their end of the field. Finally, the return team must block the cover men to open a running lane for the returner.

There are three basic elements in a successful kickoff-return scheme. First, the initial alignment must allow the return team to field any type of kickoff. Second, the return-team blockers must be able to get into position to block the kickoff cover men with the correct timing as the returner brings the ball upfield. Third, the blockers of the return team must execute and maintain their blocks so that the returner has a running lane.

Kickoff-Return Alignments

Several possible alignments will satisfy the first important element of kickoff returns. The most common has five men lined up 10 to 15 yards off the kickoff restraining line, with two more about 15 yards back and two more behind them near the 25-yard line (figure 13.11). The two remaining men are the returners; they line up anywhere from the goal line to the 10, depending on the kicker's leg strength.

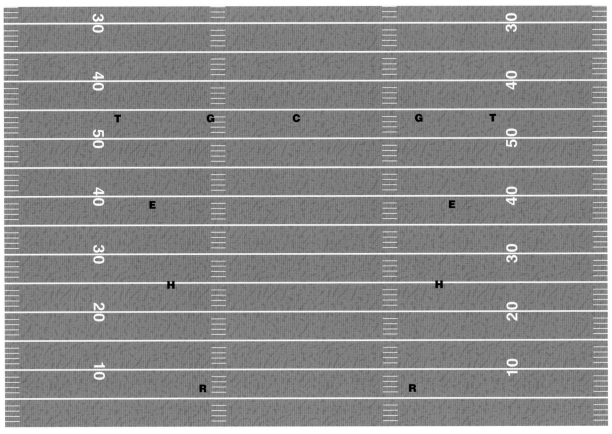

Figure 13.11 Kickoff-return alignment.

Two other common kickoff alignments are the 5-3-3 alignment (figure 13.12a) and the 4-2-3-2 alignment (figure 13.12b).

Kickoff-Return Blocking

Getting into position to block is the key for the front-line blockers. They must run back to a position where they can make their blocks with the right timing. Too soon, and they'll have to hold their blocks longer than might be possible. Also, if they leave their alignments too soon to get back, they'll risk the possibility of an onside kick by the kicking team. Too late, and they won't be able to get to the right spot to make the block before the cover man gets by.

MISSTEP

The front-line blockers on the kick-return team turn to run back to their block points before the ball is kicked, allowing the kick team to cover a short surprise kickoff.

CORRECTION

The front-line blockers must see the ball being kicked before they turn to run back to their block points.

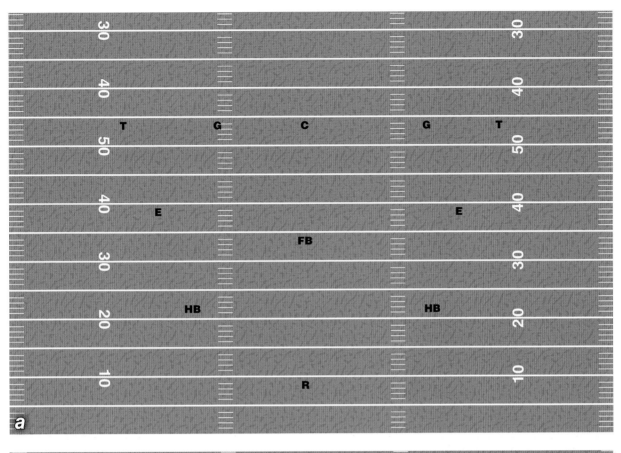

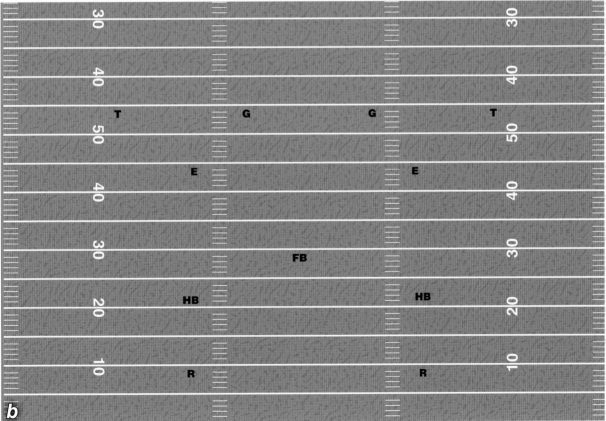

Figure 13.12 Kickoff returns: *(a)* 5-3-3 alignment; *(b)* 4-2-3-2 alignment.

From his initial alignment, each front-line player keeps his eyes on the kicker and the ball. He holds his position until he sees the ball is kicked and makes sure it's a deep kick. Once he sees this, he turns and sprints back to his designated spot. As he runs, he glances back at the cover team, keeping an eye on the man he's assigned to block. As he drops, he moves at an angle that will put him in the correct position to block his man away from the returner's intended path.

As the cover men approach, the blockers settle and stop their backward motion. When the cover men get within 5 yards, the blockers start moving toward their assigned men. Each blocker makes contact on the cover man using his hands, placing the hand closest to the runner's path on the cover man's near shoulder. The blocker's other hand aims at the cover man's chest. As he makes contact, the blocker needs to be in a good football stance, with his body between the cover man and the runner's path.

After contact, the blocker moves his feet, taking quick shuffle steps to keep his body between the cover man and the returner. The block doesn't have to be violent. He doesn't need to knock down the cover man, just to stay between him and the returner as long as possible.

The remaining blocks will depend on the design of the return. The main coaching point for the remaining blockers is to use their hands to contact the cover man and move their feet once contact is made to stay on the cover man as long as possible.

Kickoff Catching and Running

Obviously, catching the ball is a critically important part of a successful kickoff return. Sometimes the ball won't go directly to one of the designated returners. One of the returners should be designated the call man. He'll make a "you" or "me" call to the other returner, telling him who should catch the ball. This must be an assigned responsibility, so both returners don't go for a kickoff catch at the same time. Likewise, if a kickoff is short and the returners can't get to it, they need to communicate to the return men in front of them that they should catch the ball. Use a "short" call to communicate this. As with any call, they should repeat the call three or four times in a row, loudly, to make sure the other men hear.

No matter what kind of return is planned, the returner can help his blockers and set up the return in the way he begins to return the ball once it's caught. Whether returning the ball to his right or left, the returner should start running straight upfield for 4 or 5 yards. This tends to get the cover men to veer in that direction toward him. After this, the returner can break right or left to his designed lane. This gets the cover men slightly out of position and might give the blockers a better angle to block them.

Figures 13.13, 13.14, and 13.15 show examples of kickoff returns. Note there are many other possibilities. As with any scheme, execution is the most important element for success. If the return is too complicated, or is changed every week to something new, the return team might not be able to master it well enough to be successful. A simple system well executed is always better than a complex system poorly executed.

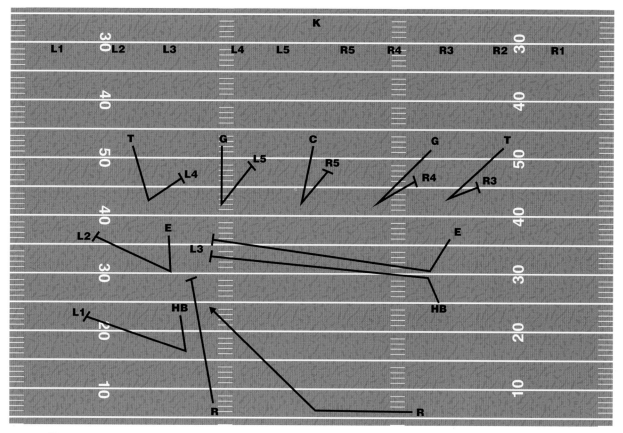

Figure 13.13 Side kickoff return out of 5-2-2 alignment.

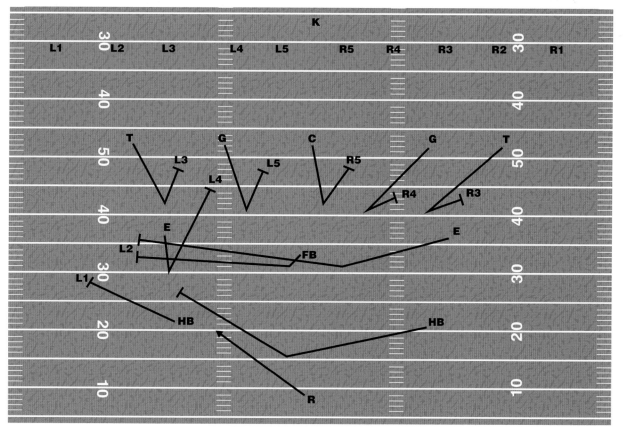

Figure 13.14 Side kickoff return out of 5-3-3 alignment.

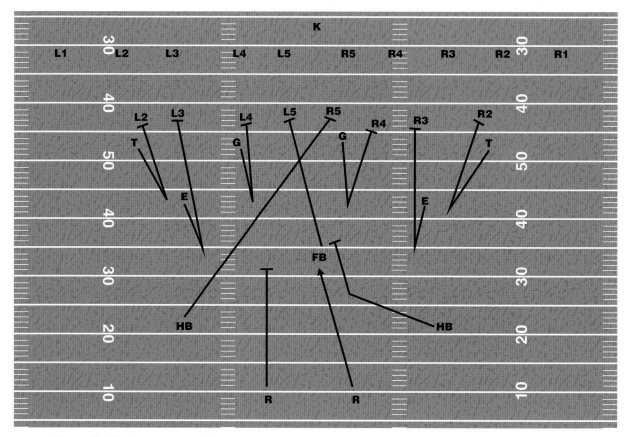

Figure 13.15   Middle kickoff return out of 4-2-3-2 alignment.

FIELD GOAL AND PAT ATTEMPTS

Most field goal and point-after plays are critical. These are points that need to be on the board.

There's not typically much complexity in this play, although the threat of a fake should keep the defense alert. Figure 13.16 shows the most common alignment used by most teams.

A variation of this alignment is used by some teams when the ball is on the hash mark, especially if it's close to the goal line (figure 13.17). In this variation, one of the linemen lines up to the wide side of the field to create a long side of protection. This is sometimes called an unbalanced field goal formation. The idea behind this involves the flight of the kicked ball. Because the kicker will kick the ball to the middle of the uprights, when the ball is on the hash, the angle of the kick will be over the guard or tackle to the field side. It might be possible for an outside rusher from the field to get to the ball because its flight is farther to that side. Moving a player to that side forces the outside rusher to come from a farther point.

The offensive linemen align foot to foot with inside foot back and inside hand down. The wings can align facing forward or at a 45-degree angle to the line based on their technique. The holder is on one knee (the front one) and marks a spot on the ground (or for high school, on a tee) 7 yards from the line of scrimmage. Setting the ball at 7 yards is critical to allow room for the ball to get height over the line. The holder marks the spot with his back hand (left hand for a right-footed kicker) and signals to the snapper that the kicker is ready. As he catches the ball, the holder places

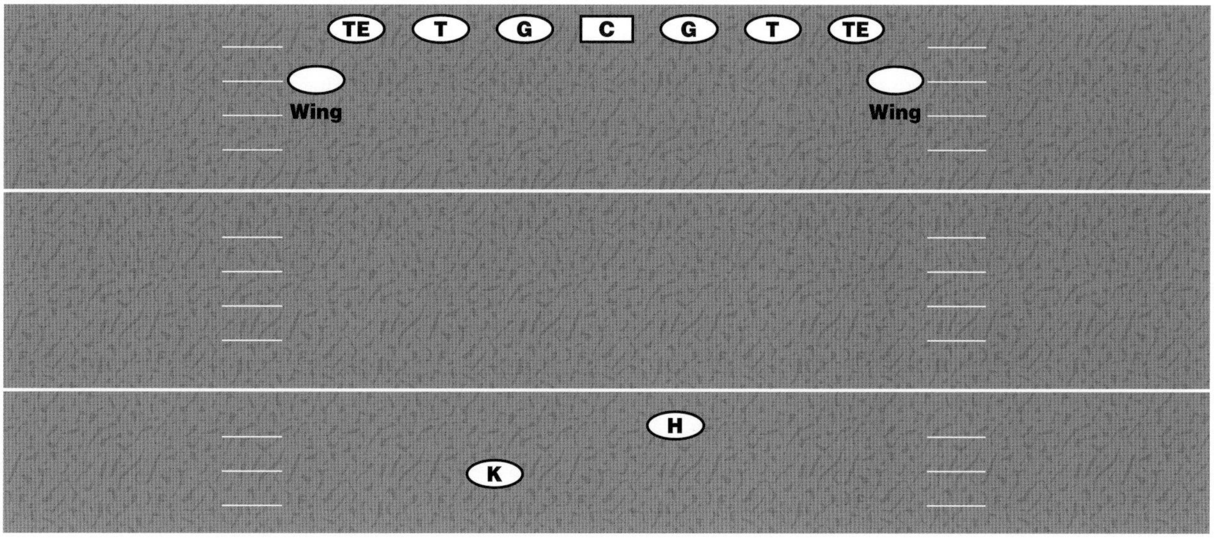

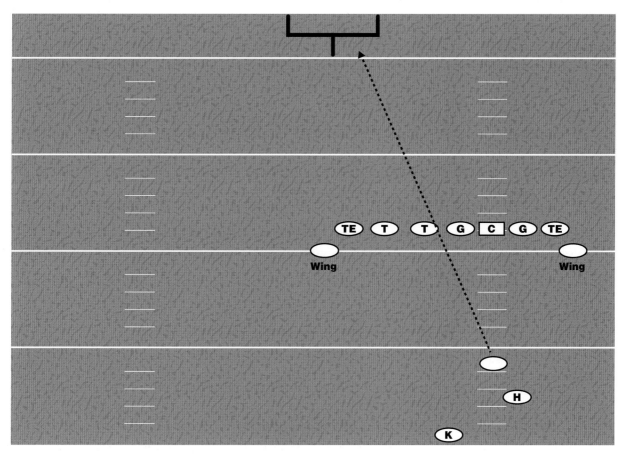

Figure 13.16 Field goal and PAT attempt alignment.

the ball on the spot indicated and tilts the ball in the position desired by the kicker. The kick needs to get off in 1.2 to 1.3 seconds to prevent rushers from having a good chance to block it. If off in 1.2 seconds, it should be nearly impossible for an outside rusher to block the kick, even if he's not blocked. The snapper, holder, and kicker must work in sync, executing the snap, hold, and kick quickly and smoothly every

Figure 13.17 Unbalanced field goal alignment.

time. This part of the field goal or PAT attempt should be practiced until mastered. Once mastered, it should still be practiced every day.

On the snap, the offensive linemen and tight ends step with their inside feet back behind the men to their inside. At the same time, they block anyone trying to rush through the gap to their inside. Having everyone block his inside gap prevents any inside penetration by rushers directly in line with the flight of the kicked ball. As they step and block, the linemen must keep their heads up, be solid in their stance so they won't be knocked back, and keep their shoulders square so no one can slip through a gap.

The wings can block in several ways. The most common is for the wing to first block anyone attacking his inside gap. If someone is also rushing outside him, he can punch out on that rusher after securing the inside gap. This is sometimes called a double-bump technique. Another way is for the wing to line up about 2 yards in back of the tight ends. On the snap, the wing steps forward toward the tight end and blocks the gap just off the tight end's butt. At the same time, the wing keeps his outside and back foot set in its original spot, forcing any outside rusher to run over the leg. This should slow down the rusher enough to make it impossible to get to the kick and block it. Figure 13.18 shows the gaps each man should be blocking.

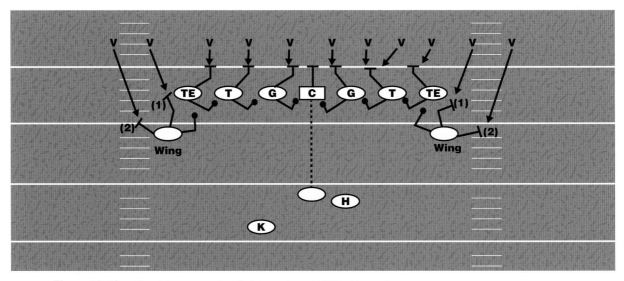

Figure 13.18 Blocking gaps for field goal and PAT attempts.

The alignment and blocking are identical whether the kick is a PAT attempt or a field goal. The only variation would be the unbalanced formation shown in figure 13.17 for a short field goal.

If the snap and hold are not executed properly and the kicker can't get the kick off, the offense must have an emergency play that occurs immediately so they still have a chance to score points. This play would involve the holder picking up the ball and attempting to pass it to one of the tight ends or wings. The holder uses a code word to trigger the play once he realizes the kick cannot occur. Many teams use the word "fire." Whatever the code word, it must be repeated three or four times loudly. Figure 13.19 shows an example of a fire-call play. There are many possible variations.

When the fire call is made, both tight ends and wings release downfield. As they release, they glance back at the holder to see which direction he has rolled out to. The direction depends on what happens with the hold. The holder should roll in the direction the ball takes him. Once they see the holder's direction, the ends and wings run their routes accordingly.

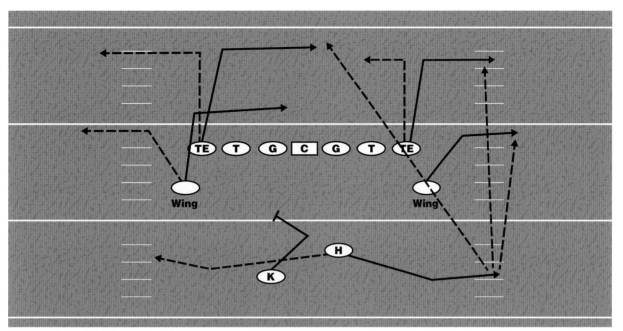

Figure 13.19   Fire call on a field goal or PAT attempt.

An alternate fire call would have each side running their routes to the outside, so they wouldn't need to know which way the holder rolled. This simplifies the play but cuts down on the holder's options.

FIELD GOAL OR PAT BLOCK

Field goal and PAT attempts are also important plays for the defense. A block of a field goal or PAT usually prevents a score. Odds are against the defense on these plays because stopping these kicks is difficult. However, they are not 100 percent effective and can be stopped in several ways. The kick might get blocked. The holder might mishandle the snap. The kicker might be forced to miss. But because the odds are against stopping the kick, many defenses tend to relax on this play. Not a good idea. They might miss an opportunity to take advantage of a mishap. Many football games are won by one or three points, so the defense must always give its best effort.

In most cases, the defense lines up to execute the attempted block versus the field goal team. In some cases, substitutes might be sent in to serve specialized jobs on the blocking team. For example, a taller player or a player who can jump higher might be subbed in for a defender. Likewise, a faster player might be sent in to attempt to block the kick from the outside. In any case, there are many ways a defense can line up to attempt to block a kick. The only basic requirement is to make sure they cover any potential receivers in case the kicking team runs a fake or resorts to the fire play. Care should be taken when designing a kick-block so that gaps aren't left open for a possible fake. As teams study film of their opponents, weaknesses in alignment can be noted and taken advantage of. A coach should design his field goal or PAT block with this in mind.

Regardless of the design of the block, several things must occur for the defense to have a chance to block a kick. First, rushers coming from the inside must come out of their stances and attempt to get a strong push on the offensive line to drive it back as far as possible. Keying the movement of the ball will help the rusher do this. If he can beat the offensive blocker to the punch, he might be able to get an extra push. As he comes off, the rusher must stay low and get as much leverage as possible as he drives his legs for two or three steps. Once he does this, he must get his hands up in the air as high as possible to try to deflect the ball. The more push the defender can get, the more likely he'll get a piece of the ball. Some blocks are designed for two or three defenders to get this push while a third or fourth tries to split a gap between blockers.

Defenders assigned to cover potential receivers must watch their man throughout the play. A defender covering a receiver should not try to block the kick. The defenders should line up in the correct gaps, as designed, so they don't open up a fake with an undefended gap. Figure 13.20 shows a block designed for three defenders to get a push on a guard so they can get enough push to block the kick from inside.

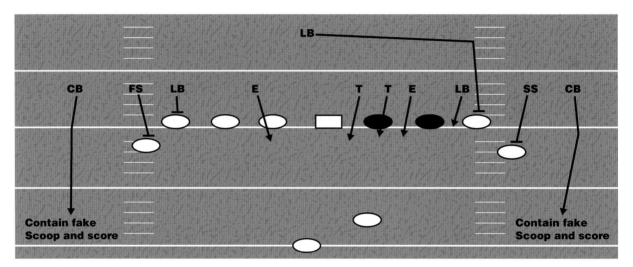

Figure 13.20 Field goal block attempt: push on guard with three defenders, inside block.

In this block, the two tackles and the right end attempt to drive the guard and tackle back as far as possible. A three-on-two push should make this happen. The important aspects of this block are that each eligible receiver (tight ends and wings) are covered by a defender who's not rushing. Each run gap is also covered by a defender, including those who are rushing. This block is designed to attack the kick from the inside. Figure 13.21 shows an outside block.

If the designed block is coming from the outside, the man coming must remember that the shortest distance between two points is a straight line. When he rushes outside the wing, he must stay as close to the wing as possible, flattening his path toward the blocking point once he gets to the edge. The blocking point will be about 1 yard in front of the ball as it's being held on the ground. This is a critical point—the blocker must pass in front of this point so he doesn't collide with the kicker. Running into the kicker is an infraction that will result in the kicking team getting another play or the offense getting another set of downs. The free safety must do a good job of forcing the wing to block down on him, so the corner can come around the edge tight. If the wing does not block down, the free safety should come free and attempt to block the kick.

In several situations the blocking design should be based on the game situation. First, if a fake is suspected, the blocking team wants to put everyone on alert and place players in positions where they can react to a fake (figure 13.22). Note that

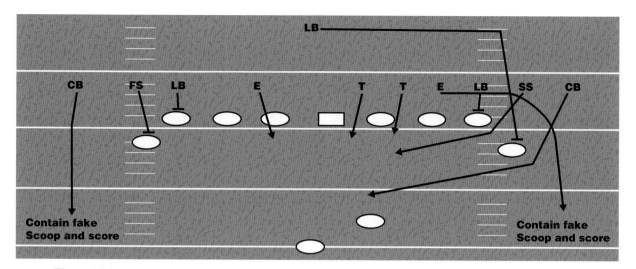

Figure 13.21 Field goal block attempt: outside block.

players who have coverage responsibility have backed off so they can see their men better and are in position to react if a fake is run.

Another situation in which a team's normal blocking design should be tweaked is at the end of a game when the kicking team is attempting a field goal or PAT to win the game (figure 13.23). Chances are good that the kicking team won't risk running a fake in this situation, so the blocking team can send everyone without worrying about coverage. In this situation, everyone is rushing to block the kick, with one exception. The corner in figure 13.23 is running upfield in case the ball is blocked. If the block occurs, it's his job to scoop up the ball and run for a score. Everyone else tries to block the kick. The blocking team is gambling that the kicking team won't risk running a fake when they must score to win.

The key to a blocking team's success is effort. Players must go full-force, believing they will get the block. Coaches must cultivate this mindset in all their players. Make it happen by believing it will happen, and by putting in the work. Many techniques and skills are required in football, but none is as important as effort, positive attitude, and a strong work ethic.

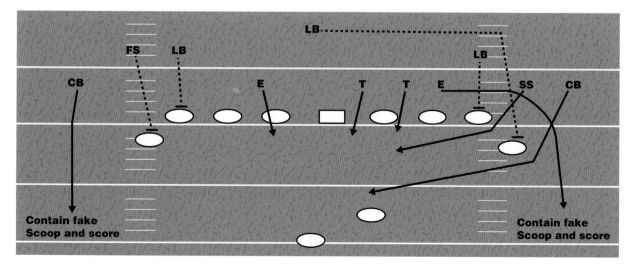

Figure 13.22 Field goal "safe"—look for fake.

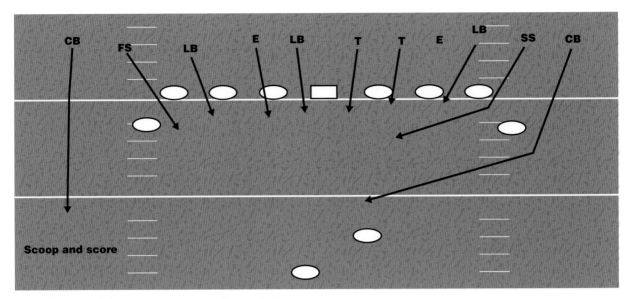

Figure 13.23 Field goal "max"—end of game.

SUCCESS SUMMARY

In step 13 we have discussed the basic elements of special teams, including formations, potential schemes, fundamentals, and variations. It's not uncommon for special teams to be relegated to second-class consideration, after offense and defense. This is a mistake. Solid play from your special-team units will win you football games, as any experienced coach will tell you.

To ensure you have a solid grasp on special-team play, answer the following questions.

Before Taking the Next Step

1. Which special teams play can be responsible for more yardage within a game than any other phase?

2. What are two types of blocking schemes that can be used with the punt unit?

3. What are the four main elements of a successful punt-return unit?

4. What are the four main elements of a successful kickoff coverage unit?

5. What are three basic starting alignments for the kickoff return? Which do you prefer and why?

6. Why is the field goal and PAT unit so important?

7. What is a "fire" call?

8. When attempting to block a PAT or field goal, what must the blocking team do to ensure the kicking team cannot run a fake?

Glossary

angle tackle—A tackle made on a running back who is aiming at a point on either side of the tackler. The tackler must angle his aiming point to intersect the runner.

back block—A block in which the lineman blocks the first man to his inside, while the offensive man over that defender pulls to the outside to block someone else.

blocking—Obstructing an opponent by contacting him with any part of the body.

blocking zone—A rectangle centered on the snapper that extends 5 yards laterally and 3 yards longitudinally in each direction.

boot pass—A play in which the quarterback fakes a running play in one direction and then rolls out in the opposite direction to throw the ball.

chop block—A high–low combination block performed by two offensive players against a defender. This type of block is illegal at all levels of football.

clip—An illegal block in which initial contact is made from behind or below the waist.

contact point—The point on the field in front of the punter where his foot makes contact with the ball.

corner back—A defensive back who usually lines up on the widest aligned offensive receiver.

counter play—A play in which the offense fakes a running play in one direction and then runs the ball in the opposite direction. Usually run somewhere near the tight end position.

curl passing zone—The area from the offensive tackle to the outside approximately 10 yards up to 15 yards deep from the line of scrimmage.

cushion—The space a defensive coverage man has between himself and the offensive receiver he is covering.

cut block—A block in which the blocker makes contact on the defender around the waist or below.

deep 1/2 passing zone—The area 15 yards from the defensive side of the line of scrimmage to the defense's goal line, spanning 1/2 of the field.

deep 1/3 passing zone—The area 15 yards from the defensive side of the line of scrimmage to the defense's goal line, spanning 1/3 of the field. Can be deep outside 1/3 or deep middle 1/3.

deep 1/4 passing zone—The area 15 yards from the defensive side of the line of scrimmage to the defense's goal line, spanning 1/4 of the field. Can be deep outside 1/4 or deep inside 1/4.

deep out passing route—A passing route in which the receiver runs 10 to 20 yards downfield and breaks to the outside away from the quarterback.

defensive back—A defensive player who lines up to defend passing plays. Defensive backs usually line up 5 to 14 yards from the line of scrimmage. Safeties and corner backs are defensive backs.

defensive end—A defensive linemen who usually lines up on either the offensive tackle or tight end.

defensive tackle—A defensive linemen who usually lines up on either the offensive guard or center.

double-team block—A block by two offensive men on one defender at the same time.

down—A play opportunity given to the offense; the offense has four downs to move the ball 10 yards by running or passing the ball.

drive block—A block by an offensive man on the defender directly in front of him. The blocker drives the defender straight back.

drop kick—The action of kicking the ball after it has been dropped onto the ground. Contact with the ball takes place immediately after the ball hits the ground. Very rare in football today.

encroaching—An offensive player moving into the neutral zone prior to the snap of the ball after the offensive center touches the ball. An exception to this rule is the center. He can be in the neutral zone when he touches the ball.

eye control—Refers to a defender looking at the proper key or opponent during a play.

fair catch—The catch of a punt or kickoff in which the receiver waves his hand above his shoulder to indicate he will catch but not advance the kick; the kicking team is not allowed to hit or tackle the receiver after he signals the fair catch.

field goal—A scrimmage kick that may be attempted from anywhere on the field; if the ball is successfully kicked through the uprights, it earns the kicking team 3 points.

field of play—The area inside the sidelines on either side of the field and the goal lines on either end.

fire call—An impromptu play run by the field goal kicking team after a bad snap when the kicker is not able to kick the ball.

flat passing zone—The area from about 10 yards outside the offensive tackle to the sideline up to 15 yards deep from the defensive side of the line of scrimmage.

football stance—A body position in which the player has his knees bent slightly, weight on the balls of his feet, with his head up and chest pointing straight ahead.

forward pass—A ball thrown either overhand or underhand that travels toward the defense's goal line.

frame—A player's body from the shoulders down, used to determine if a block is legal or illegal.

free kick—A kick made after a safety.

fullback—A running back who blocks on most plays. The fullback may also run with or catch the ball.

fumble—Occurs when the player in possession of the football loses the ball during a play, making the ball a free ball that may be recovered, and sometimes advanced, by either side.

gap scheme offensive play—An offensive play in which the blockers make their blocks at angles inside or outside of their aligned positions.

gunners—The players on a punting team who are aligned split out away from the main body of the punting team. Their main job is to get downfield as quickly as possible to cover the punt returner.

handoff pocket—The position of the running back's hands to receive a handoff from the quarterback.

hang time—The time a punt is in the air from kick to catch.

hook passing zone—The area from offensive tackle to offensive tackle, up to 15 yards deep on the defensive side of the line of scrimmage.

inside linebacker—A linebacker who usually lines up over the offensive tackle or guard at a depth of 3 to 5 yards.

interception—Occurs when a defensive player catches a thrown pass, giving his team possession of the ball.

isolation play—An offensive running play in which a linebacker is not blocked by a lineman but is then blocked by a lead runner (e.g., a fullback) in front of the ball carrier.

kicker—The special-teams player who kicks the ball on kickoffs, field goals, and PAT (point after touchdown) attempts.

kickoff—The kick that starts each half and follows each touchdown, successful field goal, and safety.

lateral pass—A ball thrown either overhand or underhand that travels parallel to or away from the defense's goal line.

leg lock—Refers to a kicker's or punter's leg position at ball contact when the leg is fully extended with the knee locked.

linebacker—A defensive player who lines up directly behind the defensive linemen, usually 3 to 5 yards from the line of scrimmage.

line of scrimmage—The imaginary line between the offense and defense prior to the snap. The line of scrimmage runs through the near point of the ball as it lays on the ground and extends from sideline to sideline.

long snapper—The special teams player who snaps the ball on punts, field goals, and PAT attempts.

low shoulder—Refers to a pass defender's position as he covers a receiver. Being low shoulder means the defender is positioned between the receiver and the quarterback.

man coverage—A pass-coverage scheme in which the defenders cover a specific offensive player wherever he goes on the field.

man free coverage—A type of man coverage in which defenders cover a specific man, with the exception of one or two defenders who defend an area on the field.

muff—An unsuccessful catch of a punt or kickoff in which the receiver touches the ball but fails to catch it; once the receiver touches the ball, it becomes a free ball that can be recovered by either side.

neutral zone—The space between the two lines of scrimmage, extending from sideline to sideline.

offensive center—The offensive player aligned on the ball, responsible for snapping the ball to start the play.

offensive guard—The offensive lineman aligned just outside the offensive center on either side.

offensive tackle—The offensive lineman aligned two positions outside the offensive center on either side.

offsides—At high school level and below, when a defensive player moves into the neutral zone prior to the snap. At the college and professional levels, when a defensive player moves into the neutral zone prior to the snap and is in or beyond the zone when the ball is snapped, contacts an opponent beyond the neutral zone before the ball is snapped, or threatens an offensive lineman, causing an immediate reaction by that lineman before the ball is snapped.

one-gap defense—A defensive scheme in which each player is responsible for only one running gap versus a running play.

open-field tackle—A tackle made on the field with no other tackler around to help.

option play—A play in which the quarterback has the option to hand off the ball to a runner, keep it for himself to run, or pitch it to another runner.

outside linebacker—A linebacker who usually lines up over the offensive tight end or wider.

pass block—A block used by offensive men on a passing play in which the blocker catches the charging defender and shields him from the quarterback.

pattern match zone coverage—A technique used by defensive players as they drop back into zone coverage in which their initial aiming points are based on the alignment of the offensive receivers.

place kick—A field goal or point after touchdown (PAT); the ball is placed on a tee or on the ground and is held by a teammate for the kicker.

point after attempt (PAT)—The play that immediately follows a touchdown. The scoring team may attempt a kick from the 3-yard line worth 1 point, if successful, or run a play from the same yard line worth 2 points, if successful.

pooch kick—A kickoff that is higher and shorter than a normal kickoff, designed to be kicked in an area not covered by the return team.

pooch punt—A punt that is higher and shorter than a normal punt, usually used when the punting team is on the opponent's end of the field and the punting team doesn't want the punt to go into the end zone for a touchback.

post passing route—A passing route in which the receiver runs 5 to 9 yards downfield and breaks at a 45-degree angle to the inside. Post refers to the goal post and can be used as the aiming point on the break.

power play—A play in which the offense runs the ball off tackle with both a pulling guard and fullback blocking ahead of the runner.

punt—A kick in which the punter drops the ball and kicks it before it strikes the ground; a punt is usually used on fourth down if the offense has not been able to move the ball 10 yards.

punt returner—The player on the punt-return team whose job is to catch the punt and run with the ball.

quarterback—The offensive player who lines up directly behind the center anywhere from a foot or two to 5 yards back. The quarterback calls the offensive plays in the huddle, calls the snap count for the play to start at the line of scrimmage, and is usually the first player to handle the snap from the center.

quarterback sneak—A running play in which the quarterback takes a direct snap from the center and attempts to run through the guard–center gap on either side. This is usually a quick hitting play designed to surprise the defense or to pick up very short yardage.

reach block—A block by an offensive man in which he moves right or left to block the next defender in that direction.

reception point—The point on the field at which a receiver will end up as the pass arrives.

reverse play—A play in which the offense fakes a play in one direction and then runs the ball in the opposite direction. A reverse is usually run outside the tight end position.

run gap—The area a defensive player is responsible for defending on a running play. The gap is usually from the nose of one offensive lineman to the nose of the next offensive lineman.

running back—The offensive player who carries the ball on running plays but may also catch passes. Running backs primarily line up behind the offensive line.

safety—A defensive back who usually lines up over the receivers who are closer to the offensive line

safety—A two-point score by the defense that occurs when one of its players tackles an opponent in possession of the ball in his own end zone. Following a safety, the team just scored upon must kick off to the other team.

scrimmage kick—A kick or punt that begins with a snap of the ball.

shallow crossing passing route—A passing route in which the receiver runs across the field to the inside past the quarterback 4 to 10 yards deep.

short out passing route—A passing route in which the receiver runs 5 to 7 yards downfield and breaks to the outside away from the quarterback.

snap—The motion of the center or long snapper, moving the ball from its place on the line of scrimmage to start the offensive play.

soft hands—Refers to catching a ball with a slight give in the hands and arms to avoid the ball bouncing off.

spot drop—A zone-coverage drop technique in which the defensive players drop to a specific spot on the field regardless of where the offensive players line up.

squib kick—A type of kickoff in which the kicker sends a line-drive kick along the ground, causing the ball to bounce in an unpredictable way.

stalk block—A block by a wide receiver in which he attempts to shield the defender from the ball carrier.

stem—A movement by a receiver in which he starts in one spot in relation to the defender and then runs to either an inside or outside position.

tackle—The act of grabbing and bringing the ball carrier down to the ground.

tailback—A running back who usually lines up directly behind the quarterback and offensive center.

three-step pass—A passing play in which the quarterback drops back only three steps before throwing the ball.

thud—A tackle that doesn't take the ball carrier to the ground. This is used in practice to limit injuries.

tight end—The offensive player who may be lined up three players outside the offensive center on either side. The tight end may be lined up in any position on or off the line of scrimmage.

touchback—A kick play (kickoff, field goal, or punt) in which the balls falls into the receiving team's end zone, resulting in the receiving team getting possession of the ball on its own 20- or 25-yard line (depending on level of play).

transition—The point at which a defensive back changes from a backpedal to a backward run.

trap block—A block in which an offensive lineman pulls to his left or right and blocks a defender from the inside out. The defender is usually two or more gaps away from the blocker's original alignment.

two-gap defense—A defensive scheme in which several of the defensive linemen are responsible for both gaps on either side versus the run.

wide receiver—An offensive player who usually lines up split out away from the offensive line on or off the line of scrimmage. The wide receiver's primary job is to catch passes.

zone coverage—Pass coverage scheme in which the defenders cover anyone in a specific area on the field.

zone play—A running play in which the offensive blockers step to one side and block whoever shows up in that gap while the runner looks for the open gap to run to.

zone read play—A zone play in which the quarterback reads the reaction of an unblocked defensive lineman to decide whether to hand off the ball or keep it.

About the Author

Greg Colby has coached football for 34 years, including 27 years as a collegiate coach and 10 years as a defensive coordinator at the NCAA Division I level. He has been on staff for two Big Ten Championships and 12 collegiate bowl games. In his nine years as a high school football coach, he won a pair of state championships. Colby was named the new defensive line coach at the University of Illinois in February 2013, after spending five years as the head coach at Millersville University in Pennsylvania and six years as defensive coordinator at Northwestern. Before his time at Northwestern, Colby spent four seasons as the defensive coordinator at Kent State University. From 1995 to 1997, Colby served as an assistant coach at Michigan State under head coach Nick Saban, and from 1988 to 1995, he was assistant coach for outside linebackers and special teams at Illinois. He also played football and baseball at the University of Illinois, where he was a three-year starter for the Fighting Illini football team and a three-year starter in baseball. Greg was team captain of the baseball squad in 1974.